THE PENGUIN BOOK OF THE ROAD

Delia Falconer is the author of two novels, *The Service of Clouds*, shortlisted for major Australian awards including the Miles Franklin, and *The Lost Thoughts of Soldiers*. An acclaimed essayist, short-story writer and critic, she holds a PhD in English Literature and Cultural Studies from the University of Melbourne.

THE PENGUIN BOOK OF THE ROAD

EDITED BY DELIA FALCONER

VIKING

an imprint of

PENGUIN BOOKS

VIKING

Published by the Penguin Group
Penguin Group (Australia)
250 Camberwell Road, Camberwell, Victoria 3124, Australia
(a division of Pearson Australia Group Pty Ltd)
Penguin Group (USA) Inc.
375 Hudson Street, New York, New York 10014, USA
Penguin Group (Canada)
90 Eglinton Avenue East, Suite 700, Toronto, Canada ON M4P 2Y3
(a division of Pearson Penguin Canada Inc.)
Penguin Books Ltd
80 Strand, London WC2R 0RL England
Penguin Ireland
25 St Stephen's Green, Dublin 2, Ireland
(a division of Penguin Books Ltd)
Penguin Books India Pvt Ltd
11 Community Centre, Panchsheel Park, New Delhi – 110 017, India
Penguin Group (NZ)
67 Apollo Drive, Rosedale, North Shore 0632, New Zealand
(a division of Pearson New Zealand Ltd)
Penguin Books (South Africa) (Pty) Ltd
24 Sturdee Avenue, Rosebank, Johannesburg 2196, South Africa

Penguin Books Ltd, Registered Offices: 80 Strand, London, WC2R 0RL, England

First published by Penguin Group (Australia), 2008

10 9 8 7 6 5 4 3 2 1

Cover design by Cameron Midson © Penguin Group (Australia)
Text design by Marina Messiha © Penguin Group (Australia)
Cover photograph by Rick Lew/Getty Images
Typeset in 12/16.5 pt Fairfield Light by Post Pre-press Group, Brisbane, Queensland
Printed and bound in Australia by McPherson's Printing Group, Maryborough, Victoria

National Library of Australia
Cataloguing-in-Publication data:

The Penguin book of the road / editor, Delia Falconer.
9780670071517 (pbk.)
Short stories, Australian.
Travel – Fiction.
Roads – Fiction.
Falconer, Delia C.

A823.010832

penguin.com.au

CONTENTS

INTRODUCTION

Roads, in Australia, have never been the 'glossy black dance floors' of Nabokov's America. We have produced no home-grown Whitman or Kerouac to sing the freedom of the open road or riff on the exhilarations of the highway. On the whole, roads make us uneasy. If we celebrate them at all, it is for their strangeness; their Big Pineapples, desert hermits and marauding hoons. Our pleasures are more likely to be found off-road, ranging through trackless bush like the Wild Colonial Boy or forging empty beaches in a four-wheel drive. In our collective imagination the road is usually a place traversed on the way to somewhere better. While the American road speeds forward, Australian tracks tend to wind back. Even our iconic song 'Along the Road to Gundagai' is less about the road itself than the nostalgic home comforts ('old-fashioned shack', mother and father, childhood friends) at its end.

Yet our roads, with their fringes of yellow railway flowers and mysterious unpaved turn-offs into bush, are the unsung backdrops for the defining moments of our lives. As an island nation, in which the majority of our population clings to the coast, we spend more time on the road than almost any other country. Learning to drive is an essential rite of adolescence; just as, for women of my mother's generation who learned to drive late in life, the road was a literal passage to liberation. Undulating, heath-flanked roads take us to coastal holidays and family reunions and secret sexual trysts. Grevillea-lined tollways flash by on the way to work or school or hospital. We argue in traffic jams on highways cut through sandstone. At night the monotony of cats' eyes reflected in the high beam challenges the long-haul truckie, weekend skier, or police officer to stay awake. Roadside shrines, with their homemade crosses, remind us that a sudden curve is where our lives all too often come skidding to an end.

Our history has also played itself out along our roadways. Convicts in Botany Bay whispered about illicit tracks through the bush that led all the way to China. Explorers left lines of marked trees to be dug into roads by the convict teams and bullock carts that followed. Roads were the powerful war machinery of the early colony; implacable replacements for storied indigenous paths that had left the earth unscarred. They brought the squatters and selectors who claimed the land for themselves. And, as the colony grew, they played host to the travellers who literally made this nation: Afghan camel traders, travelling photographers and itinerant pickers; domestics, drovers and Chinese miners; bushrangers, doctors, lonely graders and surveyors.

Our country roads channelled the great Cooee marches of conscripts, farm boys from towns like Gilgandra and Dubbo, to the city camps that would train and ship them to the First World War; they witnessed the return of broken men, setting out for their cramped selections, from the next. During the recessions of two centuries city-dwellers have tramped the highways looking for work. In 1965 Freedom Riders passed by bus through the segregated towns of New South Wales and struck one of the first major blows for

Aboriginal civil rights while, at the same time, the appearance of the shiny government car was still putting fear into the hearts of the Aboriginal families who were to become the Stolen Generations. Roads have paved the way for some of the most significant alterations of our landscape: mines, dams, forestry, and nuclear tests at Maralinga. More recently, they have supported growing populations of grey nomads, backpackers, and jaded city-dwellers on the way to a sea- or tree-change.

But while the Australian road is an unglamorous and ubiquitous backdrop to our lives it would be a mistake to think it has no literary traditions of its own. Look at our fiction and non-fiction and you will soon see that roads are everywhere, a major preoccupation of our writers. Our road stories may not subscribe to the triumphalist grandeur or existential wildness of the American tradition, or share its generic self-awareness (they are often part of other stories rather than 'road stories' *per se*), but they do something different and perhaps more interesting – they seem to always look back over their own shoulders.

In our literature the road appears as something haunted and hyper-alert. Things shimmer, sensations are heightened; relationships become slightly unreal, even characters' relationships with themselves. The unfolding landscape is often intense, mirage-like and perturbing. Even at its sunniest our road writing is on guard; it does not take progress for granted. It is on the lookout for danger, aware of other paths that cross its own. The traveller's mind frequently finds itself in overdrive, dogged by memories or unfulfilled desires. There is a sense in so many of our stories that the road has its own unusual presence. It brings an odd quiddity to the journeys that take place upon it. It stirs things up.

Although the fiction and non-fiction in *The Penguin Book of the Road* has been chosen primarily for its quality, it is my belief that road writing forms a unique and under-appreciated sub-genre of our literature. Each of the writers in this anthology – whether recounting the search for an expedition's lost botanist, the memory of a beloved carriage horse, or the disappearance of a drover down a mysterious 'nowhere road' – is part of an unnoticed tradition that reflects in sharp and fascinating ways on the way we live in this country. Each depicts the road as a place that demands something of us; which, in rushing forward, leads us strangely to the past.

In 'A Bloody Expat,' the opening story in this collection, Robert Hughes passes in and out of consciousness on a highway in the remote Kimberley, the wreck of his car folded around him 'like crude origami'. Among the Aboriginal residents of the Bidyadanga community who stop to assist him is the teenage daughter of Joe Fishhook, first at the scene. Later she claims to have seen a spirit-apparition: 'It was of no particular colour. It looked in all respects human, except that it moved through the bush soundlessly, with a sort of elusive lightness.' According to Hughes, this may have been a feather-foot, an Aboriginal guider of souls that turns up at the site of an impending death. The 65-year-old atheist likes to imagine, in retrospect, that this spirit may not have found him 'entirely unacceptable'.

Why do so many of our road stories hover on the brink of horror and the supernatural? Our most famous ghost tale, John Lang's 'The Ghost Upon the Rail', is after all also a road story in which the phantom of a murdered farmer appears to travellers on a lonely public highway. Even our unofficial national anthem, 'Waltzing Matilda', ends with the spirit of the swagman in a billabong who 'may be heard' by passers-by. In *The Penguin Book of the Road* the threat of violence is just around the corner – it is there in the stories by Robert Drewe, David Malouf, Tara June Winch, Christina Stead,

Dorothy Hewett and Tim Winton and comes to terrible fruition in the autobiographical pieces by Peter Rose and Roberta Sykes. Even when the road holds no potential murderers, rapists or ghastly accidents, the very trees and breezes of the bush seem filled with terrors. A more diffuse sense of anxiety assails the protagonists of stories by Barbara Baynton, and D'Arcy Niland; and echoes, more gently, in Patrick West and Gillian Mears's stories.

The strangest of these stories is William Hay's 'An Australian Rip Van Winkle', which must be one of the most unsettling ghost tales written in this country. At the beginning of last century, the narrator tells us, the South Australian coast was riddled with little 'nowhere roads', early colonial tracks now superseded by a new traffic causeway. It is up one of these eerie white sandy tracks that the stockman Jake rides to spend the night in the house of the dead eccentric Biddy Laurence, who may have been his lover. His reasons for going there remain unclear, though there is some suggestion that he has come to suspect his shady co-executors of stealing, as Biddy's possessions are so often shifted and disturbed. When Jake enters he is attacked – or possessed – by something that sends him staggering, disorientated, into the overgrown garden. The surrounding bush is now brimful of footsteps and presences. He wakes to the 'voice' of the river that fills his head with the line: 'The poetry of the earth is never dead.' He returns home, battered and half-dead, to discover that almost three weeks have passed.

In 'The Search for Mr Cunningham', the explorer Sir Thomas Mitchell's account of the loss of his expedition's botanist in the western New South Wales bush, we can find one origin for the supernatural eeriness that threatens to engulf the road in William Hay's story. Ignoring Mitchell's warnings not to stray from the fragile path the expedition has been making through the mountains, the impulsive Mr Cunningham wanders only metres into the bush – and disappears. Mitchell's painstaking account of trying to find this lost member of his party unwinds with the terrible inevitability of a fairytale. It is a kind of primal scene for the bush vertigo that can overcome us even today as we travel along a lonely track deep into the country. Like the girls at the centre of another of our most iconic stories, *Picnic at Hanging Rock*, Mr Cunningham seems to have been literally swallowed up by the landscape.

One of the traditional folk forms this fear of a hostile landscape has taken is its transformation into dozens of stories of lost children in the bush. It is this fear that D'Arcy Niland plumbs so effectively in this collection's extract from his much-loved novel *The Shiralee*. Four-year-old Buster has been tramping with her resentful father since he separated from her mother. When he tries to abandon her she braves the terrors of the night-time highway to search for him. The pluck and devotion of this tiny girl in facing up to a landscape that can unsettle us even as adults is heartwrenching. Barbara Baynton's strange story, 'A Dreamer', also exploits this fear of the night-time road, as a pregnant woman battles an almost-animate storm-ravaged countryside to see her dying mother. This story has the quality of a nightmare in which our longing for sustaining home comforts, for a mother or father waiting at the end of the road, is horrifyingly prolonged and postponed.

At the same time there is no shortage of real threats on our roads. 'St Valentine's Day', Peter Rose's moving account of driving with his mother to his brother's bedside, is a reminder of our terrible road toll. Peter, the gay, bookish younger brother, learns that Robert, a star football player who has been in a car accident, will spend the rest of his life in a wheelchair.

Our huge, unpopulated landscape and the mobile anonymity of the car also make our roads ideal hunting grounds for the criminally violent. In 'The Bodysurfers' and 'Lone Pine', Robert Drewe and

David Malouf explore our fear of the criminals who move among us. Drewe and Malouf's protagonists face the anxieties of comfortable travellers. Yet the road is most dangerous of all for the least powerful members of our society. In the introduction to her famous novel *The Battlers*, researched by tramping the road with the homeless in the 1930s, Kylie Tennant recalls the callous attitudes of the general public towards her companions, a hostility that borders on violence. In the extract from the first volume of her autobiography *Snake Cradle*, Aboriginal activist and academic Roberta Sykes tells the appalling story of being raped and left for dead on the night of her seventeenth birthday celebrations by a carload of men after being abandoned without a lift at the pictures.

Of course there is another 'poetry of the earth' whispering from the edges of our roads that gives so many of our road stories an extra charge, and that is the history of Aboriginal presence in this land. Thousands of years of paths and tribal boundaries also account for the uncanny sense of being haunted that dogs our travellers on their journeys. Looking back from the twenty-first century, part of the horror of Mr Cunningham's ordeal is that he has become helplessly lost among an invisible skein of indigenous passageways. We do not have to read far between the lines of Mitchell's account to see – as the smoke from the Aboriginals' fires surrounds him – that the fragile track the explorer's party has been making is through an already populated land. As 'country', we now know, this area would have been covered by conceptual 'roads', a complex organic poetry of dreaming tracks.

It was only in the late 1980s, with the publication of Bruce Chatwin's controversial *Songlines*, that the presence and significance of these indigenous 'road stories' exploded into the public consciousness. Nevertheless one can't help wondering if their ancient presence is what speaks so mysteriously through Jake the stockman in William Hay's story. Certainly, 'An Australian Rip Van Winkle' is about a disturbing *something* that lurks among the ruined churches and overgrown orchards left by the early colonists where 'by all human conjecture there is *nothing*, and never was anything of permanent consequence'. Hay's transplanted story is weirder and more horrifying than the northern-hemisphere original because whatever it is that overcomes Jake seems to come from deep within the 'empty' bush, which exudes a pervasive sense of enchantment. Jake experiences so many strange visitations, both human and animal, that this landscape in the middle of 'nowhere' feels busy and supersaturated with threat – as if haunted by hauntedness itself – to the point where the present buckles. This sense is exaggerated by the second story within the story, of a young boy who experiences his own time-slip at the property. It may be a guilty sense of the unacknowledged violence done to Aboriginal culture by the building of roads that fuels our fascination with them as brooding sites of danger. One of the saddest road trips recorded in this country must surely be that of the English linguist R. M. Dixon through north Queensland in the 1960s, which he recounts in *Searching for Aboriginal Languages*; at the end of these humid roads he continually encountered the last ageing speakers of 'language'.

This repressed history of violence may be the 'feather-foot' that stalks the edges of our roads. The writer Ross Gibson makes this claim in *Seven Versions of An Australian Badland*, his meditation on the notorious 'horror stretch' of the Pacific Highway between Rockhampton and Mackay. This section of road is known as a 'badland' because of its myriad unsolved murders and terrible accidents; but it is also the site of unacknowledged massacres of the indigenous population. Gibson claims that areas of unmourned violence attract stories of violence to themselves, because myth steps in to resolve what rational means will not, repeating over and over again the broken and disrupted nature of the land. This sense of unfinished business may be why we are so preoccupied by the killers on our roads: from Ivan Milat, who launched a systematic program to lure and kill backpacking hitchhikers, to Anita Cobby's murderers who struck in the deserted and poorly lit streets of Sydney's western suburbs. Part of the horror and legendary force of these stories is their incompleteness. We wonder, for example, what variety of superhuman strength or persuasion was used by the Victorian-era Gatton killer, who subdued and raped a brother and two sisters on their way to a dance. The broken rail, the empty field, the mutilated carriage horses, the mute bodies – these leave a dreadful space for the imagination that our horror stories probe.

And yet to entertain the possibility, even subconsciously, that the road is pre-owned and resistant to settlement is also to flirt with a terrible sense of loneliness and existential threat. This accounts in part for the great nothingness that thrills at the edges of our road stories and films. Patrick West's 'Nhill' – whose very title suggests emptiness – is a gentle exploration of a middle-class white couple's sense of not belonging to this landscape. Although they travel to the centre of the Little Desert of western Victoria, its 'heart of salt', everything in this gorgeous haze of a story conspires to convey a sense of fragility and unreality. Husband and wife are never entirely sure that they have quite 'left' the desert, since, in an oddly dreamlike detail, their exit seems 'not to have registered' on the carpark's turnstile counter.

This nothingness finds its most disturbing shape in the famous story of the death of Carl Strehlow at Horseshoe Bend, as told here (in abridged form) by his son T. G. H. Strehlow. Forty years earlier, the German Lutheran and his wife had taken over the Hermannsburg Mission north of Alice Springs in an attempt to Christianise the Aranda people of the central Australian desert. When Strehlow became gravely ill with dropsy the church elders in Adelaide quibbled over the cost of sending a car. And so his final odyssey began, a story of tribulation in the desert so excoriating it might have been conceived of by Patrick White.

Grotesquely swollen, barely able to fit into his clothes, Strehlow set out for the south in a dray as friends rallied forces to meet him. Three hundred kilometres later, unable to travel further, he took refuge at the hotel at Horseshoe Bend. Suffering in the stifling heat of his room, and hiding the inevitability of his death from his wife, this devout Christian found himself alone with his God. In a landscape pregnant with the Aranda people's gods and stories, Strehlow came to the terrible conclusion: 'God doesn't help.'

But for many of the writers in this collection the road is also a place of heightened pleasure. The Australian road story is distinguished by a hypnotic and visceral sense of the joys the road offers. In 'Virginity and its Promise', extracted from his novel *Summerland*, Malcolm Knox invokes an almost cellular memory of the most iconic of Australian journeys, the drive through remnant suburban bush to the summer beachhouse. In this case, the journey is also toward adult sexual knowledge. Frank Moorhouse's 'Across the Plains, Over the Mountains, and Down to the Sea' suffuses another coastal road with the sensuous memories of a lost relationship. 'The car sang along the stones,' the narrator tells us, while 'the sticking bitumen was a-kissing our tyres.' The peanut-butter sandwiches picked up from a country store tasted 'as no other sandwiches have ever tasted to me.'

In Helen Garner's 'A Happy Story' a 41-year-old woman discovers the sweet delight of driving her new car around the streets of Melbourne. She has been feeling self-conscious and old next to her teenage daughter but, in the simple act of flipping on the cassette player and turning the car into the grey dusk-light of the city, her heart lifts, and the story turns into a sharp stab of joy. For all its dangers, the road seems to offer women in particular new vistas of freedom and sex. Dorothy Hewett's 'Nullabor Honeymoon', a story of *amour fou* between a woman and her new sailor husband, plays itself out against the vast backcloth of the moonlit desert. For the ideologically sound feminist heroine of 'The Road to Gundagai', taken from Linda Jaivin's comic erotic novel *Eat Me*, pleasure arrives in the shape of rough sex with a truckie beneath Goulburn's kitschy Big Merino. In the extract from Miles Franklin's *My Brilliant Career*, headstrong Sybilla discovers the joys of ditching her male companion and taking the reins of the property's buggy herself.

For the young men in Robert Bropho's 'The Great Journey of the Aboriginal Teenagers' joy arrives in the form of a spree stealing cars and gunning them away from the camps across the desert. For Clive James, growing up in Kogarah, Sydney, in the 1950s, it takes the shape of makeshift billycarts careering through the beachside suburb's sleepy backstreets. Rolf Boldrewood, in 'The Horse You Don't See Now', pays a delightful tribute to his favourite carriage horses, Steamer and Railway. They were 'such a pair as few people were privileged to sit behind,' the author of *Robbery Under Arms* tell us. Their pace was exquisite: 'For four years I enjoyed as much happiness as can be absorbed by mortal horse-owner… they were simply perfect as to style, speed and action. I never was passed, never even challenged, on the road by another pair.'

It is interesting that of all the stories in this collection, Bropho's is the only one that comes close to the American road tradition in which outlaw buddies, doomed to eventual capture, share the existential thrills of freedom and speed. But even when the teenagers drive off-road the police are never far behind. This is also the case in my own story 'Republic of Love', in which Mary the Larrikin recounts her doomed love affair with Ned Kelly. For all his heroic glamour, Kelly has been marked by the law from a young age; he can only truly escape its grip in dreams. Both stories suggest that the freedom of the road is only a temporary illusion. The law's reach stretches far across the continent, to the point of denying citizenship to those who fail to keep to the beaten path.

Because of this our off-road pleasures are often the most intense. Part of the bushranger's appeal as one of our most enduring folk heroes is that he (sometimes she) spurns the road and the authority it embodies. Kelly, roaming the Victorian High Country's Puzzle Ranges, possesses a superior bushcraft that allows him to melt into the bush. His command of the untracked wilderness makes him a kind of white superman, the mythic opposite of lost, pathetic Mr Cunningham. Similarly, it is the Aboriginal teenagers' ingenuity that thrills us as they carve their own route through the desert near the rabbit-proof fence, their epic mid-century journey anticipating the 2001 cult television hit *Bush Mechanics*, in which Warlpiri men perform astonishing feats of feral engineering with clapped-out cars in the Northern Territory desert. This reminds us that Australian road stories often put a high value on ingenuity and making do, perhaps as a reflection of our not-so-distant status as a remote colony. Even Clive James's story plays delightful mock-heroic tribute to this tradition, as the children's billycarts are joined into a makeshift train, babies in the 'chuck-wagon' at the back.

An uncanny, dreamlike beauty imbues the rural backroads of Western Australia in 'July 1921', the extract from Brenda Walker's *The Wing of Night*. Joe, a Light Horseman, makes the long tramp home after surviving an explosion in a sniper's hole at Gallipoli. 'On the road, he floated above himself as the fenceposts drifted by . . . He was light as a fist. His eyes were almost closed. Vast wings seemed to open beside him.' In 'North', the extract from *Dirt Music* in which Fox hitchhikes to the town where his father mined the asbestos that would kill him, Tim Winton's description of the passing landscape of north-Western Australia – its 'gibber plains' and 'late crops that stand brassy in the sun' – is oddly ecstatic. The men who pick up Fox also feel the road in their viscera, smoking monster rollies and stuffing their cavities with opium suppositories as they overtake trucks in 'slipstream blasts'. Yet there is a sense in both Walker and Winton's stories that the road's exaggerated, uncanny radiance is an attempt to fill an aching emptiness. Joe and Fox are hollow men who use the landscape to give shape to what is missing in themselves. Drugged by his companions, Fox experiences the land in his body as a kind of Technicolor harrowing, while Joe tries to put himself back together by concentrating his mind on the smell of water and the rhythm of his footsteps on the road.

It is extraordinary how many of our road stories, like Tara June Winch's 'Territory', in which a girl hitches a lift with a truckie through the Queensland cane fields searching for her father, revolve around the search for lost lovers or parents. While the road in America is celebrated as an escape from family or emotional commitments, the quest to solve family or romantic rifts is a striking feature of our road writing (and also of our road movies such as *True Love and Chaos*, *Mad Max*, even the flamboyant drag extravaganza *The Adventures of Priscilla, Queen of the Desert*.) In part, our geography forces our road stories to turn inward, since our highways have never had the American associations of a better life in the west, circulating instead around the edges of the continent. But as Frank Moorhouse's story suggests there is a more Freudian side to all these backward gazes. As an ex-colony and nation of immigrants our history is recently marked by traumatic separations from lovers, family and homeland. But our emphasis on the domestic, our huddling into the past, and our difficulties in moving forward, may again be symptomatic of a sense of even more profound loss that marks the landscape.

Gillian Mears's elegiac 'The Burial and the Busker', in which a young girl in a country town contemplates the new highway that will resume her friend's plot in the graveyard, is also about loss. Mears's story suggests that our tendency to build highways that allow us to travel faster across the country by turning space into time occurs at the cost of the intensely local, accumulated life of small towns. And yet, as the new highway slowly bears down on the town, 'The Burial and the Busker' also meditates on the way the road's power to obliterate everything before it makes perceptions more radiant. Mears's narrator shores up physical impressions – like the rosellas that 'come shattering' to eat the berries on the graves – against oblivion. 'Everything gets sadder', she writes. 'And almost too clear.'

Of all the stories in this collection, Peter Carey's weird fable 'American Dreams' is perhaps the most self-consciously reflective about what roads mean to us in this country. Along with Linda Jaivin's it is also one of the very few to embrace the kinds of kitschy roadside attraction – the African lion safaris and giant beer bottles and berry farms – that were an iconic joy of a seventies childhood. When a local eccentric builds a perfect scale-model of his town it attracts Americans with cameras and money. But it soon turns out that they expect the townspeople to remain frozen in time, just as they were when their portraits were taken.

Carey's story raises a host of complex questions that hover over this anthology. Is it such a bad thing to be a backwater? What is the cost of turning your home into a tourist attraction? But his fable also works on a national level. Carey seems to agree with the character in Wim Wenders' German road movie, *Im Lauf der Zeit* (*Kings of the Road*), who says that America has 'colonised our subconscious': that the road is defined in the world's dreams as American. So are we driven, his story slyly asks, by the subconscious fear that our own roads are the backroads of the world? Is this part of the odd pathos and sense of unreality that clings to our journeys? And yet – and this is the kicker – if we play up our Australianness for outside eyes, do we risk becoming even less real to ourselves?

The road stories in *The Penguin Book of the Road* are shaped by the road itself, unrolling moment by moment. Their characters' lives are prone to chance, the end of their journeys uncertain. Each minute on the road has the potential to be heaven or hell, a delight or a disaster. This sense is expressed beautifully in Christina Stead's 'The Milk Run'. From a child's point of view, as a bully lurks in the neighbourhood, a dirt road in a new suburb is magnified to an epic scale. The simple act of collecting the milk is terrifying. David Brooks's 'The Line' – in which a sentence from the author's manuscript leaves his desk to tour the night streets of the neighbourhood – makes the road's make-it-up-as-it-goes-along nature playfully explicit. Road stories are always improvised. On the road, every moment of the future is in doubt, teetering between Strehlow's 'God doesn't help' and Helen Garner's '*Habe Dank!*'

It is this unpredictability that makes our road stories so resonant and such an important sub-genre. Literal dispatches from the ground, they take place at the raw edge of life in this country. Because they inhabit the step-by-step *now* they are essentially antiauthoritarian; instead of rehearsing the smug certainties of the national story they put us in a mindset of doubt and revelation. They are also, as Kylie Tennant points out, where we are most likely to encounter people who fail to fit our most self-congratulatory stereotypes.

At the same time, road stories make an extraordinary connection with the landscape which appears alive, radiant, full of possibility, and haunted. Continually forced back on themselves, they carry some of our most profound feelings of joy, sensuality, love and loss. They also remind us of the great crowds who have gone along the road before us: lost botanists, Light Horsemen, and bush mechanics; lovers, urbane gay men, and hitchhiking girls; itinerant horse-stealers, honeymooning brides, and frightened children.

So fasten your seatbelt, and enjoy the ride. While *The Penguin Book of the Road* sets out to include a broad range of different travellers and road trips, it does not offer itself as a definitive historical collection. Instead, it aims to capture something of the feel of the Australian road – sexy, dangerous, nostalgic, harsh, mysterious and unnerving. It aims to rekindle the sense that sometimes strikes us – whether we have just passed the turn-off to the Belanglo State Forest or driven into an eerie haze at the vanishing point between two paddocks – that we are not quite at home.

A BLOODY EXPAT

Robert Hughes

The most extreme change in my life occurred, out of a blue sky, on the 30th of May, 1999, a little short of my sixty-first birthday.

I was in Western Australia, where I had been making a TV series about my native country. I had taken a couple of days off, and chosen to spend them fishing off the shore of a resort named Eco Beach with a friend, Danny O'Sullivan, a professional guide. We went after small offshore tuna, with fly rods, in an open skiff. It had been a wonderful day: fish breaking everywhere, fighting fiercely when hooked, and one – a small bluefin, about twenty pounds – kept to be eaten later with the crew in Broome.

Now, after a nap, I was on my way back to the Northern Highway, which parallels the huge flat biscuit of a coast where the desert breaks off into the Indian Ocean.

After about ten kilometres, the red dirt road from Eco Beach ended in a cattle gate. I stopped short of it, got out of the car, unhooked the latching chain, swung the gate open. I got back in the car, drove through, stopped again, got out, and closed the gate behind me. Then I hopped back in the car again and drove out onto the tar and concrete of the Great Northern Highway, cautiously looking both ways in the bright, almost horizontal evening light. No road trains galloping toward me: nothing except emptiness. I turned left, heading north for Broome, on the left side of the road, as people have in Australia ever since 1815, when its colonial governor, an autocratic laird named Lachlan Macquarie, decreed that Australians must henceforth ride and drive on the same side as people did in his native Scotland.

It was still daylight, but only just. I flipped my lights on.

There was no crash, no impact, no pain. It was as though nothing had happened. I just drove off the edge of the world, feeling nothing.

I do not know how fast I was going.

I am not a fast driver, or in any way a daring one. Driving has never been second nature to me. I am pawky, old-maidish, behind the wheel. But I collided, head-on, with another car, a Holden Commodore with two people in the front seat and one in the back. It was dusk, about 6:30 p.m. This was the first auto accident I ever had in my life, and I retain absolutely no memory of it. Try as I may, I can dredge nothing up, not even the memory of fear. The slate is wiped clean, as by a damp rag.

I was probably on the wrong (that is, the right-hand) side of the road, over the yellow line – though not very far over. I say 'probably' because, at my trial a year later, the magistrate did not find that there was enough evidence to prove, beyond reasonable doubt, that I had been. The Commodore was coming on at some 90 m.p.h. (144 k.p.h.), possibly more. I was approaching it at about 50 m.p.h. (80 k.p.h.) Things happen very quickly when two cars have a closing speed of more than 130 m.p.h. (209 k.p.h.) It only takes a second for them to get seventy feet closer to one another. No matter how hard you hit the brakes, there isn't much you can do.

We ploughed straight into one another, Commodore registered 7EX 954 into Nissan Pulsar registered 9YR 650: two red cars in the desert, driver's side to driver's side, right headlamp to right head-lamp. I have no memory of this. From the moment of impact for weeks to come, I would have no short-term memory of anything. All I know about the actual collision, until after almost a year, when I saw the remains of my rented car in a junkyard in Broome, is what I was told by others.

The other car spun off the highway, skidded down a shallow dirt slope, and ended up half-hidden in the low desert scrub. Its three occupants were injured, two not seriously. Darren William Kelly, thirty-two, the driver, had just come off a stint working on a fishing boat and was heading south to Port Hedland to find any work he could get. He had a broken tibia. Colin Craig Bowe, thirty-six, a builder's labourer, was riding in the front seat and sustained a broken ankle. Darryn George Bennett, twenty-four, had been working as a deckhand on the same boat as Kelly, the *True Blue*. Kelly and Bowe were mates; they had known each other for two years. Neither had known Bennett before. He had heard they were driving south to Port Hedland, and he asked for a ride. He was a young itinerant worker in his mid-twenties, whose main skill was bricklaying.

Their encounter with the world of writing only added to their misfortunes. All three were addicts and at least two were part-time drug dealers. At the moment of the crash, Bennett, in the back-seat, was rolling a 'cone' of marijuana, a joint. It may or may not have been the first one to be smoked on what was meant to be a thousand-kilometre drive south.

In any case, they had things in common. They had all done jail time. They were young working-class men living now on that side of the law, now on this: sometimes feral, sometimes bewildered, seldom knowing what the next month, let alone the next birthday, would bring.

Not long after he had recovered from the injuries of the collision, Bennett tried to tear the face off an enemy in a bar with a broken bottle. Bowe, as soon as his injuries had healed, attempted an armed robbery, but was arrested, tried, and sentenced to ten years in jail.

Bennett was by far the worst hurt of the three. The impact catapulted him forward against the restraint of the seat belt and gave him a perforated bowel. He had no skeletal damage. All three of them were able to struggle out of the wreck of the Commodore, which had not rolled over. The effort of doing so was agonising for Bennett, who collapsed on the verge of the road, his guts flooded with pain.

If the Commodore was badly smashed up, my Nissan Pulsar was an inchoate mass of red metal and broken glass, barely recognisable as having once been a car. When at last I saw it in Broome on the eve of my trial, eleven months later, I couldn't see how a cockroach could have survived that wreck, let alone a human being.

The car had telescoped. The driver's seat had slammed forward, pinning me against the steering wheel, which was twisted out of shape by the impact of my body, nearly impaling me on the steering column. Much of the driver's side of the Pulsar's body had been ripped away, whether by the initial impact or, later, by the hydraulic tools used by the fire brigade and ambulance crew in their long struggle to free me from the wreckage. It looked like a half-car. It was as though the fat, giant foot of God from the old *Monty Python* graphics had stamped on it and ground it into the concrete. Later, I would make derogatory noises about 'that piece of Jap shit' I'd been driving. I was wrong, of course. The damage had saved my life: the gradual collapse and telescoping of the Nissan's body, compressed into milliseconds, had absorbed and dissipated far more of the impact energy than a more rigid frame could have done.

Now it was folded around me like crude origami. I could scarcely move a finger. Trapped, intermittently conscious, deep in shock and bloodier than Banquo, I had only the vaguest notion of what had happened to me. Whatever it might have been, it was far beyond my experience. I did not recognise my own injuries, and had no idea how bad they were. As it turned out, they were bad enough. Under extreme impact, bones may not break neatly. They can explode into fragments, like a cookie hit by a hammer, and that's what happened to several of mine.

The catalogue of trauma turned out to be long. Most of it was concentrated on the right-hand side of my body – the side that bore the brunt of the collision. As the front of the Nissan collapsed, my right foot was forced through the floor and doubled underneath me; hours later, when my rescuers were at last able to get a partial glimpse of it, they thought the whole foot had been sheared off at the ankle. The chief leg bones below my right knee, the tibia and the fibula, were broken into five pieces. The knee structure was more or less intact, but my right femur, or thigh bone, was broken twice, and the ball joint that connected it to my hip was damaged. Four ribs on my right side had snapped and their sharp ends had driven through the tissue of my lungs, lacerating them and causing pneumothorax, a deflation of the lungs and the dangerous escape of air into the chest cavity. My right collarbone and my sternum were broken. The once rigid frame of my chest had turned wobbly, its structural integrity gone, like a crushed birdcage. My right arm was a wreck – the elbow joint had taken some of the direct impact, and its bones were now a mosaic of breakages. But I am left-handed, and the left arm was in better shape, except for the hand, which had been (in the expressive technical term used by doctors) 'de-gloved', stripped of its skin and much of the muscular structure around the thumb.

But I had been lucky. Almost all the damage was skeletal. The internal soft tissues, liver, spleen, heart, were undamaged, or at worst merely bruised and shocked. My brain was intact – although it wasn't working very well – and the most important part of my bone structure, the spine, was untouched.

That was a near miracle. Spines go out of service all too easily. The merest hairline crack in the spine can turn a healthy, reasonably athletic man into a paralysed cripple: this is what happened to poor Christopher Reeve, the former Superman, in a fall from a horse, and it eventually killed him. The idea of being what specialists laconically call a 'high quad' – paraplegic from the neck down, unable even to write your own end by loading a shotgun and sticking its muzzle in your mouth – has always appalled me.

But I wasn't thinking clearly enough to be afraid of that. What I was afraid of, and mortally, was burning to death. Some are afraid of heights, others of rats, or mad dogs, or of death by drowning. My especial terror is fire, and now I realised that my nostrils were full of the banal stench of gasoline. Somewhere in the Nissan a line had ruptured. I could not move. I could only wait. There seemed to be little point in praying; in any case, there is no entity I believe in enough to pray to. Samuel Johnson once said that the prospect of being hanged concentrates a man's mind wonderfully. The prospect, extended over hours, of dying in a gasoline fireball does much the same. It dissolves your more commonplace troubles – money, divorce, the difficulty of writing – and shows you what you really want to use your life for.

At one point I saw Death. He was sitting at a desk, like a banker. He made no gesture, but he opened his mouth and I looked right down his throat, which distended to become a tunnel: the *bocca d'inferno* of old Christian art. He expected me to yield, to go in. This filled me with abhorrence, a hatred of nonbeing. Not fear, exactly: more like passionate revolt. In that moment I realised that there is nothing whatever outside of the life we have; that the 'meaning of life' is nothing other than life itself, obstinately asserting itself against emptiness and nullity. Life was so powerful, so demanding, and in my concussion and delirium, even as my systems were shutting down, I wanted it so much. Whatever this was, it was nothing like the nice, uplifting kind of near-death experience that religious writers, particularly those of an American-style fundamentalist bent, like to effuse about. Perhaps the simple truth is that, near death, you have visions and hallucinations of what most preoccupies you in life. I am a sceptic to whom the idea that a benign God created us and watches over us is something between a fairy story and a bad joke. People of a religious bent, however, are apt under such conditions to see the familiar kitsch of near-death experience – the tunnel of white light with Jesus at the end, as featured in the uplifting accounts of a score of American Kmart mystics. Jesus must have been busy with them when my time came: he didn't show. There was, as far as I could tell, absolutely nothing on the other side.

So I was stuck; unable to move, and no more than intermittently conscious. Later, Kelly would testify that despite the injury to his leg he was able to make his way to my car and ask me what had happened; that I asked him the same question, and said, 'I'm sorry, mate, I'm terribly sorry, I'm not sure if I fell asleep.' It has always been my habit to apologise first and ask questions later, and Sgt. Matt Turner, the Broome officer who was the first policeman at the scene, would later recount that I showed an almost silly degree of courtesy as rescue workers tried to extract me from the wreck, apologising again and again for the inconvenience I was causing him and them.

It would be some hours before these rescuers got to the crash site. The person who set the machinery of rescue going had already been there. He was a middle-aged Aborigine named, rather fittingly, Joe Fishhook. He and his family lived nearby, at an Aboriginal settlement not far from Eco Beach named Bidyadanga. He was driving south in his truck, with his wife, Angie Wilridge, and their teenage daughter Ruth, along with a few members of their extended family, when the Commodore overtook them, zooming past at what he guessed to be about a hundred miles an hour. (Later, a police observer at the scene of the crash looked at the speedometer of the Commodore and saw that the needle was stuck by the collision impact at 150 k.p.h.)

Shortly afterward Fishhook came upon the wreck and saw the remains of my Pulsar straddling the centre line of the highway. He stopped, got out, and tried but failed to free me from the wreck. I was crushed into it, like a sardine in a can squashed by a hammer. Fishhook gingerly checked that I was still breathing, but he couldn't find any document that identified me. He checked the back of the Pulsar – the hatch door, at least, opened – and looked inside the cooler, finding the little tuna. Something snagged his attention. The fish was fresh, newly caught, but there was no tackle in the car. So I must have been fishing with someone else's gear. That meant a professional guide. And how many such pros were there on this stretch of coast? Only one that Fishhook knew of – Danny O'Sullivan, a few kilometres away at Eco Beach, which was also where the nearest phone was.

After this excellent deduction, leaving his wife and daughter at the wreck, Fishhook spun a U-turn and drove back to the Eco turnoff. Twenty minutes later, burning red gravel all the way, he found Danny in the resort bar. Did he have a client who was taking a little bluefin home to Broome? Sure, said Danny: my mate Bob

Hughes. Well, said Joey Fishhook equably, you better get up the road quick smart: he's wrecked on the highway, he's in deep shit, your mate is.

Danny rang the Broome police. He rang the Broome hospital. He sprinted downstairs, with Joey Fishhook close behind him. The two men took off in their cars, Danny accompanied by a former ambulance officer who now worked at the Eco Beach resort, Lorraine Lee. When the heat is on, Danny has a foot on the accelerator heavier than a rhino's, and he reached the crash site in almost no time at all, by 6:45 p.m. He checked me out. I was as white as dirty skim milk and my breathing was shallow; I was sliding into a coma. 'Bob, Bob mate, come on, bastard, wake up.' I could hear him, but he seemed very far away, as though we were in mutually distant rooms of a large, echoing house.

Lorraine Lee had brought some towels, with which she stanched the flow of blood from my head and left hand. I kept straining to hear Danny, but the effort was frustrated by waves of pain from my collarbone. Danny has a hand tough enough to strangle a crocodile. Fishing with him in the past, I have seen him reach lightning fast into a small line of breaking water and seize a passing shovelnose shark by the tail, hoicking it out of the wave with a feral grin of pleasure. Unfortunately, he now had my shoulder in a vice-like grip. It was meant to be comradely and reassuring, but he was squeezing broken bone. 'You're going to be fine, mate,' he was saying encouragingly. The pain was taking me over. 'Oh Danny,' I whined, 'it hurts, it hurts so much, it's really bad, make it stop.' He kept squeezing the broken bone, sending bolts of fresh anguish through me. 'She'll be right, cobber,' he said. 'She's going to be right as rain. Just hang in there.' Squeeze from him, squawk from me. It took a few minutes to get cause and effect straightened out.

Then something passed between us that may never have

happened; I am still not sure. I kept passing out and waking woozily up, and whenever I surfaced into consciousness I could still smell the petrol, that sickly smell building up to finish me off with one spark. I didn't want to die at all, but most of all I didn't want to die that way. I thought Danny owned a .38, and I implored him to finish me off if the car blew. 'Just kill me,' I kept saying, or thought I did. 'Just take me out, one shot, you know what to do.' And he, I think, swore that he would. But I do not know, and, looking back on it, I realise that I had asked the morally impossible of my friend, so perhaps I had never really asked it at all. I don't know, and on a very deep level I remain uncertain and afraid to ask. But the desire to die before I could burn was very strong.

The absurdity made me sick. I thought of dying without ever seeing my sweetheart Doris again, never feeling that silky skin or hearing that soft voice in my ear. I had been through so many erotic miseries and matrimonial weirdnesses to reach Doris, the first woman ever to make me completely happy – and now it seemed that I would never revisit the paradise of the senses and the ecstasy of mutual trust to which she had granted me access. Instead there would be the opposite of paradise. It wasn't dying as such that I feared, but dying in a hot blast, the air sucked out of my lungs, strangling on flame inside an uprushing column of unbearable heat: everything the Jesuits had told me about the crackling and eternal terrors of Hell now came back, across a chasm of fifty years. I could envision this. It would look like one of the Limbourg brothers' illustrations to the *Très Riches Heures du Duc de Berry* – the picture of Satan bound down on a fiery grid, exhaling a spiral of helpless little burned souls into the air.

But the fire didn't come. Neither did the fire brigade, nor the police, nor an ambulance. Some passing traffic stopped, including a semitrailer truck. Quite an array of vehicles was beginning to build up to the north and south of my Nissan, and these included some cars and four-wheel-drive utes driven by Aborigines. It being Friday night, there was meant to be a dance at the Bidyadanga settlement, and by twos and threes a curious group of Aborigines began to accumulate by the wreck.

They were behind me, so I couldn't see them. I could hear them, though: a thin chanting, to the beat of handclaps, to which I could attach no meaning. Later I was told that the Aborigines had assembled in a half-circle behind my car, and were trying to sing me back to life. It must have seemed unlikely that they would succeed, but one person who was convinced they would was Joey Fishhook's teenage daughter. She later said she saw what she stubbornly insisted was a spirit-apparition, not far from the Nissan. It was of no particular colour. It looked in all respects human, except that it moved through the bush soundlessly, with a sort of elusive lightness.

This creature, or entity, is known to Aborigines as a featherfoot. It is not easy to say what a feather-foot is, or what it does. It is definitely not an animal spirit. It is a native equivalent of the Greek manifestation of Hermes as an emissary of Hades, in his role as Hermes Psychopompos, the 'guider of souls'. It is neither hostile nor friendly: it just turns up at the site of an impending or possible death, and passes judgment on the soul and its prospects of survival in further incarnations. I didn't see it, of course; even if it had been there, my vision was too blurred to see anything quick moving, and I couldn't turn my head. But I like to think that perhaps it was a feather-foot, and that it had not found me altogether unacceptable.

Whether it could boast a real feather-foot or not, the Bidyadanga settlement did have its own nurse, a Filipina Catholic religious sister named Juliana Custodio. As soon as word about the collision reached her at Bidyadanga, she drove to the site to see if there was anything she could do. In the event, there wasn't much. She found me, according to the police report, 'trapped in the car, awake and talking, asking about his fish, swearing with the pain and then apologising. Juliana said, "He was such a gentleman!" She saw that his hip and chest bones were out of alignment . . . he was sweating and cold but his heart and pulse rate were very strong and his blood pressure normal.'

Sister Juliana did her best to get a saline IV into one of my veins, but they had collapsed. She wiped off the worst of the blood and applied some dressings to my head wounds. I kept sliding into patches of insensibility and she struggled to keep me awake, not with drugs, but simply by talking to me. Our conversation can't have kept my wandering attention, because I soon gave up on it and started, as I was told later, to count aloud, backward from a hundred, one number slurring into the next – 'forry-five, forry-four, forry-three . . .' Then I would lose track and have to start again, at a hundred. I thought I was trying to stay conscious, but Sister Juliana thought I was counting off my last moments; bystanders saw this good and devoted woman weeping with pity and frustration. Maybe we were both right. Later she would ask the Catholic priest at Bidyadanga, Father Patrick da Silva, to say a Mass for my recovery. 'Juliana rang the hospital in Perth a few times during his stay,' the police report concludes, 'and followed his progress with interest. She kept saying, "He was such a gentleman!"'

Meanwhile, a sea fog had rolled in from the Indian Ocean, slowing the sparse traffic to a crawl. It must have been two hours after the crash, close to nine o'clock, when a rescue team of volunteers from the Broome Fire Brigade at last reached the spot. Its men tugged and twisted at the door, but it would hardly budge. Eventually, they brought out the drastic solution to crushed car

bodies – the so-called Jaws of Life, a massive pair of shears pow-
ered by hydraulic pressure. I was only dimly aware of this tool as
it chomped through the Pulsar; I felt apprehensive but curiously
distant as its blades groaned against the metal. Would they slip and
chew my leg off? I didn't much care; all I wanted was to be out of
the danger of fire, away from the reek of gasoline. I was vaguely
aware of skilled hands wiggling the lower parts of my legs, working
them free. I felt, rather than heard, a resonant crunch deep down
in my frame, at some level of my skeleton that had never been
disturbed before, like the deep crack of an extracted tooth breaking free from the jawbone, as the shears bit off the spokes of the
steering wheel whose rim was crushed into my thorax. The wheel
was lifted free; one of the firemen tossed it in the back of the car,
where I would find it nearly a year later. My whole chest felt light
and empty now that the pressure was off. There was surprisingly
little pain in it: this was due to shock, of course. Concerned faces
were all around me. 'I'm sorry about this,' I kept babbling. 'I'm sorry
to be so much trouble.' 'You'll be right, mate,' one of the firemen kept
saying. 'We'll have you out of this in two ticks.' And they did, to my
eternal gratitude. I felt a delirious sensation of lightness as I was
lifted clear of the car. They slid a stretcher under me. My head felt
swollen on its feeble stalk of a neck, lolling like a melon. Was my
neck broken? I couldn't frame the words of the question. At least
I knew I could see and feel, and was alive. Luminescence was all
around me: flashing, stuttering lights, red and orange punctuated
by magnesium flashes, burning in haloes through the fog. In their
intermittent flare I saw the face of Danny O'Sullivan, bending over
me. His mouth turned down hideously – no, it was upside down,
so he must be smiling.

'You'd have to be the toughest old bastard I know, cobber,' he
said encouragingly.

Oh no, Danny, I wanted to say; you know dozens of guys who are tougher than me; dear God, I'm old and fat and I'm not going to last it through. 'No, no, bullshit,' I managed to croak.

Danny reflected for a moment. 'Ah well,' he conceded, 'you'd have to be the toughest old art critic, anyway.'

That'll do for me, I thought, and promptly swooned, like some crinolined Virginian lady in a novel. The stretcher locked onto its rails in the ambulance; it slid in with a clunk, the door slammed, and the medicos bent over me. I would not wake up for several weeks.

The first doctor to reach me from Broome had been Dr Barbara Jarad, who was on call for the Aboriginal Medical Services at the Broome hospital that night. She had set off with the police in what she laughingly called 'a high-speed pursuit vehicle' – creeping along, because of the fog, at 60 k.p.h. She talked on the police radio with Sister Juliana, who said she'd had difficulty getting a needle into me to administer saline. My veins are weak and recessive; under shock, they become almost impossible to find, rolling away from the needle. In the ambulance, Dr Jarad got a saline needle in my arm, but on the road it ceased to work long before we reached the Broome hospital; I wasn't tied down properly and the rolling of my body and the jolts of the vehicle kept pulling the needle out of the vein. I kept talking, not very lucidly; I gave the doctor my name and a few other details, but told her I had been born in 1995. It's normal procedure to keep a trauma patient talking if you can, so that you can easily tell if he passes out. At the hospital the medical head, Dr Tony Franklin, got another saline feed in my other arm, and Dr Jarad did what she called a cut-down on my left, intact ankle, opening up the skin and flesh with a scalpel to expose a vein; not the easiest of manoeuvres with a fleshy, overweight subject like myself.

It was now somewhat past midnight, almost six hours since the crash. The Broome hospital had been on the radio to the Flying Doctor Service. It could fly me more than 1600 kilometres south to Perth, the capital of Western Australia, which had a bigger hospital than Broome's – one that included an Intensive Care Unit.

And intensive care was what I was going to need. The doctors in Perth had me on the operating table for thirteen hours straight and, I was told much later, they nearly lost me several times. Their work was extraordinary. All the odds, I take it, were against my survival, and without these doctors and the immense devotion and skill of their work I could not possibly have survived. I ended up in semi-stable condition, with tubes running in and out of me, and a ventilator doing my breathing.

I was in intensive care for five weeks, in a semiconscious delirium, while the doctors and nurses of Royal Perth Hospital laboured to put me together and bring me back, detail by detail, to life. I don't know that I'd recommend to the unwary foreigner that he or she ought to live in Western Australia. But I do know that, if one has the misfortune to undergo a near-fatal car smash, Western Australia – and, specifically, the Royal Perth Hospital – is an extremely good place to be.

From *Things I Didn't Know* (2006)

THE GREAT JOURNEY OF THE ABORIGINAL TEENAGERS

Robert Bropho

Robert Bropho tape-recorded the story 'The Great Journey of the Aboriginal Teenagers' for his granddaughter, Dotty; a transcription of that tape is reproduced here.

The days of old, back there in the yesterdays, in the past . . . for us, Aboriginal teenagers then, in the fifties, in the late forties, up into the early sixties . . . back there in the past.

Today is the closing stage of the day . . . it's eight o'clock p.m. in the evening, twenty-third of the first month of nineteen hundred and eighty-five. I decided to make this tape in the darkness, in the quietness of the evening. I'd like to talk about us, the teenagers, the Aboriginal teenagers . . . then . . . in the days back there in the past. Of what we encountered and what we went through, being teenagers.

My family was living in camp life . . . it was really bad in them days for us. The teenagers today, they're of a different generation . . . white and black, they songs and musics and they beats of today is entirely different, it's fastened up. They in a different time and age now. But for us it was really rotten, really bad. We used to be bored with ourselves, nothing to do, no work. There was hardly any social services around in them days for us, the teenagers then. If we found ourselves in a starving situation, we'd have to go and steal. Oranges, fowls from the white man's fowl pens, this is after hours in the darkness. Steal bread, milk, we had to do it to survive. There is many times that we sat around the campfires, where our camps was – in the scrub, in the black, dirty filthy sand. Dry. When the east wind would blow the dust, the black dust from the sand would hit our eyes and out of that would come sore eyes, watery, red, sore and overnight the matter would build up and your eyelashes would clamp together. We'd be drinking bitter tea . . . if we had no tea we'd burn sugar till it's brown in a spoon and then put it in the boiling water and drink that.

It was idleness then for us, there was nothing for us going. That then caused us to do what we did then, to go around stealing. It got that bad that we used to get in mobs and go. One such occasion I'd like to talk about now is . . . it's a big great journey of ours which ended in disaster for us. The long arm of the white man's law, elastic law that stretched so far across the breadth and length of this country – grabbing up and snabbling up Aboriginal people who put their foot wrong in the eyes of the white man's law, the Ten Commandments.

Anyway, the great journey started off with us pinching an old Vanguard van and doing a real tour of the metropolitan area after hours, early hours of the morning. Breaking into pubs, stealing large quantities of whisky and rum, beer and wine, all kinds, and barrels of wine and picking up money if we could out of the tills. On this occasion we took all this stuff. The strangest part of it all is I was senseless drunk to some extent, before we started off on this thing and all through this breaking and entry for all this white man's spirits – which is the wine and things – I slept right through

17

it until I woke up in the morning surrounded in the back of the van with bottles of wine and beer of all kinds all around me . . . and cigarettes and things. When I became wide awake we was parked in the scrub. All my mates was with me – William Bodney, Man Mippy, Ted Bropho (Gubbi's his Aboriginal name), and Donald Wallam and his brother, the one that's noortch, dead now, who's laying in the South Guildford Cemetery who died young, twenty-eight. Anyway, the police got the wind of it that we might have been connected with the crime. So we said (this is at the Lockridge-Eden Hill area now where the camps was) 'Oh well, we'll give them a run for their money now.'

So we waited till the late hours of the night, in the darkness. Just before twelve o'clock we drove the van down to Bassendean station and abandoned it there and then got onto the station and under the darkness got onto the train and went down to the East Perth area where the line branches out and goes to Bunbury. We waited for the goods train to come then. We had a bit of swags rolled up, a few rugs with a bit of rope tied around it. We made some sort of a shape of a handle with the rope, chucked it over our shoulders so it'd give us two free hands and two free legs and free movements of the body when the train'd come. Anyway, the goods train rolled up, with all the coal trucks, pulling the coal trucks to go down to Brunswick Junction (the junction that's about seventeen miles out of Bunbury) and there the train would automatically change lines and go back through to Collie. We all boarded the train, climbed along and got into one of the empty train trucks, made our beds down and laid down and went to sleep, for some part of the journey right down through to Brunswick Junction . . . arriving down there in the early hours of the morning before daybreak.

We went up into the hills to my auntie's place . . . and had something to eat very early and went back further up on the high points of the hills so that we could get a good view of all around the flat lands. We knew the cops'd be after us. Yes, end of the day we seen them coming to the camp, to Donald Alfred Wallam's camp, to his mother's camp, who was alive then, his father. So we went down and asked after they (the cops) left and they said 'Yes, they came looking for youse.' So we decided to stick to the hills and the valleys. We walked from Roelands right back along the scrub, under the cover of the scrubs, and waited on the Collie line at a big hill and the train came. It was coming up the hill at a slow pace to climb the hills, and we runned along the side. Each and every one of us we knew exactly what we had to do, we was experts in jumping trains – we could jump onto a moving train, we could jump off a moving train – that's the hardships of being born what you are, in poverty. Anyway, we rode the train through to Collie, arriving there still under darkness, and we decided to steal a car from there.

The car we picked was a Holden ute. We got onto that, and went right through Darkan, through Williams, right down to Pingelly. My brother who's dead now was living then, was working for the PWD, the water supply, down at Pingelly. He got the job through an office in Perth here and was stationed down there. We called on him early in the morning, got some food and than had a feed. Went up to the bush and hid until darkness – we always travelled under cover of darkness, that was our protection, that was our strategy that we used . . . travelling through Corrigin, right through to Bruce Rock. Arriving there, Bruce Rock, still under darkness and seeing Bruce Rock Co-op was there, we all decided to go in there and store up with whatever food we could snabble up from the supermarket. It was our choice to pick what we wanted. We got into the place there and the first thing we looked for was torches. Everyone had a little torch, and it was strange . . . the bloke who was left outside to watch, to keep nick and see if anybody was coming, he told us after that, he said 'You was all like . . . you could see all little lights walking around in the darkness, in the darkness of the supermarket.' So we got tins of meat, and fruit, and smokes and things, and cool drinks and cordial and water bags, and we dumped them in the ute, loaded up and went through. We had to pass through Merredin before the daybreak.

We moved along very quickly and pulled right off the road down from Bulla Bulling at the siding just down from Southern Cross, and we got into the bush there. We decided to lay off all day, playing two ups for cigarettes, just lazing around in the scrub there. We was well hidden off the main highway. When it was time to go we decided that we must leave now and try to get along . . . it was getting near sunset. Just after dark started to fall we found that we had a flat tyre and no spare, so we had to abandon the ute there. We rolled up a few of our belongings and a bit of tucker and we decided to Shank's pony – that means walk – along the line, we wouldn't hitchhike on the road. We walked up to Bulla Bulling siding. We arrived there and were sitting down in the darkness, spelling ourself waiting for a goods train to come. Yes, we could hear it coming, from the Merredin area. They had steam engines then, the whistle blowing, you could hear 'em coming from a long way. Anyway, when it arrived at Bulla Bulling it wasn't going to stop, it slowed down to pass through there. So what we had to do was run along the side at the speed of the train, which wasn't travelling too fast, and board the train. To board a running train you must pick where the joining of the empty rail cars are 'cos there's always a foothold there and a handhold. That's the way you board a train. But you don't abandon a moving train from that position because it's pretty dangerous between the trucks. You must alight or jump from the centre of the train trucks when you're getting off a moving train and always fall away from the train. Anyway, we arrived in Kalgoorlie early in the morning just before sunrise. We didn't ride the goods right into Kalgoorlie, we waited until it slowed down coming into town and then we jumped from the moving train on different sides. And (when you do something like that) always explain where you're gonna head for, where you're gonna meet. That's the main thing because if you get split up then you know exactly where everybody's gonna meet.

We got off the train and was all standing together in the scrub deciding what to do and we could see this smoke rising a little way down the line, away from the line. We went down and it was an old Aboriginal man and his wife sitting down there. They had a fire going and was just finished cooking a damper in there and had a black billy of tea. So we walked up to the camp. Straightaway they offered us a drink of tea and a piece of damper each. We sat down for a while talking to them and then we decided to move further back into the scrub and wait for the cover of darkness again. So this time . . . it was a big town, Kalgoorlie then, a fairly sized big town . . . so we decided to send two people down to search for a car. The persons that had to go down was Man Mippy because he was the driver, experienced driver, and another physically fit young bloke with him, Donald Wallam's brother. So they went down and we sat and wait. After a while we could hear a lot of bloody shouting going on and cars whizzing up and down there. Someone had surprised these two fellows (Man Mippy and Donald Wallam's brother) who were trying to steal his car, and they ran up the lane, they got away from him. While the police was looking for them this end of the laneway they was further up. They went right up the top on the other side and pinched a car up there, drove back down, picked us up and we headed north from Kalgoorlie, past Broad Arrow. We had to move fast to get to Menzies because the daybreak was getting close. We

21

decided that we'd pull right away from Menzies out in the scrub and wait there until darkness again so that we could go down and see if we could pinch a bit of petrol. So we hid the car.

Through the day we was, we got on a high point east of Menzies so we could see down. We could see the road coming in from Kalgoorlie, we could see it going out towards Leonora. So we waited there, the pinpoint we could see all the movements of the trucks and things, and cars down in the town. We had binoculars that we pinched – and that helped a little bit so that it would give us the distance away and we could see things from a long distance. Anyway when night fell we went down and found a depot. We got in there and there's drums of petrol up on these stands. So we filled the car up, filled the small drums of petrol and put them in the car and then we headed for . . . Wiluna now . . . we went through Katherine Valley. That's a little place but it's long-gone now, it's closed down. We passed through there and we got to Wiluna. Again, we pulled off the road before we got to the town and waited. And we cased that joint again and we seen a surveyor's truck – we didn't know it then, but it was a half-ton truck – seen it parked, the truck in the yard. So we decided we would visit that place under cover of darkness and try and get that, to give us two – a half-ton International truck and we had the ute then, the ute from Kalgoorlie. And anyway, we succeeded in getting that half-ton truck, we loaded that up also with a forty-four gallon drum of petrol. And then we was looking for a rabbit-proof fence ran through Yandl station heading north – it's supposed to go right up to Port Hedland.

We got on the rabbit-proof fence and we followed it through, we went through Yandl station and Roy Hill and Bonny Downs. And there was many times we got bogged in creek beds. If the Holden ute got bogged and the half-ton International truck was stronger than that and would get through the bogs, we'd have to unload everything, pull that (the ute) out. We'd go on to the next creek bed, we'd get bogged again. It was a full day going along like that. We'd come to a big water tank where the windmill was – where the sheep's supposed to come – and it was really stinking hot. And in this International truck that we stole there was one of those long binoculars like those olden day pirates put out . . . right out. So we got up on the windmill then, we sent one bloke up there to keep nick from the top of the windmill and we give him this long spy-glass and he could see right back miles down the track where we'd been, and right ahead. He'd be scanning the area for dust – dust was sign of movement, whether it be cattle, kangaroos or cars or whatever – while the rest of us stripped off and had a swim in the tank. After having a swim we decided that we'd move along now and find a camping spot. So we drove along as fast as we could, we got a flat plain where all was hard clay, but dusty. And the boys started to have a bit of fun with the half-ton truck and the Holden ute, zigzagging through the trees and making the dust rise. We did this for at least an hour or so, having a bit of fun, and then we went right along. We came about sundown to this spot where all the ghost gums was, flat country . . . and the place was full with kangaroos. So we decided to camp there.

We sent the Holden ute around, chasing the kangaroos around and they knocked one over, brought it back and we skinned that and we ate a meal of kangaroo and some dry biscuits and things. We all bedded down. We made a big fire and let the coals die down so that there wouldn't be no light. We thought it'd be safe, that far out. Plus we could see any lights coming if any cars were coming along the fence where we came, or if there was cops looking for us, trailing us. We was all sitting down around the coals of the fire, talking and planning out . . . and talking about where we came from and how far we travelled and what we did. But you must bear in mind that we had no drink, we wouldn't touch the drink. We could hear these camel noises in the distance . . . and I know from experience of my Dad and what he's told me about camels, if a camel knocks you down he'll lay on you until you stink. So everybody started to get a bit scared and so they all decided to climb up on the half-ton truck and all squeeze in there. Made beds and laid down there.

We got up the next morning and we headed for Port Hedland. We got so many miles out, travelling in the dark, and we took a chance on getting bogged and running into difficulties through the night. We drove for endless hours and we lay down and we went to sleep. And it was the early hours of the bloody morning and we didn't know we was close to the gravel road, where the rabbit proof fence come in. And the Holden ute was hidden out of sight but the International truck, half-ton truck, was in sight. And one white bloke going into Port Hedland seen it. He didn't come near us, he went and told the bloody cops. Anyway, this was unknowns to us, the fugitives. We was laying there sleeping and I came out of my sleep and I could hear this 'Bang!' . . . this bloody rifle shooting. When I woke up there was a cop standing there pointing a rifle at me. 'Don't move,' he said, 'you black bastard. You the bastards we've been looking for.' I could hear the rifles going off. 'Bang!' getting further and further into the distance. They were chasing Johnny Wallam and Donald through the spinifex. They came out of their sleeps seconds before the police got out of their cars and they started running across this red sand with the spinifex, the spinifex was all this sharp grass in different spots but not all over the ground and they never had time to get their shoes and they bloody runned. They runned so many miles, so what the bloody cops went and done they brought in some black trackers . . . and those buggers was cantering along on bloody horses tracking Johnny Wallam and Donald, followed by cops on horses until they found 'em. By the time they found 'em I was already taken into custody, put into the Port Hedland lockup. Man Mippy was with me and William Bodney. Then they brought in Donald and Johnny handcuffed, blisters all on their toes and on their heels and soles of their feet from this hot sand. Gubbi (my brother Ted) was already in there with us.

Anyway they kept us there for days on end until the magistrate came, the visiting magistrate. In the meantime they had us out working like bloody horses – cleaning all around the gaol, outside, cleaning around the sergeant's house – but they gave us freedom, they wasn't standing over us watching us. They'd just open the doors up and say 'Alright, work now today.' When it was getting near twelve o'clock they'd call us back, we'd go in and leave the doors open. We'd go in and have something to eat, the sergeant's wife used to cook it – a very thin meal. Same applied to suppertime and then they'd lock us up for the night.

It went on for a while there and we decided that we'd make a break from there. We opened the side gate with a knife, got out, went down to the bloody jetties. Before going to the jetty we broke into the bloody pub and got some beer and wine. We'd decided 'Okay we'll have a bloody . . . we'll have a spree up now' (that means have a good time while it lasts). We all got these cans of beer and things and then went down to the mangroves . . . because when the tide goes out the mangroves become higher, you're standing on the dry ground then. And we stole a little rowing boat. 'Righto, we're going to row to Singapore now.' They loaded everything on the boat. And the best part of it is, everybody else could swim but I couldn't. So I explained it to them and they said 'Oh, you'll be all right. If the boat goes down we'll save you.' So we got in the boat and started rowing out. We got a bit of distance from the shore and the waves started to get rougher. Each time a wave'd hit a certain drop of water would come into the boat and they started emptying it out with a tin. And I said 'Turn back, I want to go back.' 'No you'll be all right, Singapore's not far away.' Anyway while this was going on we heard some shouts from the foreshore – it was the bloody sergeant and the two constables, the black trackers and a few civilians from the town – and the sergeant's voice was singing out 'Come back . . . Co . . . me ba . . . aaack.' So we decided to row back. We rowed so far back. The sergeant red face was chest deep in the water coming out, trying to paddle out to us . . . and the two constables, they couldn't wait until the boat got into shallow waters, the moment they got us in arm's reach, they started wrestling with us. William Bodney, they handcuffed him to me. Of course William started pushing the constable and the constable started pushing him – because William Bodney was a bit of a fighter – and me at the same time was tiptoeing because each time they'd wrestle they'd go down a bit, and I was tiptoeing to keep my head out of the water.

And anyway, they got us all back into the cells and double-locked the doors and they gave us our sentence then, took us to court and gave us our sentence. I ended up with thirty-two month. The rest of them twelve month and six month and whatever.

They put all us on one of the old DC planes with the propeller engine and brought us right back down to the Guildford airport. Arriving there . . . and the police paddy wagon van was still going then, was waiting there, and the police constable. Out of the plane, into the van and down to Roe Street and down to Fremantle Gaol. And that's where the journey of the teenage Aboriginals – that's us – in the late forties through the fifties and early sixties ended up . . . and that's what us the teenagers in them days went through.

(1985)

VIRGINITY AND ITS PROMISE

Malcolm Knox

Pup, not I, was the storyteller. When I sit here and wonder which thread to pick up and, as one says, *run with*, I turn to Pup's advice, which was unfailingly wry and wise, arch and pessimistic. I would ask her how she began her stories. Had anyone else asked, she would have refused to answer. 'Go ask someone who can write,' she would have said. To me, her one rose-glassed *fan*, she would respond. To me she would say: 'It doesn't matter where you start, because you need to write the story before you know what it's about and where it should begin. So just get on with it.' That is, I imagine her telling me that before she stopped talking to me about her stories. I like to remember the good times, even when I'm only making them up.

I start, then, where I fall.

When you leave St Ives on the Mona Vale Road, you are leaving civilisation. Rarely do you hear St Ives spoken of as civilisation; nor, in these days of business parks and brand-new 'country clubs' and cancerous neo-Georgianism, the outer Mona Vale Road spoken of as wilderness. But in my memory there was a clean break: the pale Brady Bunch limits of St Ives behind, the fire-ravaged

27

ocean of wild bush ahead. The stages of the drive to Palm Beach replay like an opening theme to a favourite television show. Up past the cop speed traps to scrubby old St Ives Showground, speeding the raceway through Terrey Hills, down Tumbledown Dick Hill, whose name made us giggle until Pup lost an uncle at a hundred and sixty kilometres an hour over the rise, where it breaks to the left just as the car leaves the earth, up again to the Baha'i Temple, pink and white and gold in changing sun, our suburban Taj Mahal, careering down to the flats of Mona Vale cemetery – these sights are my overtures. By the time we reach Mona Vale and the big left turn past Nat Young's surf shop – its giant curling dumper painted onto the exterior wall – onto the Barrenjoey Road, my stomach is a murder of tiny flapping birds.

Each northern beach, like characters in a story, is a separate colony, where the colonists have inscribed the marks of their social standing. Mona Vale is a junction of shops and hospital and final provisioning, the last suburb. Newport, with its famous peak and reef, is the working man's northern haven, the surfers' surf where the Barrenjoey Road fronts crudely onto carpark and sand, eschewing the niceties of landscape. Rise from Newport to the twin serpent roads of Bilgola, plateau or beach, a deep rainforested basin where the architects arrived in the 1960s and stole carte blanche to perch their creations in the view-from-every-room gully. Out of darling little Bilgola, tightly held Bilgola, Avalon shields its proud 'village' life. Avalon pretends the main road doesn't exist. The shops and houses are set inland, the beach protected by high dunes. The main road is quarantined. Avalon doesn't want the tourists to stop, and the tourists could indeed drive straight through Avalon without knowing what is hidden away to left and right, and without knowing the locals' territoriality. Beyond Avalon the peninsula narrows, and the Pittwater introduces itself to your left. Still-water enclaves – Clareville,

Careel Bay – behind casuarina curtains, modest girls peeping out of upstairs bedrooms. Hidden to the sea side are the high cliffs of Whale Beach, another surfers' haven, where the rich who could not quite afford Palm have built their weekenders and left them, fifty weeks of the year, for the hardcore waveriders to piss in their own nest. At Whale, the road narrows and winds and my anticipation rises in cold jewels. The rainforest closes around the car. Hairpin bends and concealed driveways – here, in the 1970s, I first saw those circular convex mirrors, outside our friends the Vickers', as in Vickers Pharmaceuticals, which told them when it was safe to pull out onto the road – and on to the final stage, into a place you only approached if you had a destination. The road flattens out for a brief straight on the Pittwater side of Palm Beach, where Mr Bowman would stop the giant green V12 Jaguar, with its uphol-stery that always smelt new and slightly sickening, to buy the last supplies. We waited in the car, and Hughnior fought with his two little sisters while Mrs Bowman lunged at them between the front bucket seats, brandishing her open palm but never striking. And they knew it. 'You wouldn't have the guts,' they taunted her. Soon Mr Bowman would return with a small plastic bag of pawpaws, a large paper bag of eye fillet and sausages, a case of beer, and Weis bars for us. I had never tasted Weis bars before. Hugh liked rock-melon, I mango. Hugh punched his sisters until they gave him bites of their fruitos. We sang: 'Weis bar, Weis bar, la la-la la la la la' to the tune of that 'Moscow' song at the time of the Olympic Games. 1980. There it is. I have fixed a date to an ice-cream.

We disdained the plebeian road all the way to the north end of the peninsula, where the mere tourists drove. We took a shortcut up over the ridge, barriered by more hairpins, Mr Bowman plac-idly swinging the wheel in one hand and changing the automatic gears – Drive, Slo, Lo – with the other. I was fascinated that Mr

Bowman drove his automatic as a manual. At the top of the ridge, Palm Beach would open out before us. We would fall silent, even Hugh and his querulous siblings, as if in a cathedral's vestibule. Palm Beach. Our holiday. There.

The aisle of our church was Ocean Road. Having paused at the top of Sunrise Road, and seen what kind of surf awaited us (always Big in those days), our impatience would return and we would screech down the hill and howl to the right. Onto Ocean Road, the avenue of Norfolks down the southern end, coated with resinous pine scree and pink-gold sand. Mr Bowman would switch back to Lo, and we'd cruise past the clubs – Surf, Cabbage Tree, Pacific – then the Packers', and what was to become the Murray Steyns house. Murray didn't buy it, and turn it into a keep with an electronic polo pony, until some years after I first went there. Big Murray was a latecomer. There was the scandal when he tried to buy his way into the Cabbage Tree Club. You couldn't belong to the Cabbage Tree unless you had been a working member of the Surf Club. Nor could you belong to the Pacific next door, the women's equivalent, unless you had been a clubbie. Murray, who had grown up skulking in the shadows of Centennial Park, making soldiers out of pieces of bark while hiding from his father, was no surf sprite. There was uproar when he tried to buy membership of the Cabbage Tree. Murray had bought mountains of iron ore – wasn't that enough for him? The locals wouldn't sell, but Hugh Bowman Senior ran against the grain: he liked Murray, and couldn't see any reason why his new neighbour should be barred from enjoying the beach. 'Bygones be bygones,' Mr Bowman said, as if he invented the saying. Mr Bowman had a way of staking ownership over commonplaces. And Steyns was allowed in. His wife and daughter were allowed into the Pacific Club, too. That was twenty years ago. Nowadays, you'd never guess they'd been the despised migrants.

We dipped into the cul-de-sac at the end of the beach and swung past the ocean baths that sat below the Bowmans' driveway. The children who had the doors – invariably Hugh and I – would dash out and swing open one half each of the rusty old gate. It never had a lock on it until the mid-eighties, when the Bowmans' cousins arrived at the house one day to find it crawling with squatters. In those innocent pre-squatter days, Hugh and I would leap out, swing the gate open and race ahead to the swing that hung from the great fig in the lower front yard. This was my first memory of Palm Beach – climbing the slats of wood nailed into the trunk, a precarious ladder; Hugh went first, grabbing the knotted rope and jumping from the tree onto the top of the fence dividing us from next door. On the fence we had the rope at a good acute angle from the part of the branch to which it was tied. But the knotted rope seemed to shrink each year. At first you could comfortably slip the twelve-by-three-inch piece of wood that was the swing's seat up between your thighs, lean back, and then let your feet slip off the fence's top rail. As the years went on, the rope shrank mysteriously and the slat became a tighter squeeze. Finally, the rope was so short that you actually had to jump and insert the slat between your legs simultaneously, a dangerous manoeuvre which ended with the inevitable Mercurochrome and parental proscription.

The Bowman house was the finest on Palm Beach. The front yard was shaped by the sea into a steep wave, covered in grass, the kikuyu in mortal combat with the softer couches and clovers. Down the centre of the bank was the set of broad-tiled stairs up which we lugged our sleeping bags. We could run back down those steps, over the driveway, leap the fence and jump straight into the ocean baths. The house had a face. It looked over the baths and back along the beach to Barrenjoey. Tourists on Ocean Road wheeled to the end of the cul-de-sac and, instead of U-turning back down the beach, stopped at that house to exchange regards. Built in the 1920s, the house had the stucco walls, curved particolour tiles and Moorish touches typical of the Hollywood style of the time. Which is not to say it was garish. Ostentation was foreign to the Bowmans, and they had managed to allow the arched windows, bougainvillea trellises and rounded front veranda to become just sufficiently decrepit to pass off the impression of tasteful tattiness. The little stone fountain in the upper front yard hadn't bubbled for a generation; to have a fountain was one thing, to operate it quite another. Below the veranda, partly concealed behind some crusty hibiscus and succulents, were the lovely golden sandstone foundations and basement rooms. Those rooms were packed with discarded surfboards, beds, furniture, surf skis, windsurfers; three of them, around the northern side, were showers. It was in the storerooms, and on the veranda, that the squatters were found.

We usually arrived at night, so there was only a brief celebration on the swing before Mrs Bowman got us ready for bed. The veranda, open to the air, was where we slept. There were four beds at each end. The house, inside, was symmetrical and deceptively simple. Two small bedrooms at each end, back from the veranda; French windows led into the broad living room; to its right, behind, was the corridor leading to the inside bathroom; to its left, the kitchen. That was it. Behind the house was a shamrock-shaped saltwater pool, an excess perhaps, but Mrs Bowman loathed and feared the sea and her husband preferred to swim and sunbathe away from prying eyes. The bottom of the pool twinkled with a mosaic of imported Moroccan tiles. Beyond was a triangle of Santa Ana couch grass, always cut to a carpety nap, a barbecue and a Hills Hoist; the yard was bordered by a screen of lantana reaching into the lush gully up to Florida Road. The house's furnishings were not cheap, but were beach-shack staples: floral couch, two big deep claret-coloured armchairs, a bookshelf, a dining table and chairs. There was always sand on the tiles and floorboards, and the Bowman children would fight about whose turn it was to sweep. Hugh, the eldest, tended to win. I never knew siblings to fight as they could. When they fought, they could remain enemies for days, for an entire holiday. Sometimes their father would take them to his bedroom and strap them. When it was Hugh's sisters being strapped, this would embarrass me, because I knew it was always Hugh's fault, and he knew I knew, and he and I would be sitting at the dining table with Mrs Bowman in awkward silence while Mr Bowman's stern reprimands or the cracks of his strap would echo from the bedroom, and Hugh would be kicking my shin under the table to make me laugh. He could get away with anything. Once, he decided to become a vegetarian after watching some nature program. He loved nature documentaries, and took them seriously. We were having a barbecue that day. Hugh crossed his arms over his sausages and chops and said no. Everyone yelled for a while, and Mr Bowman took Hugh to the bedroom to strap him. I sat and waited, and ate my meat with the others. Within minutes, the sound of laughter came from the bedroom: Mr Bowman's deep, disbelieving laughter. Hugh had done it again. At the dining table, over the chewing of meat, I could feel the dismay from his sisters, even from his mother. 'Hughnior,' she shook her head. 'Hughnior.'

Let me pause. Pup, for all of her tolerance about starting points, would be screwing up her nose and asking me to get to the point. But I'm not sure the point is not buried in those rambling early summers, before Pup, before Helen. Perhaps I shall discover this point, and regret a childhood wasted, again. I could sit here and go on all night about things that happened between Hugh and me. But that would be an evasion, wouldn't it? That would repeat what I have always done: when I set out to tell the truth about the four of us, and about Hugh in particular, when I seek to expose what he was, I end up diverting myself with misty-eyed memories of the times when it was just him and me. I forgive him too easily. He must not be allowed to get away with it this time.

So those childhood years must be relegated to scene-setting, or prehistory, or preamble, or context, whichever you will have. They will be glossed over; the cure lies in the most recent blink.

Briefly, then. I spent every holiday, from the age of six to seventeen, with Hugh at Palm Beach. How did it start? How had we become friends? I cannot recall. Hugh had boarded at my prep school since kindergarten; I arrived in second grade. He told me once that when I arrived, a boy from a public school, he noticed that everyone was talking about me. That I seemed popular, in the way you can be popular with six-year-olds, as an a priori fact. Hugh said that one day he called my name across the playground. Just like that: he was with his friends, they were talking about me, he saw me and wanted to meet me, so he called out to me. I came over, and we were friends. The next school holiday, we did what new lovers do: we went on a holiday together.

What was Palm Beach before girls? Hugh and I hid in the stormwater drain on Ocean Road and egged cars. We explored the rainforests and gullies, and diverted ourselves with military fantasies. We watched Midget Farrelly and Nat Young surf. We dived off the anvil-shaped point and heard stories from Karim, the little nut-coloured Ethiopian prince who taught us how to snorkel and fish. We loved to go out with our rods in Karim's dinghy and fish for luderick and bream off the point. We poked sticks at crabs in the rock pools. We found a blue-ringed octopus and stayed with it for hours, daring each other to offer it a sacrificial toe. We went to swimming school with Barry Lister, a tyrant whom everyone loved but I hated because I couldn't swim very well and because he knew

I wasn't one of the children of the locals. I was only a blow-in, and Barry Lister couldn't see the point in the likes of me. He didn't know where I'd come from, as if I were an unwashed hand. We made friends with other boys around Palm Beach and played tip football on the beach. We hung around at the tiny kiosk and ate Redskins. We walked around to the Pittwater shops on errands for Mrs Bowman. We never stopped talking. We set fires in the lantana. We tortured Hugh's younger sisters. Hugh's father brought home a computer game, an Atari, which we could program using a cassette recorder. We awoke to music: top forty, disco, punk. And scrawled down the words of songs as if discovering an important archaeological find, a Rosetta stone. We believed we discovered the New Romantics; we heard the first Duran Duran song, 'Planet Earth', and liked it. When the movement mushroomed after that, Hugh and I would wink at each other: *We Made Them Giants*. We expressed our hatred of Billy Joel one afternoon by me holding the cassette on the veranda and Hugh pinching the tape between his fingers and running it down the lawn, across the ocean baths, onto the rocks and into the Pacific Ocean. I held the cassette, helped it unspool, and watched Hugh run with the seaweed sliver of tape. I could barely see him through tears of laughter. We listened to talk-back radio and made crank calls to Father Jim McLaren. When the house was empty, we took out a many-folded centrefold from the tin of Throaties where Hugh kept it. It was some shred of evidence from the incredible world of pornography, left by some careless or beneficent stork in a rubbish bin. In fact, I had found it. But it had become Hugh's, because he had the Throaties tin. He was Throaties custodian. When we knew the house was going to be empty, we'd start to make conversation about 'Miss Throaties'. How she was, whether she'd like us to call her up, what she'd be doing this afternoon. Once alone, we'd go and sit on our beds and unfold her. She was crisscrossed powdery white along the lines of the folds. We learned how to wank, turning modestly from each other, burying our faces in our pillows, holding our separate conversations with Miss Throaties while she, papery, fell unattended to the floor. We did other things. We watched a lot of television. We got stupidly sunburnt and caught in rips. Hugh surfed (I bodysurfed). We set up a slip 'n' slide down the steep front yard and played on it. Dozens of tourists stopped outside the gate and watched us and cheered. When Hugh was given a windsurfer, we took up windsurfing. When he was given a Laser, we took up sailing. Or surf-skiing. With the arrival of each new toy, we dropped whatever we'd been playing with the holiday before. When Hugh was given a video camera, we scripted and acted and shot a detective film of our own. This life was a necklace of non sequitur passions.

If I saw girls as a threat, as invaders, it was not because I disliked girls. Far from it. I was as possessed as any boy-adolescent by the dream of girls. I wanted girls in our little cell. I was not possessive of Hugh. I had no fear of losing him to girls. The way I saw it, there were plenty to go around.

As I think I've said, my good times with Hugh were interspersed with a low-lying anger towards him. I recall clearly, around the age of fifteen or sixteen, being so offended by something he'd done that I was prepared to 'break up' with him. 'Breaking up' was a new term, a new thing people did. It seemed a logical step. I would be ready to try this new thing and 'break up' with Hugh. But a mercenary notion would intrude: Hugh was rich, charming, handsome, and I was not. What hope had I of a girlfriend if I didn't crumb one off Hugh? He was the shark, I the dowdy pilot fish. I had no sisters, no cousins, no entree to girls. At our private school, girls might as well have been on another planet, our teachers and parents more than happy to keep them there. What hope had I without Hugh?

None. So I would stay with him in the hope that he would attract enough girls to himself that one might spill over and be mine. I'd be happy with just one. Chooser, meet thy friend Beggar.

But girls did become a threat, and it was Hugh's fault. It was the fault of his secrecy, his single-mindedness, his disease. This is how it happened. We would be walking along the rocks at Palm Beach and some other boy from swimming school would swagger up to Hugh and ask what So-and-So, a pretty girl from the pool, had been like to *pash*. Hugh would laugh and deflect the question. Or something like this: he and I would be sitting on the beach talking, as always. No change. I'd go up to the house for suncream or something. Two minutes later, when I'd cross the road coming back, my heart would stop: a clutch of girls standing ten metres away from Hugh. He'd be smiling and tossing a word to them over his shoulder. They would ripple with excitement, their hands at their mouths, their elbows crossed over their breasts. When I returned, they would run away. Or like this: I'd see a school-friend, back in class after summer holidays, and he'd ask me how often Hugh had *gone off* with his sister the last few weeks at Palm Beach. I'd say, 'I didn't know he'd gone off with her at all.' The brother would give a don't-shit-me smile and say, 'Have it your way. You know everything he does. Just tell him to quit it.'

In these few exchanges lay everything about Hugh and me. We were the tightest, closest friends, who shared anything, who adored each other, and yet I kept my most important thing – my rancour – a secret from him, and he decided to make his most important thing – this *new* thing – a secret from me. He had a life where he *went off* with girls. Who knew how many? Not me – hardly me.

Once we acted in concert. Only once. This exception proves the rule. Hugh and I were on the phone to each other, and got a crossed line. At the other end of the crossed line were two girls,

Lana and Tina. They liked us, and the four of us had a lot of laughs. This one conversation went for about five hours. Hugh and I told lies about ourselves, pretending to be older than we were – pretending to be the same age as them, about sixteen. We swapped phone numbers. Hugh and I went down to Palm Beach the next weekend to lay down our strategy. I'd told my parents I would be supervised by Hugh's, and in a way I was: Mrs Bowman was quite happy to give us the keys to the beach house whenever Hughnior asked. We had more long conversations with Lana and Tina, and decided to pair off. I'd take Lana, Hugh Tina. It was good: we had no idea what they looked like, nor they us, so our pairings were to be decided by 'personality' alone, or personality as judged from a string of increasingly antic four-way telephone conversations. I seemed to click with Lana, Hugh said, and he felt comfortable with Tina. We started shrieking when we realised how earnest we sounded. Finally we set up a date with them. We'd go to a movie in town. Lana and Tina described what they looked like, and what they'd be wearing. We did the same – and, for insurance, lied. Tina was tall and blonde, Lana short and brunette. Hugh told them he had a fair beard and would dress in a flannelette shirt. I told them I had long dark hair and a touch of American Indian. God knows, they believed us. So, insurance in place, we went to the cinema. We caught the 190 bus all the way from Palm. We strategised. As soon as we got near the cinema, we agreed, we would split up. We could not be seen together. Even though they didn't know what we looked like, we were sure that if we walked anywhere near the cinema together we'd stick out like dog's balls. And we'd arrive late, to make sure they were there first.

So we got there, late. Lana and Tina had told us they'd be sitting on a lounge in the foyer. Hugh went first. The plan was for him to walk along the street, look into the foyer, check them out, and keep walking. Then I'd follow, about a minute behind, and do the same. We'd keep walking to the end of the block and confer. I watched Hugh go first. He had that gawky, lanky walk that cracked me up. (Anything could crack me up at that moment; a passing car could crack me up.) He passed the foyer. He had a po-assed walk; he didn't show a thing. I followed. I turned my eyes to the left. Oooh yes, Lana and Tina were there. They were looking out to the street. Blushing, I looked away. Before I passed the entrance entirely, I stopped and pretended to read a poster. I examined them. They hadn't lied about their clothing, nor about their appearance. Tina was tall and blonde. She was about six foot two. She had a tiny pin head and yellow crimped hair with dark roots. Her eyes were scored like a raccoon's. She had braces of the kind that stop a girl from completely closing her lips. Lana, beside her, was a square-set dark-haired girl who looked as if she spent a lot of her life sitting in a favourite chair. I wanted to cry, a fist in my throat. I moved on. Even Hugh looked grim. We didn't say much. It wasn't disappointment for our sakes: had Lana and Tina been as gorgeous as models, we still wouldn't have had the guts to go up and see the movie with them. In a lot of ways, beauty would have been more troubling than plainness. But they were so plain. I saw, in one glance, the chasm between their lives and ours. That was what made me so sad: that we'd fallen for them on the false pretext that conversation, sense of humour, shared interests and disembodied affection were in any way feasible grounds for forming a relationship with a girl.

We did end up seeing a movie that day, a B-thriller called *When a Stranger Calls*. I remember nothing of the film except a scene where the babysitter is terrorised by the murderous caller who croaks chillingly: 'Have you checked the children? Have you checked the children?' The babysitter gets the police to trace the source of the calls. She is in darkness, holed up in a downstairs room, when the police get back to her. The police say: 'The calls are coming from inside the house. Get out of that house.'

Hugh thought it was hilarious. For a few months after seeing that film, we'd call each other up at night and rasp: 'Have you checked the children?' Or: 'Get out of that house! The calls are coming from inside the house!' It was a craze of ours, for a while. To be honest, Hugh found it funnier than I did. I needed him to make it funny for me. When the line came to my solitary idling mind, without Hugh to draw out my bravado, those words scared shit out of me. Even now, the memory of that scene, cheap and pungent as a cream biscuit, can still prickle my skin. The calls are coming from inside the house. I wish he were here to translate it for me, to make it funny again.

From *Summerland* (2000)

JULY 1921

Brenda Walker

One day Joe crossed an old wooden bridge and found that he was home. The bank was thick with the dead stems of a vine. He spotted geese on the Blackwood River. He was thinking of a beer. He wondered why he had left it so long to come home. Settling into one job after another, keeping his head and his shovel down, trying not to think of how he'd failed Bonnie.

The doors of the pub where he'd once worked so steadily, rising in darkness to sweep the night's filth from the floor, were closed. The stables were empty but the water trough was still there. And there was the hitching post where the publican had once tethered the thoroughbred that was to be Joe's. Joe had followed his boss out to the street intending to sluice down the gutter outside the entrance. Instead he was given the horse, which had been neatly brushed, its hooves blackened by the stable-boy. The animal stepped up close to him with a kind of nervous hopefulness.

The post office was open and a woman he'd never seen before told him there were abandoned houses along Chapel Creek where he could set up camp. Chapel Creek fed into the Blackwood River, snaking its way through the established properties in the district.

Joe knew the group of houses, some five miles out of Bridgetown. He could follow the road or he could take a shortcut on a track that skirted the old properties. He decided on the shortcut, where he could walk among the old trees that bordered the pastures. He hoped he might see a flock of black cockatoos.

— -

There weren't many doors on the row of derelict houses by the creek. Mostly you could walk right in. Poke a stick through the rust in the side of the stove. Pick up a child's shoe by a chewed strap and put it on the table. The dirt was clean. It smelled like turned earth. Joe thought this was probably because of the cold and the solid roofing of the deserted houses that kept the rain out. Through the cracked windows, clouds shredded in the wind. The sky was a cold, cold blue.

One house had smoke rising from the chimney. He knocked to introduce himself. He planned to camp in one of the empty houses and he didn't want to frighten any women who might live nearby. The women in the country were all wet-eyed from the smoke that drifted under their unsealed oven doors. They smelled of the clean sap of hardwood. Children stood about their knees.

This woman was called Annie Crane. Joe explained to her that he was just taking shelter for a night or two. If she needed any small jobs done she should let him know. She thanked him. Her sons took care of the wood-gathering and the milking, she told him.

He set himself up in the house next door, unrolling his swag on a long table with a split down the centre, as if someone had jammed an iron wedge into the join of the wood and struck it with the back of an axe.

He lit a fire in the stove. There was no door. Air sucked through the rust-holes and bled out everywhere. The cold pushed back hard against the fire. Joe's fingers ached. For a moment he thought of Bonnie, of the way they had once fitted together like the stones in a fireplace.

There were solitary chimneys all over the district. Chimneys and old wattle trees. Tanks rusted, roof beams fell or burned, but a stone fireplace settled more strongly into itself through the years.

— —

He woke to the sound of breathing. It was dark; the fire was low. Two children dressed in nothing but dirty, collarless men's shirts were sitting on the bench beside the table where he lay. A boy with red hair and a boy whose bruised fingernails were black to the quick, as if he'd had an accident with a hammer. They scuffed their bloodless feet against the floor.

Joe recognised them as Tom and Robbie, who had been standing behind Annie the previous afternoon, listening while he explained that he was looking for work in the district, that he was tired and planned to camp and rest for a couple of days. The boys had been in trousers then, and oversized boots. Their ankles were crusted and weeping under the tough leather of the boots.

Did he have any leftovers? No. Not even the crust of a damper? Joe forgot about food for days on end. But he could boil up water for tea.

Tom, the redhead, and the older of the two, told him that they used to live in this house when their dad was still alive. After he was shot in France their mother moved in with their granny next door. There'd been a stuffed fox on top of the dresser. Their father killed it but its hair fell out and it got burned.

43

The wood in the wall was speckled and rotting. Something was making a home inside the planks.

Joe swung his legs down from the end of the table, keeping the blanket bunched around his waist. A white dawn showed through the window. He could feel the boys watching him as he blew on the crumpled paper in the firebox. He stepped behind a door and buttoned himself into his pants.

Joe gave the boys enamel mugs. Sugar, a crumpled gumleaf: tea. They talked. Their mother had burned a lot of old stuff when she left the house, they said, mainly newspapers. She put the fox on top of her bonfire. Robbie told Joe about the shock of sparks lifting from the fur, He was a big bright fox, as big as this – the boy stretched out his arms – and you had to screw up your eyes to look at him. Had Joe ever seen a fox that big?

Joe blew across the surface of his tea. The handle of his mug was heating up. The weight felt good in his fingers. It took so little to feel good. 'Oh, my word,' he said. 'I once saw a fox so big he set a whole army galloping.'

'Were you a Light Horseman?' asked Tom, reaching for Joe's tobacco under cover of the question.

Yes, he was with the Light Horse. He was in Cairo, in Gallipoli, in Jerusalem and Damascus. In Cairo boys their age sold oranges. Boys their age sold themselves too, though Joe wasn't going to mention that. The look on their faces told him that if they had an orange they'd have trouble parting with it. He swept the tobacco tin back to his side of the table.

Had he been wounded? the boys wanted to know. He said no, but a camel had once stood on his foot. They liked that. They forgave him for not sharing his tobacco with them. He rolled himself a thin dry smoke. He was running low.

'Tell us about the fox,' Robbie said.

Yes. The fox. The tea was almost cool enough to sip.

'When you go without drink your tongue hardens up. Your eyes get dry.' Joe thought about how far he should go. Your lips break open in the wind. Your nose dries, inside, and cracks and bleeds. You're breathing the dust of your own blood.

'Your eyes play tricks on you, especially when you're short of sleep.' It was a lie. He believed what he had seen.

'Did you kill anyone?' asked Robbie.

'Lord, no. My sights were out.'

It was a funny thing. Joe couldn't remember shooting anyone. He must have killed someone. If he'd shot wide for the whole war Brazier would have had a word or two to say to him.

'Did you win a lot of ground?'

'We were fighting for water. Dirty water. And we won. Then we turned back. It was Christmas, just before Christmas. The horses were working hard in the sand. It was a long night. Every man had his chin on his chest. You can sleep on a good horse. When we woke we were riding into a city and the moon was up. We put the horses through stone doorways and over shallow stairs. It was an old city, older than Jerusalem. They didn't put glass in their windows. They had stone shaved so fine it let through light.'

Joe remembered suddenly that the stone was drilled and carved so that every man was marked with shadows, making a pattern he could never understand.

'Each horse in the file was staggering at the same point on the stairs and shaking himself when we passed through the last gateway and out across the sand.'

Joe drank his tea. Back at El Arish they'd been told they were mad. Briefly mad. Through lack of sleep. There was no city; the city they rode through had not existed for a thousand years.

The men were taken one by one into a tent and given a cigarette each and told to keep it all to themselves.

'A fox likes a bit of human company.'

A fox liked a grave or two: a place where the work of digging a den had already been done for him. A fox liked a ruin.

'We weren't far out into the sand when a fox came up behind us from the city walls. The fox was running low on black paws like burned matches and his tail was like a big flame. We saw him first, then the horses saw him. He ran under their hooves. Tired horses were stumbling everywhere. Then one put his ears forward and set off at a gallop and the others were right behind him. The men were grabbing for their rifles and stirrups and settling into the pace, fast and smooth across the sand under the moonlight. Christ, it was good. Pelting over the sand. We made it into El Arish, flecked with froth and blood.' The men back in the camp hadn't wanted to hear that a fox had brought them home.

It was daylight outside. The boys were glancing at one another. 'Thanks for the tea, mister.'

Joe walked them to the end of the hallway. The floor tipped down to its failed stumps. He could smell the sweetness of rotten wood. The hall was a crate and he was boxed up like an animal. In the small tunnel of darkness he remembered the black cold of Anzac Cove at night. Not the faces of the men, not the conversations or the orders, just the cold. The feeling was bigger and closer than memory. Under his loose worn clothes he felt the breath of that unhealthy cold. His eyes hurt.

He turned back inside the house. When he was facing the window, looking down to the creek, he allowed himself to cry.

—▪—

Joe had found his pocketful of tiles after one of those quick, swerv-
ing engagements with the enemy that had seemed very slow at the
time, as if some mouth other than his own were shouting, as if he
were watching his rifle in another's hands. The sky could be white
in the desert; the sand was white. The horses broke the surface
and you might be riding through burning snow.

When the fighting was over they discovered pieces of an old
mosaic floor that had been blasted into the light by an enemy shell.
Centuries of earth flew aside.

'Priceless,' said the Padre. 'Maybe it's a piece of the early Church.'
He had turned his back and the fellows helped themselves to the
tiles.

Joe remembered the design of the mosaic: the fish rising up, all
throat and gills; the thin hound with his ribs sticking out, closing
on a wide-eyed hare. Almost too lovely to walk across. This square
of desert, at least, had been solid underfoot for more than a thousand years. Joe had wanted to unlace his boots. Slip off his socks
and close his eyes and let his bare skin fall upon these swimming
running animals.

He had worked the tiles free with his pocket-knife, trying not
to chip them as he edged his way underneath. He had scraped his
fingers raw. Now that the tiles were freed from their pattern, they
moved about randomly in his pocket under his touch. They were
never still.

There had been bones under the mosaic tiles. A shoulder blade,
hard and pale. Someone else had taken the bones.

He laid his pieces of mosaic on the table of the deserted house.
He could hear Annie speaking softly next door. She had planted
sunflowers beside the creek and through the window he saw their
stalks standing tall and grey. The leaves hung down like tobacco. A
black-eyed man had once given him tobacco, and grapes. A handful

of each. It was in one of their cities. Jerusalem. Damascus. Joe couldn't remember.

He built up the fire. Chickens were cackling hard outside as if the day were a big surprise. It was a blue-grey day. A day for remembering. He put two chairs opposite each other, in line with the window so he could look out at the stalks of winter sunflowers. He settled in one chair and put his feet up on the other. It was good to sit still with an empty belly and wait for the shreds of memories.

There were such black drifts in his memory. Sometimes when he rubbed his eyes dark clots slid around in his vision. A doctor who explained it to him in the camp in Egypt said it had something to do with the inside of the eye. What Joe saw as immense, as shadows moving before him, was in fact the smallest imperfection deep inside his eye. It meant nothing. It would come and go. He wondered if his memory might be like this. Some small clotting within him made black shadows on his memory, and when he was rested they would clear. He thought it would be a gradual thing.

Outside, the boys were running through the reeds by the creek, laughing, slashing at one another, falling to the ground to roll and then springing up again, calling out that the other was dead.

Joe suddenly remembered being inside a barn with stripes of light cutting through the gaps in the planks of the walls, and dust floating in the light. He was sitting on a stack of timber, sliding a peeled twig along a line of dirt, like a child would, and Bonnie was sitting next to him. She smelled like fine dust on a hot road. He could feel her mouth on his bare shoulder. He could feel her light smile against his skin.

An aeroplane cartwheeled through the sky, up behind the sunflower stalks, behind the grey branches of the winter trees. He saw the small plane come in straight and level, then it banked and tipped and flipped slowly three times, and disappeared. A circle of black smoke hung in the air.

For a moment the aeroplane had looked like a horizontal windmill. There was something they used to say in camps, on railway platforms, wherever they met up with other fellows – boys from Glasgow or Lancashire or other places they'd never heard of. The Tommys would say they were from Glasgow or Lancashire and ask where you were from, and the Australians would say, 'Between the windmill and the sea.' That covered it. A whole country between a windmill and the sea.

Because, Joe would explained doggedly inside some tent, in some forgotten camp, there was a problem with water in Australia. You could settle along the sea and the river mouths, but that didn't give you much of a country. You had to peg the country back into the interior to give yourself a bit of space. Sink wells. Pull the water up to the light with a windmill. Your sentry posts, the edges of your territory, weren't settled with a fence-line. Sand buried fences. The real borders, deep inside, were marked with troughs and windmills.

He remembered how the dry wind had hissed against the sides of the tent. And the cry of the camels, or of strange birds. 'We still put up fences, though,' he'd explained. In the night, on horseback, it seemed you could ride over every sand dune in the Middle East without striking a good wire fence.

The pilot must have pulled out low along the creek, because there was no crash and no sign of the plane in the sky. The smoke was gone. He blinked. Suddenly he understood that there had been no aeroplane, just as there had been no fox.

Joe got up and crumpled more newspaper into a ball and fed it to the fire. It burned for a moment. He'd load up the firebox with wood soon. But the paper burned with a brief white heat, very hot, which was what he wanted.

He had seen a real aeroplane go into the desert once. After three days of fighting in a cactus thicket. Punching bullet-holes through big fleshy plates of cactus and getting shot at yourself, white wet stuff turning up across your face and chest with the odd cactus spine. Fellows crouched down and flicked it across at each other. In the middle of it he looked up and saw an aeroplane, theirs or ours, spin across the sky. The sand had no spring, no give in it. When something hit, it hit. He felt it, hard. If he could have chosen the thing he'd keep with him later, the thing his mind would reproduce for him, it would be pitching a handful of cactus pulp through the air, not watching an aeroplane come down.

Rats had been living on the beam above the stove. He saw their small beads of waste. He put his hands halfway into the firebox for what was left of the warmth. These things were real. The rats, the coals, the soft drift of ash from the newspaper. The aeroplane wasn't real. He might be mad.

They said the men were mad, after the reports of riding through the old stone city. Maddened by thirst, they said. A drink of water would set them right. He had been mad after he was blown out of his sniper hole as well. He was strapped into a bed and talked into getting better. Or was he strapped? Did he just lie still? A nerve doctor talked and talked to him. Laid a hand flat on his breastbone.

Being mad was only a problem if you talked. If you kept to yourself you could watch an aeroplane out of the corner of your eye. It wasn't breaking any branches because it wasn't real. You could feel the shadow of stonework across your back. You could hope to be standing somewhere, anywhere, standing with your hands in a firebox and a neat pile of animal shit before your eyes and a woman might step up behind you bringing an old sweetness, an old smell of sweetness with her that you thought had vanished from the face of this earth and she might slide her hands across your belly as you stood at the stove feeling the pressure of the side of her face between your shoulderblades and it would be well worth being mad for that. But it could only happen if you kept to yourself, kept your mouth shut and your head clear and open to the sound, the taste, the visions.

— · —

'Mister,' Robbie said when he and Tom appeared again the following morning, 'did you shoot your horse?'

Joe's horse was a kissing horse. It was a trick a few of them learned for a laugh in the camps. The horse would stretch its neck out and bring its big square nose up to Joe's face and hold it there while someone got a camera.

This wasn't the horse he'd gone over with. Not the horse from the bank of the Blackwood River, from home. That horse died while he was at Gallipoli. This one was issued to him like a new hat or a rifle. Part of his equipment. But they were close, the uneasy horse and the man who taught it to lift its chin up for a kiss.

'No,' said Joe. 'Just before the horses were shot, mine broke her tether and wandered off to the Nile. She waded in for a drink and slipped and nobody could haul her out.'

Robbie waited.

'She drowned.'

He shot his horse. A horse has a big brain and it flew everywhere. Men were moving through the lines, steadying the horses with old kind sounds, the sounds their mothers used for frightened children. They had even organised a race meeting, wearing out the animals with a hard run and a rub-down afterwards. It didn't work. The horses dragged at the ropes. They stamped in the sand. They were taken up to a high plain, one by one. After the first shot there was no keeping it from them. Joe squatted next to his dead horse and rubbed his hands along its neck. He wept without shame.

When they sailed someone saw horses following in the wake of the boat.

'A horse can swim,' said Tom.

'Not mine,' said Joe. 'My horse couldn't swim.'

He pulled his shaving gear out of his kitbag and set it up on the enamel sink. A bowl. Cracked soap. A razor and a mirror. A scrap of towel. Stuff you could pick up anywhere. Joe didn't even have a postcard picture of Cairo. He had his slouch hat and a handful of mosaic tiles to remind him of what they called the great adventure of war. He moved a tin with water in it to the hottest part of the stove.

Robbie was watching him sharply. 'You shot your horse,' he said. He was keen for Joe to have shot something.

'Yes,' said Joe. 'I shot the horse. I had to shoot her. She would have starved, or been flogged along in front of a plough.'

They weren't allowed to bring the horses home. He pictured them in Egypt, legs splayed, sniffing the dirt, or whipped through the heat of the day. Horses eating the shit of other animals. Eating scraps of wire. Anything.

Joe's water started to boil. He folded the piece of towel and used it to pick up the hot tin, ignoring both boys. Steam rose from his shaving bowl. Chickens scrabbled after insects in the space below the floorboards.

He was right to shoot his horse. There were fellows who'd broken in their own horses in stockyards — hours and hours of turning in a slow circle with a rope in one hand and a stick in the other, the horse pacing neatly on the end of the rope until you were both soothed. Give it more time and you could throw the stick away. All you needed was a voice and a rope. There were fellows, and horses, who didn't even need a rope. One horse had carried four men out of trouble, two on its back and one on each stirrup, standing up. They called that horse Bob the Bastard. Running under fire with four men. Nobody touching the reins.

Men who still had the horses they brought with them from Australia were most determined to shoot them. But there was something else, something that Joe recognised apart from the worry about hunger and cruelty and the bewildered hearts of the deserted horses. It was a great strain, the ending of the war. You shot your horse and there was an end to all that was bad. Or so you hoped. You could shoot yourself. Or you could shoot your horse. There were fellows who did both, given a little time and the opportunity.

The water was hard. Joe couldn't get much of a lather from the soap. He heard a chicken cackle. The deep note of a dairy cow. 'Tell you what,' he said. 'Would your mum sell me a bit of milk?'

The boys looked at one another. 'We'll ask.'

He heard them down on the bank, then later, up high above the houses, among the granite and the blackberries, calling and calling for someone.

—●—

Joe was stirring sugar into an enamel mug of tea when he heard someone knocking softly on the open door. He turned from the window. It was Annie Crane, standing hesitantly at the threshold.

'Come in,' he said. 'Please.'

He pulled across a chair for her. She didn't sit down.

'There's a dead woman up in the bush,' she said. 'My mother. She wandered off this morning. We thought, because you've been in the war, we thought you could go and get her . . .'

He had heard someone chopping and stacking wood for the

night. He'd heard the boys calling from the ridge. They had climbed up the granite outcrops behind the house and found their granny. Joe saw that there wasn't going to be an end to it. He could shoot half a dozen horses and sail across an ocean and he'd still find himself face to face with a corpse.

'Yes,' he said. 'I'll take care of your mother. Just let me finish my tea.'

Annie sat down and fanned out her fingers in front of the stove and told him the story of how her husband had been pressured into enlisting. The envelopes of white feathers delivered to the front door in the night by people too cowardly, she said, to show their faces.

Joe finished his tea. At least he was warm; deep inside his body he was warm.

——

It was a steep climb. Halfway up the ridge he turned and looked down at the red road and the black creek. He saw the burnt-out tree where Annie Crane must have had her bonfire, destroying all the newspapers with their accounts of the progress of the war.

He climbed over flat rock, carrying the old blanket he'd brought to lay the body in. It began to rain. He sat down, put his head in his hands and felt the rain on his shoulders like fingertips. Then he went on.

With all this talk about foxes Joe half expected to find gnawed flesh. But the body was intact, covered by a floral dress. The woman lay on her back on a wide sheet of stone. Her hair had come loose. A calico bag of mushrooms had fallen from her hands.

Joe rolled himself a smoke and sat down next to her. The dead face did not frighten him. He cupped his hand around his

smoke. It was raining again. She was on the inside now, with the
Padre at Gallipoli who said life was just a waiting room. He imagined everybody milling around, waiting to die and be let inside.
Joe thought of a railway station. A crowd circling in front of the
departures board, shoving their way across to one platform after
another. You got off the train and you kept walking until you arrived
at a mansion. Stone gateposts, a tunnel of trees. A mate who had
been blown up on the beach at Anzac Cove opening a heavy door
to welcome you in.

He smoked the cigarette until it was nothing more than a wet
brown slip of paper, stinging his lips. He tucked it under a rock.
Then he opened out the blanket and pulled the body over. The old
woman's head bumped against the rock. He slid his arms under
her shoulders and her knees and lifted her onto the blanket. Her
daughter would want her rings. He slipped them free. Joe used
the blanket like swaddling cloth, bringing it up over the feet and
wrapping it tight around the sides as if he were calming a child.
Then he picked her up and walked down the hill with her.

——◆——

Joe put the body on the table in the house where he was camping.
The blanket had worked loose at the side of the old woman's face.
There should have been candles. Instead he opened the firebox of
the stove and viewed her in the gold light, the shadows.

'You don't need to sit with her.' Annie was at the door.

'I haven't always had the chance to sit with the people I brought
in,' said Joe. He got to his feet slowly, tucking in the edge of a cigarette paper, rolling it backwards and forwards. He put it up to his
mouth and smoothed it down with his tongue.

'Her eyes are pointing in different directions,' said Annie.

'It happens sometimes.'

Outside, the leaves of the sunflowers rattled in a little wind. He heard a parrot calling, a clear sound like the note of a bell. It was their foraging cry, a cry of hope and discovery.

'She was from England,' said Annie. 'She always said that in her village the cobblestones looked just like little grey potatoes.'

Take me back to dear old Blighty, Blighty is the place for me. Some of the fellows had played it on the harmonica. Joe suddenly remembered bending close to the wounded somewhere – on the floor of a trench or in the sand at Anzac Cove – to catch their final ordinary words about the countryside, the hawthorn and the hedges of England, or their mothers. Then the memory was gone.

— · —

He was cold from washing in the creek. Annie led him into her kitchen, where plates were piled with runner beans and chopped fried fish. The fish must be building up in the river, he thought, with so few people about. The boys were clean. Their big galvanised bath-dish was dripping out on the veranda.

Annie passed him a stone jar of beer. The neck cracked against his teeth. He gulped the beer down and it sprang back into his mouth. He gulped again. Annie was bringing a bread tin out of the oven. 'You can have a glass, if you like,' she said.

Joe held the jar in both hands. He breathed in wood-smoke, kerosene and the smell of yeast. He turned to the window. Night was closing in but he thought he could see the flat rocks up on the other side of the creek.

Annie told him that they lived on whatever they could shoot or pull from the creek. She bought flour, bullets and beer whenever she got a bit of work. She was a wonderful cook; the fish was sprinkled with some feathery herb and she had a plate of watercress in the centre of the table. She explained to Joe that she used to cook for Elizabeth Zettler, who lived on a farm an hour's walk away. Mrs Zettler was a poor useless thing, a widow who kept a big black crow as a pet and let her cattle wander through broken fences and out onto the public road. She needed a workman more than she needed a cook. But lately Mrs Zettler had been keeping to herself, although she could well afford the help, and Annie wanted the work because her money had almost run out.

Zettler. The name was familiar. There were plenty of fellows he'd known for a few days in some camp or trench but their names rose up and sank like a flame catching a dry twig in an open fire.

The boys had done a good job with the scaling knife. Joe said so, in between working small bones to the front of his mouth and picking them out with his fingertips. Annie told Joe about her plan for more fish traps, and a goat or two. The window behind her shoulder was a solid black square and there was nothing on the other side of it, no rocks, no creek, no sad dead mother.

Late that night he carried his blanket down to the grass by the bank and made himself a bed. His breath tasted stale. He began to dream about cobblestones breaking apart beneath his feet.

In the morning Joe inspected the tree where Annie had lit her bonfire. Charcoal clung to the trunk in thumb-sized squares. He didn't see the glass eyes of the fox that the children said Annie had burned. He moved around until the trunk of the tree stood between him and the house and he found a stretch of creamy bark to piss on.

Joe's arms ached. So did his ribs. He had had one good dream, after the dream of cobblestones; he couldn't remember it but he knew it had been good, and he was stupidly, easily happy. It was a loose muscular happiness that his mind was going to have trouble catching up with.

He buttoned himself and turned back to Annie's house. She was standing on the veranda, watching him.

He'd build a yard. He'd patch up the tanks.

Robbie ran down through the garden to stand at his side.

'Where do you reckon a goat would like to live?' Joe asked him.

'The last goat had a rope with a spike on the end of it. We dug up the spike and moved him along the creek. When we put him under the gum tree he ate a ball of worms.'

In the summers of his boyhood, Joe remembered, big black caterpillars clung together in writhing balls in the dirt under the eucalypts all along the Blackwood River. 'Tough goat,' he said.

'No,' said Robbie. 'He died.'

'What say we build a yard away from the gum tree and put a goat in it for your mother?'

Robbie looked down at his black and broken fingernails. Annie hadn't moved from the veranda.

'First you cut your posts.' Joe could see plenty of fine timber on this side of the creek. 'You keep an eye on which way your tree is growing because you drop the posts in upside down. Other- wise they'll strike and grow.' Joe saw a lush square of young trees gripped by old fencing wire. 'Then you sink a strainer post,' Joe explained. 'That's the end of your line. Something all fencers have in common. They're proud of their line.'

The boy was sorry he'd come down, Joe could see that. He'd rushed at Joe like a wave and now he was bored: small and flat and slipping away.

'You put your line post in next. Loose, to give you a bit of play. Then you get it nice and straight.' Joe stopped. Robbie waited until he was told to go.

Up at the house, Annie made a pot of tea and told Joe about the nugget her husband had found in the first week they moved here; about the old mine camp where they dug for flattened bullets and belt buckles, the richness of the soil along the creek. Joe described his proposed fence.

At night he lay on his back on the bank. He breathed in the smell of the water and looked at the spaces between the stars. You'd get away from that smell if you were a desert man, or a man who lived beside the sea. Joe liked the smell. He thought of his horse coming down in the darkness to the Blackwood River to drink. The horse casting a big soft shadow and blocking out the stars. Small turtles rising in the safety of the shadow. What did it matter if the horse was dead?

When he stood up suddenly he staggered, his body remembering what it was like to be flung high in the air, to turn slowly above the trenches at Gallipoli, to fall through all that fast explosive metal. Then he settled firmly on two feet on the spongy earth and the smell of the creek came to him and the smell of himself on his hands and he thought of Annie's mother lying on a piece of stone on the other side of the water. He felt the light scrape of her dead hair under his chin.

He had been blown out of a sniper's hole at Gallipoli. He had been up with the sun in the sky. Then he had fallen. In the hospital ward, in the horse-lines, on the ocean and the shore, while his body moved about obeying orders some part of him was still falling.

The earth of the bank finally broke his fall.

Once he'd built the goat pen he would roll his swag and say goodbye to Annie and her sons. This Mrs Zettler needed a workman.

On the road, he floated above himself as the fenceposts drifted by. He was as calm as a hawk. He shrank. He was as light as a fist. His eyes were almost closed. Vast wings seemed to open beside him.

He felt the rhythm of the road. The footfalls past counting. He was on his way to work, to a strainer-post and a length of fencing wire.

Somewhere on the road he was stopped in his tracks by a cat. He bent at the knees and worked his fingernails around its ears. The air was dry and the cat's fur crackled with static under his hands. He felt the light shock of electricity. When he stood up the cat called to him, small and loud, a single note coming up from the road. He picked it up and put it in his shirt and kept walking.

The cat slept above his belt and its weight rocked against him in rhythm with his footsteps, the cat in front and the billy-can behind, and he almost forgot he was carrying them.

And suddenly there was Bonnie's house, barely changed after all these years. He stood for a while, looking at it from a distance, before moving closer. The chicken-pens were empty. He longed for a complete loss of memory. The cat moved inside his shirt. He recalled a story about a boy who put a fox cub in his shirt. A Spartan boy. It ate through to his heart. Joe thought of the fox like a swift flame with black-burned paws running before the horses. The cat was asleep against his skin. He hitched his swag higher and turned.

From *The Wing of Night* (2005)

NHILL

Patrick West

As I had hoped, when we arrived at the lake we were the only people there. Neither of us had seen any other cars at the place where the road ended and the desert began. Yet perhaps there was another way in we didn't know about; or somebody had decided to camp overnight on the shore of the lake. Somebody who didn't have a car, perhaps. But there was no one.

The evening before, over a shared ice-cream dessert at the motel restaurant, my wife had told me that she would be going to bed as soon as we were finished, to be rested for our early start the next morning. Though worn out myself by the half-day drive from Melbourne, I had stayed up for some time after her: getting together the things we would need for our trip into the desert; estimating distances and times.

Our room was next door to the reception area. The manager had his TV turned up loud and kept switching irritatingly between the channels. There had been a movie on, and the local news, and it wasn't until after the movie that I had turned off the main light. Getting into bed myself, next to my wife, I lay on my back and thought of the pair of empty fish tanks on the manager's desk.

And then I think I took a long time falling asleep, because when our alarm clock went off it seemed as if the movie were still going on inside my head.

There had been no lights shining in the motel complex when I eased the room door closed behind us, and unlocked the passenger side of the car for my wife. The only artificial illumination came from the frosted lamps around one side of the swimming pool, which made the water bright green. Although I had remembered thinking, upon our daylight arrival, that I had never seen water so blue. There had been clothes-pegs on the bottom that afternoon. Children were diving for them.

Some of the fainter stars had been dimming out as we drove along the road that would soon veer right and become the main street of the town of Nhill, Victoria. Our motel was about at the point towards the end of a long stretch of highway where the speed limit begins to be lowered on white-and-black signs. We both saw a rabbit in the headlights.

A few minutes after we had departed the silently sleeping motel, my wife spotted the turn-off to the Little Desert before I did. Her vision was much keener in the pre-dawn light. The road to our destination ran alongside the railway tracks on the edge of Nhill. Our tourist map showed us that halfway to the desert the road and the tracks would diverge, meet again, then finally part for good. I slowed down to take the left-hand turn.

While the light continued to increase and alter, she had been the one to say the morning had broken. A sliver of sun flashed across my rear-vision mirror as we parked on a slope of dew-dusted earth. I turned off the engine. For the first time that morning it was perfectly quiet.

For a while we hadn't even been sure if we were really in the desert or not. Then we came to a turnstile in a short run of wire fencing, and we knew. We had arrived. The turnstile had a counter attached to it; as we went through the white numbers noiselessly turned over. It was probably part of someone's job to note how many people went into the desert. Perhaps this information was important. I couldn't help thinking about those people who deliberately went around the fence or used the turnstile more than once. My wife must have read my mind. She had said quietly, perhaps it all evens out in the end.

That had also been when we first noticed the real sand mixed with the soil beneath our feet, and that the Little Desert mainly consisted – the vegetation falling away – of a serried formation of low rises and shallow dips. We were now into a new landscape, walking across the first of its modest plateaus, incongruously headed for water.

Tucked into my shirt pocket was a map of the desert produced for walkers, and we weren't long in our progress towards the lake before the cartographic marks like the diminuendos and crescendos on a page of music became signs we could interpret. The map gave the lake a neat edge, filled in with a colour that by convention indicated deep water. But my wife and I had speculated that at that season, and at the very centre of the desert, the lake would be a salt lake. Its water would be shallow and its shore uneven, we had guessed. And we were right.

The whole morning, from the surface of the path and from the rest of the ground, the air had been rising in warm waves. What little there was of copper-coloured, needle-like grass had been the first to respond. An hour later, the same waves had brushed around our faces, slowly continuing to ascend, moving through black and blonde hair like fingers of gentleness. This was a sensation we hadn't felt before, out there in the relative flatness of the Little Desert. And then, when our watches showed that it was almost noon – hour and minute hands about to touch the twelves on our wrists – we noticed again how peculiar nature is.

Although there wasn't a breath of wind, the few trees at first appeared to be straining against their confinement in the earth, all of themselves rejecting the land from within.

The next moment, however, this had curiously seemed not to be happening. Precisely the absence of even the weakest breeze now manifested itself as decisive, as if the trees that we could see here and there on the landscape, not needing for their equilibrium to be rooted and heavy and thus not being so, were no longer rebelling against their connection with the lowest part of the visible desert, but were touching it with only the smallest possible touch, nothing of themselves actually buried into the loose soil. As if roots had withdrawn completely into trunks, as if something had turned completely and utterly around, as if the few trees were held up sheerly by the rising air – a delicate balancing act – and into its cloud-headed warm waves.

I had walked with my binoculars around my neck, seeing two eagles. Or perhaps the same eagle twice.

At times, the silence was extreme.

There had been low signs by the side of the path at irregular intervals, sometimes three or four clustered together. They had on them descriptions of the interesting aspects of the desert and its life. Here were indicated two trees that had grown into each other in a cleft of rock, and become one; there, the same thing had happened, but with one of the trees having died. A few of the signs had referred to rainfall or temperature change in the Little Desert's unique microclimate. Others said that at this spot one could often see a particular bird or furtive animal. My wife had told me that the signs looked like church lecterns springing from the ground, or tombstones made to resemble open books. (A rare parrot we read about had last been seen in 1961, by N. Green.)

Our route to the lake had taken us through a part of the desert supporting very little in the way of scrub or other plant growth. The ground had to it what my wife called an angry tone. In places the sand gathered in drifts deep enough for our legs to disappear up to the bare flesh of our calves.

At the point where our walkers' map told us that we would arrive at our lunch spot by the salt lake in just under an hour, we had found ourselves on a slightly higher plateau, where the fine sand gave only a few grains of cover to the shale beneath. In view before us was an expanse of clumpy bushes of a bleached-green colour: a prospect of palest olive. Obviously we were on the edge of fertile soil. It had almost looked as if we might walk, from where we were, right across the top of the scrub, to the next low rise; although by careful observation, if nothing else, we knew we couldn't. The surface of the scrub was even and uninterrupted, but the smallest bird to alight on it sank beneath the feathery leaves and tips. Sank to fly out of the scrub's surface bafflingly elsewhere (the same bird? or another?).

I had related to my wife what I knew about a certain type of mixed bush-growth in western Tasmania, described in forestry literature, which was often able to sustain – for considerable dis-tances – the weight of people who simply wanted to walk above the land for a while. My wife had only grimaced in response. She was becoming tired; the comparison, furthermore, was a vague one. The scrub we were faced with then was not only unable to support us, but allowed no sort of passage through its web of lower branches either. We were therefore forced to make a long detour, by the fainter trail around its stunted-grass perimeter, in order to regain our path to the lake on the further side.

For no known reason, we had each taken a different way from the other. Tiny desert mice and prodigious desert rats were in shadowy motion within the scrub, chittering among themselves without regard to size or species. Under blazing sun, it had felt nevertheless as if I were looking into darkest night.

There was orange peel on the ground where the main path took up again: the first sign of recent intrusion that either of us had seen.

We caught sight of the salt lake just a little later than my planning had allowed for.

As I had hoped, when we arrived at the lake we were the only people there. Neither of us had seen any other cars at the place where the road ended and the desert began. Yet perhaps there was another way in we didn't know about; or somebody had decided to camp overnight on the shore of the lake. Somebody who didn't have a car, perhaps. But there was no one.

Across the lake we could see three waterbirds still as statues, a little way in from the opposite shore. They did not disturb at all the few centimetres of water they were at rest in. It gave out almost nothing, that salt water: without movement and shallow at every point. Reflections from the surface of the lake were mixed with the appearance of its bottom. It was difficult even to be sure about what sort of a body of water we were looking at. An oversized puddle? Ridges of land that began well back in the desert around us continued out into the lake as thin fingers of earth, which dropped beneath the surface only when almost to the middle. They were the ribs of the Little Desert, I had thought to myself, and this was its watery heart.

The ducks' heads were nestled comfortably into the plumage of their napes. Nothing stirred. All between our words was without noise. For a moment, I almost believed that I could watch the silence that surrounded us. It had been as if the visible landscape – the few trees; the copper-coloured, needle-like grass – were listening to what we said, finding it eventually acceptable, and allowing our utterances to pass back into the quietness unhindered.

We had arrived. The two of us. At a heart of salt.

It was difficult to have to quit the lake's irregular and pock-marked shore so quickly, now that we were finally where we wanted to be. But it was past the time to have our lunch, we were both tired, and the path to the nearest shady place to eat and rest was going to take us a short distance away from the lake. My wife and I had removed our hiking boots and socks to test the temperature of the water; now we needed to sprint across the burning ground to the spot we had decided upon almost immediately after our arrival. Even several long steps from the edge of the salt lake, however, the sand was cool and moist.

Water usually darkens whatever it touches and I have read somewhere that this proves it is not really crystalline but pure black, which is to say that it makes things black by an invariable law of change and resemblance. Nowhere in even the immediate vicinity of the lake, however, did the colour of the sand vary from the salty whiteness presented by other parts of the Little Desert. Even the thin fingers of land like the spokes of a gigantic wheel had a pale and glazed hue. More than likely the same went for the bottom of the lake, although through the shallow depths of the water we couldn't tell for sure.

As we opened our backpacks, ate our sandwiches, splashed our cold drinks into our mouths, we talked about such things. A million days of evaporation, my wife said through a mouthful of bread and mortadella, had done something to the Little Desert to make its surface impervious to the effects of water. An element in the rain was not taking on the sand, I had thought without saying it.

When we had finished our lunch and felt rested again, we went back to the shore of the lake. The ducks were exactly as they had been upon our arrival. We stood on the damp sand and watched over them.

There was nothing mystical about the scene in the end. No unworldly presence suggested itself in the shallow water. There was only the salt lake precisely as it was, and a sky that all day had not been disturbed by an aeroplane. All the same, it was a place (the lake, the sky, the whole sense of it all) that you didn't want to treat like more familiar places.

When we made up our minds to go it was in sadness. A single duck's cry carried to our ears with almost no volume at all, the smallest increment imaginable before deafness begins.

—▬—

Our return hike through the desert took much less time than the journey we had begun just as the sun was rising. We walked quickly, shut out distractions, only parted company once, each of us taking the grassy route around the pale olive expanse of scrub that the other one had taken when we were still making our way towards the unknown salt lake. Our voices sang out across the even surface of the bushes so each other might hear, and perhaps be comforted.

The sign requesting visitors to leave the Little Desert around either end of the short run of wire fencing is easy to miss, as we had been guilty of, when proceeding in the direction of the water. We couldn't pretend we hadn't seen it now coming back. Climbing over the turnstile, however, would save us any further time today in the desert. It looked easy enough. Together we took hold of one of the metal arms.

Perhaps it was some chemistry of our four hands simultaneously gripping this object (palms of a man and of a woman) that made it suddenly turn the wrong way, shift backwards without warning from the salt-lake side. Whatever the reason, in an instant we were ejected from the desert and needing to pick ourselves up. My wife's pants required dusting and I was happy to oblige. Checking the white numbers – the dry bodies of insects caught between the discs of the meter – I realized, by some fluke of memory, that they were exactly as they had been after our entrance at dawn.

This seemed to mean two things: our inelegant departure had not registered on the counter; and, no one else had come through. We had always felt ourselves alone that day. Yet perhaps the white numbers had, in fact, surreptitiously registered our exit, had clicked back (once? twice?) while we tumbled out of the Little Desert, and either a single person or a couple, whom we had never seen, had entered after us. Perhaps they were still in there.

Starting the car, I suddenly thought that our trip to the salt lake was somehow never to stop happening. And then I had the impression that I was having the same thought distinctly and clearly again.

— —

The next morning, we ate breakfast sitting on the double bed in our room. A stray leaflet advertising the house-museum reputedly the Nhill home of the nineteenth-century romanticist poet John Shaw Neilson slipped between the sheets. Afterwards I swam several slow laps of the nauseatingly chlorinated pool – one clothes-peg still winked from the bottom.

Melbourne half a day away. In her reclined seat, my wife recited the back of our tourist map. The Little Desert and the Big Desert are two unique geographical and climatic regions; each is different from the adjoining countryside, and each is different from the other. She pointed to the north, without turning her head my way, and said that the Big Desert was less than 100 kilometres – pointing vaguely northwards, with splayed fingers – over there . . .

That afternoon, turning into our street in the suburb of St Kilda, I glimpsed again the brilliant green waters of Port Phillip Bay. How could such intensity ever seem so deep to us again? My wife started telling me that everything was going to be fine in a little while and I needed to listen to her with great care. Every word she used sounded as though travelling to me through both water and sand, and from much further away than she really was.

'I love you.'

(2006)

THE SEARCH FOR MR CUNNINGHAM

Major Sir Thomas Mitchell

April 17, 1835 – The sun of this very hot day, was near setting by the time I met our party, to whom I had hastened back. They had travelled two miles beyond the dry creek, which it was my intention now to trace downwards as fast as possible, followed by all our animals, in hopes that it would lead to water. While the men were unyoking the teams, I was informed, that Mr Cunningham was missing. The occasional absence of this gentleman was not uncommon, but, as he had left the party early in the day, in order to join me, it was evident, from his not having done so, that he had gone astray. At that moment, I felt less anxiety on the subject, little doubting that he would gain our camp, before I returned from the forlorn search, I was about to make for water. Leaving Mr Larmer with the rest of the party to encamp there, I proceeded eastward towards the dry creek, whose course I soon intercepted, and I hurried the bullock drivers along its bed downwards, until, after crossing many a hopeful but dry hole, they begged, that the cattle might be allowed to rest. Leaving them, therefore, I continued my search with the horses, still following the channel, until I had the happiness of seeing the stars of heaven reflected from a spacious

71

pool. We had, in fact, reached the junction of the creek with the Bogan. Having filled our kettles and leathern bottles, we hastened back, to where we had left the bullocks. Leaving them to go forward and refresh, I set off at a venture, on the bearing of south-west by south, in search of our camp. After an hour's riding, the moon rose, and at length our cooy was answered. I had previously observed, by the moon's light, the track left by my horse that morning in the long dry grass, and verified it by some of my marks on the trees. Would that Mr Cunningham had been as fortunate! At that time I did not doubt, that I should find him at the camp; especially as we heard no guns, it being a practice in the bush to fire shots, when persons are missing, that they may hear the report, and so find the party. I then made sure of a pleasant night's rest, as I was relieved from my anxiety respecting the cattle.

I had the pain to learn, however, on reaching the camp about eleven o'clock, that Mr Cunningham was still absent; and, what was worse, in all probability suffering from want of water. I had repeatedly cautioned this gentleman, about the danger of losing sight of the party in such a country; yet his carelessness in this respect was quite surprising. The line of route, after being traversed by our carts, looked like a road that had been used for years, and it was almost impossible to doubt, then, that he would fall in with it next morning.

April 18 – We continued to fire shots and sound the bugle till eleven o'clock. Our cattle were then ready to drink again, and as Mr Cunningham was probably a-head of us, to proceed on our route to the Bogan without further delay was indispensable, in order that we might, in case of need, make such extensive search for him, as was only possible from a camp where we could continue stationary.

We accordingly proceeded towards the Bogan, anxiously hoping, that Mr Cunningham would fall in with our line, and rejoin the party in the course of the day. After proceeding due north 8 miles, we came upon the bed of this river; but, before I could find water in it, I had to trace its course some way up and down. We at length encamped near a pond, and night advanced, but poor Mr Cunningham came not!

— ·—

April 19 – After an almost sleepless night, I rose early, and could relieve my anxiety only by organising a search, to be made in different directions, and getting into movement as soon as possible. The darkness of a second night of dreary solitude, had passed over our fellow-traveller, under the accumulated horrors of thirst, hunger, and despair!

It was most mysterious, that he had not fallen in with our line of route, which was a plain, broad road, since the passage of the carts; and had a direction due north and south for 10 miles. The last time, he had been seen, was 12 miles back, or about 2 miles from the dry bed of the creek (since named Bullock Creek), where I changed the direction, from north-west by compass, to due north, that I might sooner reach the Bogan, for the sake of water. It was probable, that in following my marked trees without much attention, he had not observed the turn I took there, and that continuing in the same direction, beyond the creek, he had therefore lost them, and had proceeded too far to the westward. This was the more likely, as the dry creek was on the eastward of our line; where, had he gone that way, he must have found our cattle-tracks, or met with the cattle. I, therefore, determined to examine myself the whole country westward of our line for 12 miles back. I sent the Doctor and Murray, west by compass 6 miles, with orders to return in a south-east direction, till they intersected the route, and then return along it;

and I sent two other men back along the route, in case our missing friend might have been coming on in a weakly state that way. All three parties carried water and provisions. I proceeded, myself, with two men on horseback, first 7 miles in a south-west direction, which brought me into the line, Mr Cunningham might have followed, supposing he had continued north-west. The country I traversed, consisted of small plains, and alternate patches of dense casuarina scrubs, and open forest land.

I seldom saw to less distance, about me, than from 1 to 2 miles, or at least as far as that in some one direction. We continued to cooy frequently, and the two men were ordered to look on the ground for a horse's track.

In the centre of a small plain, where I changed my direction to the south-east, I set up a small stick with a piece of paper fixed in it, containing the following words,

'Dear Cunningham,

These are my horse's tracks, follow them backwards, they will lead you to our camp, which is N. E. of you.

T. L. MITCHELL.'

Having proceeded in the same manner, seven miles to the south-east, I came upon our route where it crossed Bullock creek, and there I found the two men, who had been sent from the camp.

We then continued our search back along the west side of our route, the party, which now consisted of five, spreading so as to keep abreast at about 200 yards from each other, one being on the road. We thus ascertained that no track of Mr Cunningham's horse or of himself appeared on the soft parts of our road; and although we retraced our steps thus to where Murray, one of the men, said he saw Mr Cunningham the last time with the party, no traces could be found of him or his horse. A kangaroo dog was also missing, and supposed to be with him.

Returning, we continued the search, and particularly to the westward of Bullock creek, where the direction of our route had been changed; but I was disappointed in all our endeavours to find any traces of him there, although I enjoyed, for some time, a gleam of hope, on seeing the track of a horse near the bed of the creek, but it returned to our line, and was afterwards ascertained to have been made by the horse of Mr Larmer.

Although scarcely able to walk myself, from a sprain (my horse having fallen in a hole that day, and rolled on my foot), I shall never forget with what anxiety I limped along that track, which seemed to promise so well; yet we were so unsuccessful that evening, on the very ground where, afterwards, Mr Cunningham's true track was found, that I could no longer imagine, that our unfortunate fellow-traveller could be to the westward.

By what fatality, we failed to discover the tracks afterwards found there, I know not; but, as the sun descended, we returned once more to the camp in the hope that Mr Cunningham might have reached it. That hope was soon disappointed, and I became apprehensive that some accident had befallen him. Holes in the soft surface and yawning cracks, formed rather a peculiar feature in that part of the country; and as my horse had fallen both on this day and the preceding, when at a canter, and as Mr Cunningham was often seen at that pace, it was probable, that he might have met with some severe fall, and lay helpless, not far, perhaps, from where he had last been seen. The nights were cold, and I was doubtful whether he could still be alive, so difficult was it to account, other-wise, for his continued absence under all the circumstances.

April 20 – After another night of painful anxiety, the dawn of the *third* day of Mr Cunningham's absence, brought some relief, as daylight renewed the chance of finding him, or of his finding us by our line, as he might have endeavoured to retrace his steps on losing the party, or he might be on our route still farther back than we had looked; but I was desirous that the natives whom we had left at Bèny might be sent in search. I despatched the Doctor and Murray back along the line, the latter saying, that he knew where Mr Cunningham had turned off the road. It was not unlikely that the horse, if he had got loose, might have returned to where he had last drank water (20 miles distant), therefore, they were directed, if traces were not found nearer, to go so far back, and to promise the natives, if they could meet with any, tomahawks, &c. if they found the 'white man', or 'his horse'. No other course could be imagined. The line of route, as already stated, was a beaten road, and extended north and south. To the east of it, and nearly parallel, at two or three miles distance, was the dry channel (Bullock Creek), which led to the Bogan; on the north was our camp and the Bogan, whose general course was west, as well as our intended route, circumstances both known to Mr Cunningham. Southward was the marked route, and the country whence we had come. Still, however, I thought it so likely, that he must have gone to the north-west, when we changed our route to north, that I determined, although my sprained ankle was painful, to examine again, and still more extensively, the country into which such a deviation must have led him.

April 21 – I proceeded in a south-south-west direction, (or S. 17° W. by compass), or on an intermediate line between our route and the north-west line, by which I had explored that country on the nineteenth, the men cooying as before.

We explored every open space; and we looked into many bushes, but in vain.

I continued my journey far to the southward, in order to ascertain what water was nearest in that direction, as it was probable, were any found, that Mr Cunningham, if alive, must have reached it, and I had in vain sought his track on the other side of the country.

I soon came to undulating ground, or low hills of quartzose gravel without any grass, consisting of unabraded small angular fragments of quartz. I observed a few trees of the iron-bark eucalyptus, and pines or *callitris*, on the highest grounds. At twenty miles from our camp, we crossed a grassy flat, in which we at length found a chain of ponds, falling to the south-south-east, and also about them were recent marks of natives. At length I espied two at a distance, as I proceeded along the valley. In vain we cooyd, and beckoned to them to approach; it was clear they would not come to us; on seeing which, I left the men and horses and walked towards them, carrying a green bough before me. They seemed at once to understand this emblem of peace; for, as soon as I was near enough for them to see it, they laid down their spears and waddies, and sat down on the ground to receive me. Not a word, however, could they understand, being evidently quite strangers to the colonists. They were both rather old men, but very athletic, and of commanding air and stature, the body of one was painted with pipe-clay, that of the other with yellow ochre; and through these tints their well-defined muscles, firm as those of some antique torso, stood out in bold relief in the beams of the setting sun. The two made a fine group, on which dress would have been quite superfluous, and absolutely a blot on the picture.

No gesture of mine could convey the idea, with which I wished so much to impress them, of my search for *another white man*, and after using every kind of gesture, in vain, I made a bow in despair, and departed. They rose at the same time, apparently glad (from fear) to see me going, and motioned, as if to say, 'you may depart now, we are friends.' One of them who sat behind, and who appeared to be the older of the two, had a bone-handled table-knife stuck in the band over his forehead; one had also an iron tomahawk. The rest of the tribe were concealed about, as we heard their cooys, but no others ventured to appear. I thought, I could not give them further proof of no harm being intended to them, than by quietly going on my way, and I hoped that this friendly demonstration might remove any apprehensions respecting Cunningham, if he chanced to meet the tribe. The greatest danger to be apprehended from natives, is on a stranger first approaching them, when, chiefly from fear, they are apt to act on the offensive.

Continuing on the same line, I crossed another small water-course, falling north-east; and beyond it were hills of *micaschist* and *quartz*, which sloped rather boldly to the southward. We then entered one of the finest tracts of forest land I ever saw. It was there three miles in width, and bounded on the south by another low hill of quartzose gravel, the soil of which was indifferent. We at last tied up our horses on a little patch of forest land, and laid down under a few boughs, as it was quite dark and began to rain.

April 22 – After a fruitless ride of twelve more miles, still further southward, in pursuit of distant columns of smoke, we turned our horses' heads towards the camp, on a bearing of N. 56° E., in which direction some summits appeared. We crossed much good whinstone land, and arrived at a small ridge, where I ascended a hill, consisting of a reddish granite or porphyry. From this height I again saw Harvey's and Croker's ranges, and various hills to the southward, but I was disappointed in the view of the western horizon, which was confined to a very flat-topped woody range. I took as many angles as I could, from a round pinnacle of porphyry, which barely afforded standing room.

From this hill, we saw smoke near another eminence, which bore N. 36° E., distant about seven miles; and in that direction we proceeded (as it led homewards), but twilight overtook us, as we crossed its side, on which the bushes appeared to have been recently burnt.

This hill consisted of a rock resembling felspar, and was connected with the former, which was of granite, by low hills consisting of schistus and trap. The former had good grass about it, and produced a chain of well-filled ponds, but here we found no water, having arrived so late. The country in general was, (in point of grass at least) much better than the rotten ground on the banks of the Bogan. The water also, although scarce, was much better, and I heartily regretted, that it was not in my power to proceed, according to my original plan, along this higher ground, in my progress towards the Darling.

April 23 – Early this morning, I ascended the hill, although much incommoded by my sprained ankle, which obliged me to ride my horse over rocks, to the very summit. I could perceive no more smoke. The Canobolas were just visible to the right of Mount Juson. The height on which I stood, seemed to be the furthest interior point of this chain, whence those hills could be seen. We left the summit at nine o'clock, and proceeded towards our route on a bearing of N. 17° E. At ten miles, we halted to allow the horses to pick some green grass in a casuarina scrub; and then, after riding two miles further, we reached our marked route, at about three miles back from Bullock creek. We saw no traces on it, of the men I had sent back, for which I was at a loss to account; but I readily turned every circumstance, even my own ill success, in favour of the expectation, that I should find Mr Cunningham in the camp on my return: thus hope grew even out of disappointment. There, however, I learned, that the two men sent back, had at length found Mr Cunningham's track, exactly where we had at first so diligently sought for it, and that they had traced it into the country, which I had twice traversed in search of him in vain, and, more distressing than all, that they had been compelled to leave the track the preceding evening for want of rations! They had been, however, sent back to take it up, and we anxiously awaited the result

April 24 – Late in the evening the two men, (the Doctor and Murray), returned, having lost all further trace of Mr Cunningham, in a small oak scrub. They had distinctly seen the track of the dog with him, and that of his own steps beside those of the horse, as if he had been leading it.

April 25 – Early this morning, I despatched Mr Larmer and the Doctor, Muirhead and Whiting, supplied with four days' provisions and water. The party was directed to look well around the scrub, and on discovering the track to follow it, wherever it led, until they found Mr Cunningham or his remains; for in such a country, I began to despair of discovering him alive, after so long an absence. They did not return until the evening of the 28th, when all they brought of Mr Cunningham, was his saddle and bridle, whip, one glove, two straps and a piece of paper folded like a letter, inside of which were cut (as with a penknife) the letters N. E. Mr Larmer reported, that having easily found the track of the horse, beyond the scrub, they had followed it until they came to where the horse lay dead, having still the saddle on, and the bridle in its mouth; the whip and straps, had been previously found, and from these circumstances, the tortuous track of the horse, and the absence of Mr Cunningham's own footsteps for some way, from where the horse was found; it was considered that he had either left the animal in despair, or that it had got away from him. At all events, it had evidently died for want of water; but the fate of its unfortunate rider was still a mystery.

It appeared from Mr Larmer's map of Mr Cunningham's track, that he had deviated from our line after crossing Bullock creek, and had proceeded about fourteen miles to the north-west, where marks of his having tied up his horse and lain down, induced the party to believe, that he had there passed the first dreary night of his wandering.

From that point, he appeared to have intended to return, and by the zig-zag course he took, that he had either been travelling in the dark, or looking for his own track, that he might retrace it. In this manner, his steps actually approached within a mile of our route, but in such a manner, that he appeared to have been going south, while we were travelling north, (on the 18th). Thus, he had continued to travel southward, or south-south-west, full 14 miles, crossing his own track not far from where he first quitted our route. On his left, he had the dry channel (Bullock Creek), with the water-gum-trees (eucalypti), full in view, though without ever looking into it for water. Had he observed this channel, and followed it downwards, he must have found our route; and had he traced it upwards, he must have come upon the water-holes, where I had an interview with the two natives, and thus, perhaps, have fallen in with me. From the marks of his horse having been tied to four different trees, at the extreme southern point which he reached, it appeared, that he had halted there some time, or passed there the second night. That point was not much more than half a mile to the westward of my track out on the 21st. From it, he had returned, keeping still more to the westward, so that he actually fell in with my track of the 19th, and appeared to have followed it backwards for upwards of a mile, when he struck off at a right angle to the north-west.

It was impossible to account for this fatal deviation, even had night, as most of the party supposed, overtaken him there. It seemed, that he had found my paper directing him to trace my steps backwards, and that he had been doing this, where the paper marked 'N. E.' had been found, and which I, therefore, considered a sort of reply to my note. If we were right, as to the nights, this must have taken place on the very day, on which I had passed that way, and when my eye eagerly caught at every dark coloured distant object, in hopes of finding him! After the deviation to the north-west, it appears, that Mr Cunningham made some detours about a clear plain, at one side of which his horse had been tied for a considerable time, and where it is probable he had passed his third night, as there were marks, where he had lain down in the long dry grass. From this point, only his horse's tracks had been traced, not his own steps, which had hitherto accompanied them; and from the twisting and turning of the course to where it lay dead, we supposed he had not been with the horse after it left this place. The whip and straps seemed to have been trod off from the bridle-reins to which Mr Cunningham was in the habit of tying his whip, and to which also the straps had been probably attached, to afford the animal more room to feed, when fastened to trees.

To the place, therefore, where Mr Cunningham's own steps had last been seen, I hastened on the morning of the 29th April, with the same men, Muirhead and Whiting, who had so ably and humanely traced all the tracks of the horse, through a distance of 70 miles.

The spot seemed well chosen, as a halting place, being at a few trees which advanced beyond the rest of the wood into a rather extensive plain: a horse, tied there, could have been seen from almost any part around, and it is not improbable, that Mr Cunningham left the animal there fastened, and that it had afterwards got loose, and had finally perished for want of water.

We soon found the print of Mr Cunningham's footsteps in two places: in one, coming towards the trees where the horse had been tied, from a thick scrub east of them; in the other, leading from these trees in a direction straight northward. Pursuing the latter steps, we found them continuous in that direction, and, indeed, remarkably long and firm, the direction being preserved even through thick brushes.

This course was direct for the Bogan; and it was evident, that, urged by intense thirst, he had at length set off, with desperate speed for the river, having parted from his horse, where the party had supposed. That he had killed and eaten the dog in the scrub, whence his footsteps had been seen to emerge was probable, as no trace of the animal was visible beyond it; and as it was difficult, otherwise, to account for his own vigorous step, after an abstinence of three days and three nights. I then regretted, that I had not, at the time, examined the scrub, but, when we were at his last camp (the trees on the plain), we were most interested in Mr Cunningham's further course.

This we traced more than two miles, during which he had never stopped, even to look behind towards the spot where, had he left his horse, he might still have seen him. Having at length lost the track on some very hard ground, we exhausted the day in a vain search for it. On returning to the camp, I found that Mr Larmer, whom I had sent with two armed men down the Bogan, had nearly been surrounded, at only three miles from our camp, by a tribe of natives carrying spears. Amongst these were two who had been with us on the previous day, and who called to the others to keep back. They told Mr Larmer that they had seen Mr Cunningham's track in several parts of the bed of the Bogan; that he had not been killed, but had gone to the westward (pointing down the Bogan), with the 'Myall (i.e. wild) Blackfellows'. Thus, we had reason to hope that our friend had, at least, escaped the fate of his unfortunate horse, by reaching the Bogan. This was what we wished; but no one could have supposed, that he would have followed the river downwards, into the jaws of the wild natives, rather than upwards. His movements show, that he believed he had deviated to the eastward of our route, rather than to the westward; and this mistake accounts for his having gone down the Bogan.

Had he not pursued that fatal course, or had he killed the horse rather than the dog, and remained stationary, his life would have been saved. The result of our twelve days' delay and search was only the discovery, that had we pursued our journey down the Bogan, Mr Cunningham would have fallen in with our track and rejoined us; and that, while we halted for him, he had gone a-head of us, and out of reach.

April 30 – I put the party in movement, along the left bank of the Bogan, its general course being north-west, and about five miles from our camp we crossed the same solitary line of shoe-marks, seen the day before, and still going due north! With sanguine hopes we traced it to a pond in the bed of the river, and the two steps by which Mr Cunningham first reached water, and in which he must have stood while allaying his burning thirst, were very plain in the mud! The scales of some large fish lay upon them, and I could not but hope, that even the most savage natives would have fed a white man, circumstanced as Mr Cunningham must then have been. Overseer Burnett, Whiting and the Doctor, proceeded in search of him down the river, while the party continued, as well as the dense scrubs of casuarinae permitted, in a direction parallel to its course. Just as we found Mr Cunningham's footsteps, a column of smoke arose from the woods to the southward, and I went in search of the natives, Bulger accompanying me with his musket. After we had advanced in the direction of the smoke two miles, it entirely disappeared, and we could neither hear, nor see, any other traces of human beings in these dismal solitudes. The density of the scrubs had obliged me to make some detours to the left, so that I did not reach the Bogan, till long after it was quite dark. Those who had gone in search of Mr Cunningham, did not arrive at our camp that night, although we sent up several sky-rockets, and fired some shots.

May 1 – The party came in from tracing Mr Cunningham's steps, along the dry bed of the Bogan, and we were glad to find that the impressions continued. There appeared to be the print of a small naked foot of some one, either accompanying or tracking Mr Cunningham. At one place, were the remains of a small fire, and the shells of a few mussels, as if he had eaten them. It was now most desirable to get a-head of this track, and I lost no time in proceeding, to the extent of another day's journey parallel to the Bogan, or, rather, so as to cut off a great bend of it.

We crossed some good, undulating ground, open and grassy, the scenery being finer, from the picturesque grouping and character of the trees, than any we had hitherto seen. On one of these open tracts, I wounded a female kangaroo at a far shot of my rifle, and the wretched animal was finally killed after a desperate fight with the dogs.

There is something so affecting in the silent and deadly struggle between the harmless kangaroo and its pursuers, that I have sometimes found it difficult to reconcile the sympathy such a death excites, with our possession of canine teeth, or our necessities, however urgent they might be.

'The huntsman's pleasure is no more,' indeed, when such an animal dies thus before him, persecuted alike by the civilised and the savage. In this instance, a young one, warm from the pouch of its mother, frisked about at a distance, as if unwilling to leave her, although it finally escaped. The nights were cold, and I confess that thoughts of the young kangaroo did obtrude at dinner, and were mingled with my kangaroo-steak.

As we turned to our right, in the afternoon, in search of the Bogan, we encountered some casuarina scrub, to avoid which, we had to wind a little, so that we only made the river at dusk, and at a part of the bed which was dry. Water, as we afterwards found, was near enough upwards, but the two parties sent in the evening having by mistake both sought for it in the other direction, we had none till early in the morning.

May 2 – Five natives were brought to me by Whiting and Tom Jones, on suspicion; one of them having a silk pocket-handkerchief, which they thought might have belonged to Mr Cunningham.

The native wore it fastened over his shoulders, and seemed so careless about our scrutiny, that I could not think he had obtained the handkerchief by any violence; and still less from Mr Cunningham, as it was engrained with a smoky tinge, apparently derived from having been long in his possession. No mark was upon it, and the only information, we could obtain, as to where they got it, was the answer 'old fellow', and pointing to the north-east. As these men had been at some out-station of ours, and could speak a little English, and as they had a young kangaroo dog, called by them 'olony' (Maloney), I did not think at the time that the handkerchief had belonged to Mr Cunningham; and the men appointed to attend him, declared, they had never seen that handkerchief in his hands.

These five natives were overtaken suddenly, at a water-hole two miles lower down the Bogan. The name of him, with the handkerchief, was 'Werrajouit', those of the other four 'Yarree Buckenba', and 'Tackijally Buckenba' (brothers), 'Youimoòba', and 'Werrayoy' (youths). The most intelligent was 'Tackijally', and even he understood but little, not enough to comprehend any thing I said, about the *white man lost in the bush*.

To secure their good will and best services, however, I immediately gave them three tomahawks; and when Yarree Buckenba took a new handkerchief from my pocket, I presented him with it.

They accompanied us, when we moved forward to encamp nearer water. We passed a small pond, the name of which was Burdenda, and afterwards came to Cudduldury, where we encamped, with the intention of making what further search we could for Mr Cunningham.

While the men were pitching the tents, at this place, I rode with the natives, at their request, towards some ponds lower down. There, by their cooys and their looks, they seemed to be very anxious about somebody in the bush, beyond the Bogan. I expected to see their chief; at all events, from these silent woods something was to emerge, in which my guides were evidently much interested, as they kept me waiting nearly an hour for 'Th'unseen genius of the wood'.

At length a man of mild but pensive countenance, athletic form, and apparently about fifty years of age, came forth, leading a very fine boy, so dressed with green boughs, that only his head and legs remained uncovered; a few emu-feathers being mixed with the wild locks of his hair. I received him in this appropriate costume, as a personification of the green bough, or emblem of peace.

One large feather decked the brow of the chief; which, with his nose, was tinged with yellow ochre. Having presented the boy to me, he next advanced with much formality towards the camp, having 'Tackijally' on his right, the boy walking between, and rather in advance of both, each having a hand on his shoulder.

The boy's face had a holiday look of gladness, but the chief remained so silent and serious, without, however, any symptoms of alarm, that my recollections of him then, and as he appeared next day, when better acquainted, are as of two distinct persons.

To this personage, all the others paid the greatest deference, and it is worthy of remark, that they always refused to tell his name, or that of several others, while those of some of the tribe were 'familiar in our mouths as household words'. The boy, who was called Talàmbe Nadóo, was not his son; but he took particular care of him. This tribe gloried in the name of 'Myall', which the natives nearer to the colony apply in terror and abhorrence to the 'wild blackfellows', to whom they usually attribute the most savage propensities.

Not a word could this chief of the Myalls speak, besides his own language; and his slow and formal approach indicated that it was, undoubtedly, the first occasion, on which he had seen white men. It was evident, at once, that he was not the man to wander to stock-stations; and that, whatever others of his race might do, he preferred an undisputed sway, 'Far from the cheerful haunt of men and herds.'

Numbers of the tribe came about us, but they retired at the chief's bidding. Not one, however, except those first met with in the Bogan, could speak any of the jargon, by which the natives usually communicate with the stockmen. We could not make them understand, that we were in search of one of our party, who was lost; neither could Muirhead and Whiting, who were returning to follow up Mr Cunningham's track, prevail on any of these natives to accompany them.

May 3 – The two men having departed, to take up Mr Cunningham's track, I must here observe, that the footsteps had not been discovered in the Bogan, either at our last camp, or at this, although Whiting and Tom Jones had been in search of them, when they found the man with a handkerchief; it was, therefore, most important to ascertain, if possible, where, and under what circumstances, the footsteps disappeared. The skill, with which these men had followed the slightest impressions, was remarkable; and I fixed my hopes on the result of their further exertions.

I cannot say, that I then expected, they would find Mr

Cunningham, conceiving it was more probable, that he had left the Bogan, and gone northward towards our stations on the Macquarie, a river distant only a short day's journey from the Bogan. My anxiety about him was embittered with regret at the inauspicious delay of our journey, which his disappearance had occasioned; and I was too impatient on both subjects, to be able to remain inactive at the camp. I, therefore, set out, followed by two men on horseback, with the intention of reconnoitring the country to the southward, taking with us provisions for two days. After riding 17 miles, the first eight through thick scrub, we came into a more open and elevated country, where we saw pigeons, a sign that water was not distant, on some side of us. The hills were covered with a quartzose soil, containing angular fragments. The callitris pyramidalis, and the stirculia heterophylla were among the trees. At 19 miles we crossed some dry ponds, in open forest ground, and we then continued along fine flats for five miles more, when we again intersected the dry bed of the creek. Still pursuing the same direction, and having the water-course near us on the left, we passed (at the distance of 26 miles) some native fires; but I was too anxious to examine the country before me, to stop, although I saw some of the natives seated by them. We soon after ascended a low ridge of mica-slate; beyond which we came again on the dry creek, and after crossing it several times, we finally lay down, for the night, in its bed (which afforded the best grass), 33 miles from the party at Cudduldury. Although this water-course was perfectly dry throughout, yet it was an interesting feature, in a valley enclosed on each side by undulating hills of mica-slate; and I thought of continuing in its course next morning, in hopes, it might, at last, lead to some chain of ponds falling westward.

May 4 – Our horses had fared but indifferently as to grass, and they had no water until this morning, when we spared to each about half a gallon, of what we carried; but this supply seemed only to make them more thirsty. As soon as it was clear day-light, we continued in the direction of the creek; but, although its bed deepened, and at one place (much trodden by the natives), we discovered a hole, which had only recently dried up, still we found no water. Further on, the recent marks of the natives and their huts also were numerous; but how they existed, in this parched country, was the question! We saw, that around many trees, the roots had been taken up, and we found them without the bark, and cut into short clubs or billets, but for what purpose we could not then discover. At eleven o'clock, I changed my course to 300° from north, and, after travelling about three miles in that direction, I descried a goodly hill on my left, and soon after several others, one of which was bare of trees on the summit. After so long a journey, over unvarying flats, we had at length come rather unawares, as it seemed, into a hilly country, the heights of which were bold, rocky, and of considerable elevation. I should estimate the summit of that which we ascended, was 730 feet above the lower country at its base. The dry creek, which had led us towards these hills, from such a distance northward, had vanished through them somewhere to our left; and, bold as the range was, still we could see no better promise of water, than what this seemed to afford.

The summit, up which we forced our horses over very sharp rocks, commanded a most extensive and magnificent view of hills, both eastward and westward. The country in the north, whence we had come, was, nevertheless, higher, although the horizon there was unbroken. Southward, the general line of horizon was a low level, on which the hills terminated, as if it had been the sea. There, I had no doubt, flowed the river Lachlan, and, probably, one of the highest of the hills, was Mount Granard of Oxley. Towards the east, the most elevated hill bore 142° 30' from N., and was at a distance of about 12 miles. It was a remarkable mass of yellow rock, naked and herbless, as if nature there had not yet finished her work. That hill had an isolated appearance; others to the westward were pointed, and smoke arose from almost every summit, even from the highest part of the mass on which we stood. Some sharp-edged rocks prevented us from riding to where the smoke appeared, and I was too lame to go on foot. No natives were visible, and I could not comprehend, what they could be all about on the various ragged summits whence smoke arose; as these people rather frequent vallies, and the vicinity of ponds of water. The region I now overlooked, was beautifully diversified with hill and dale, still I could not discover much promise of water; but as smoke ascended from one flat to the westward, I conjectured that we might there find a pool, but it was too far distant to be then of use to us. The general direction of hills appeared to be 318° from north; that of the continuation westward of the flat higher land, N. 343°. A broad and extensive smoke was rising from the country where we had slept, and towards which I was about to return by a direct course from this hill (N. 56° E.). Accordingly, we travelled until night overtook us in an extensive, casuarina scrub, where we tied our horses, and made our fire, after a ride of at least 40 miles. During the night, we were made aware, by the crackling of falling timber, that a conflagration was approaching, and one of us by turns watched, while the others slept with their arms at hand. The state of our horses, from want of water, was by no means promising for the long journey, which was necessary to enable us to reach home next day; a circumstance on which the lives of these animals in all probability depended, especially as the grass here was very indifferent. We had also little more than a pint of water for each horse; and it was difficult to give that scanty allowance to any one of the animals, in sight of the others, so furious were they on seeing it.

May 5 – Proceeding in search of our first day's track, we entered almost immediately the burning forest. We perceived, that much pains had been taken by the natives to spread the fire, from its burning in separate places.

Huge trees fell now and then with a crashing sound, loud as thunder, while others hung just ready to fall, and as the country was chiefly open forest, the smoke, at times, added much sublimity to the scenery. We travelled five miles through this fire and smoke, all the while in expectation of coming unawares upon the natives, who had been so busy in annoying us. At length, we saw the huts, which we had passed the day before, and soon after, three natives, who immediately got behind trees as we advanced; but although one ran off, yet the others answered my cooy, and I went towards them on foot, with a green branch. They seemed busy, digging at the root of a large tree; but on seeing me advance, they came forward with a fire-stick and sat down; I followed their example, but the cordiality of our meeting, could be expressed only by mutual laughing.

They were young men, yet one was nearly blind from ophthalmia or filth. I called up one of my men, and gave a tomahawk to the tallest of these youths, making what signs I could, to express my thirst and want of water. Looking as if they understood me, they hastened to resume their work, and I discovered, that they dug up the roots for the sake of drinking the sap. It appeared, that they first cut these roots into billets, and then stripped off the bark or rind, which they sometimes chew, after which, holding up the billet and applying one end to the mouth, they let the juice drop into it. We now understood, for what purpose the short clubs, which we had seen the day before, had been cut. The youths resumed their work the moment they had received the tomahawk, without looking more at us or at the tool. I thought this nonchalance rather singular, and attributed their assiduity either to a desire to obtain for us some of the juice, which would have been creditable to their feelings; or, to the necessity for serving some more powerful native, who had set them to that work. One had gone, apparently to call the tribe, so I continued my journey without further delay. We soon regained our track of the first day, and I followed it with some impatience back to the camp. My horse had been ill on the second day, and as this was the third, on which it, as well as the others, had gone without water, they were so weak, that, had we been retarded by any accident another night in the bush, we must have lost them all. They could be driven on only with difficulty, nevertheless, we reached the camp before sunset.

The tidings brought by the men sent after Mr Cunningham's footsteps, were still most unsatisfactory. They had followed the river bed back for the first twelve miles from our camp, without finding in it a single pond. They had traced the continuation of his track to where it disappeared near some recent fires, where many natives had been encamped. Near one of these fires, they found a portion of the skirt or selvage of Mr Cunningham's coat; numerous small fragments of his map of the colony; and, in the hollow of a tree, some yellow printed paper, in which he used to carry the map. The men examined the ground for half a mile all around without finding more of his footsteps, or any traces of him, besides those mentioned. It was possible, and indeed, as I then thought, probable, that having been deprived by the natives of his coat, he might have escaped from them by going northward, towards some of the various cattle stations on the Macquarie. I learnt that when the men returned with these vestiges of poor Cunningham, there was great alarm amongst the natives, and movements by night, when the greater part of the tribe decamped, and amongst them the fellow with the handkerchief, who never again appeared. The chief, or *king* (as our people called him), continued with us, and seemed quite unconscious of anything wrong. This tribe seemed too far from the place, where the native camp had been, to be suspected of any participation in the ill treatment with which we had too much reason to fear, Mr Cunningham had met. As we had no language to explain, even that one of our party was missing, I could only hope, that, by treating these savages kindly, they might be more disposed, should they ever see or hear of Mr Cunningham, to assist him to rejoin us. To delay the party longer was obviously unnecessary; and, indeed, the loss of more time must have defeated the object of the expedition, considering our limited stock of provisions.

I, therefore, determined on proceeding by short journeys along the Bogan, accompanied by these natives, not altogether without the hope, that Mr Cunningham might still be brought to us, by some of them.

From *Three Expeditions Into the Interior of Eastern Australia* (1839)

AMERICAN DREAMS

Peter Carey

No one can, to this day, remember what it was we did to offend him. Dyer the butcher remembers a day when he gave him the wrong meat and another day when he served someone else first by mistake. Often when Dyer gets drunk he recalls this day and curses himself for his foolishness. But no one seriously believes that it was Dyer who offended him.

But one of us did something. We slighted him terribly in some way, this small meek man with the rimless glasses and neat suit who used to smile so nicely at us all. We thought, I suppose, he was a bit of a fool and sometimes he was so quiet and grey that we ignored him, forgetting he was there at all.

When I was a boy I often stole apples from the trees at his house up in Mason's Lane. He often saw me. No, that's not correct. Let me say I often sensed that he saw me. I sensed him peering out from behind the lace curtains of his house. And I was not the only one. Many of us came to take his apples, alone and in groups, and it is possible that he chose to exact payment for all these apples in his own peculiar way.

Yet I am sure it wasn't the apples.

What has happened is that we all, all eight hundred of us, have come to remember small transgressions against Mr Gleason who once lived amongst us.

My father, who has never borne malice against a single living creature, still believes that Gleason meant to do us well, that he loved the town more than any of us. My father says we have treated the town badly in our minds. We have used it, this little valley, as nothing more than a stopping place. Somewhere on the way to somewhere else. Even those of us who have been here many years have never taken the town seriously. Oh yes, the place is pretty. The hills are green and the woods thick. The stream is full of fish. But it is not where we would rather be.

For years we have watched the films at the Roxy and dreamed, if not of America, then at least of our capital city. For our own town, my father says, we have nothing but contempt. We have treated it badly, like a whore. We have cut down the giant shady trees in the main street to make doors for the school house and seats for the football pavilion. We have left big holes all over the countryside from which we have taken brown coal and given back nothing.

The commercial travellers who buy fish and chips at George the Greek's care for us more than we do, because we all have dreams of the big city, of wealth, of modern houses, of big motor cars: American Dreams, my father has called them.

Although my father ran a petrol station he was also an inventor. He sat in his office all day drawing strange pieces of equipment on the back of delivery dockets. Every spare piece of paper in the house was covered with these little drawings and my mother would always be very careful about throwing away any piece of paper no matter how small. She would look on both sides of any piece of paper very carefully and always preserved any that had so much as a pencil mark.

I think it was because of this that my father felt that he understood Gleason. He never said as much, but he inferred that he understood Gleason because he, too, was concerned with similar problems. My father was working on plans for a giant gravel crusher, but occasionally he would become distracted and become interested in something else.

There was, for instance, the time when Dyer the butcher bought a new bicycle with gears, and for a while my father talked of nothing else but the gears. Often I would see him across the road squatting down beside Dyer's bicycle as if he were talking to it.

We all rode bicycles because we didn't have the money for anything better. My father did have an old Chev truck, but he rarely used it and it occurs to me now that it might have had some mechanical problem that was impossible to solve, or perhaps it was just that he was saving it, not wishing to wear it out all at once. Normally, he went everywhere on his bicycle and, when I was younger, he carried me on the cross bar, both of us dismounting to trudge up the hills that led into and out of the main street. It was a common sight in our town to see people pushing bicycles. They were as much a burden as a means of transport.

Gleason also had his bicycle and every lunchtime he pushed and pedalled it home from the shire offices to his little weatherboard house out at Mason's Lane. It was a three-mile ride and people said that he went home for lunch because he was fussy and wouldn't eat either his wife's sandwiches or the hot meal available at Mrs Lessing's cafe.

But while Gleason pedalled and pushed his bicycle to and from the shire offices everything in our town proceeded as normal. It was only when he retired that things began to go wrong.

Because it was then that Mr Gleason started supervising the building of the wall around the two-acre plot up on Bald Hill. He paid too much for this land. He bought it from Johnny Weeks, who now, I am sure, believes the whole episode was his fault, firstly for cheating Gleason, secondly for selling him the land at all. But Gleason hired some Chinese and set to work to build his wall. It was then that we knew that we'd offended him. My father rode all the way out to Bald Hill and tried to talk Mr Gleason out of his wall. He said there was no need for us to build walls. That no one wished to spy on Mr Gleason or whatever he wished to do on Bald Hill. He said no one was in the least bit interested in Mr Gleason. Mr Gleason, neat in a new sportscoat, polished his glasses and smiled vaguely at his feet. Bicycling back, my father thought that he had gone too far. Of course we had an interest in Mr Gleason. He pedalled back and asked him to attend a dance that was to be held on the next Friday, but Mr Gleason said he didn't dance.

'Oh well,' my father said, 'any time, just drop over.'

Mr Gleason went back to supervising his family of Chinese labourers on his wall.

Bald Hill towered high above the town and from my father's small filling station you could sit and watch the wall going up. It was an interesting sight. I watched it for two years, while I waited for customers who rarely came. After school and on Saturdays I had all the time in the world to watch the agonising progress of Mr Gleason's wall. It was as painful as a clock. Sometimes I could see the Chinese labourers running at a jogtrot carrying bricks on long wooden planks. The hill was bare, and on this bareness Mr Gleason was, for some reason, building a wall.

In the beginning people thought it peculiar that someone would build such a big wall on Bald Hill. The only thing to recommend Bald Hill was the view of the town, and Mr Gleason was building a wall that denied that view. The top soil was thin and bare clay showed through in places. Nothing would ever grow there. Everyone assumed that Gleason had simply gone mad and after the initial interest they accepted his madness as they accepted his wall and as they accepted Bald Hill itself.

Occasionally someone would pull in for petrol at my father's filling station and ask about the wall and my father would shrug and I would see, once more, the strangeness of it.

'A house?' the stranger would ask. 'Up on that hill?'

'No,' my father would say, 'chap named Gleason is building a wall.'

And the strangers would want to know why, and my father would shrug and look up at Bald Hill once more. 'Damned if I know,' he'd say.

Gleason still lived in his old house at Mason's Lane. It was a plain weatherboard house with a rose garden at the front, a vegetable garden down the side and an orchard at the back.

At night we kids would sometimes ride out to Bald Hill on our bicycles. It was an agonising, muscle-twitching ride, the worst part of which was a steep, unmade road up which we finally pushed our bikes, our lungs rasping in the night air. When we arrived we found nothing but walls. Once we broke down some of the brickwork and another time we threw stones at the tents where the Chinese labourers slept. Thus we expressed our frustration at this inexplicable thing.

The wall must have been finished on the day before my twelfth birthday. I remember going on a picnic birthday party up to Eleven Mile Creek and we lit a fire and cooked chops at a bend in the river from where it was possible to see the walls on Bald Hill. I remember standing with a hot chop in my hand and someone saying, 'Look, they're leaving!'

We stood on the creek bed and watched the Chinese labourers walking their bicycles slowly down the hill. Someone said they were going to build a chimney up at the mine at A.1 and certainly there is a large brick chimney there now, so I suppose they built it.

When the word spread that the walls were finished most of the town went up to look. They walked around the four walls which were as interesting as any other brick walls. They stood in front of the big wooden gates and tried to peer through, but all they could see was a small blind wall that had obviously been constructed for this special purpose. The walls themselves were ten feet high and topped with broken glass and barbed wire. When it became obvious that we were not going to discover the contents of the enclosure, we all gave up and went home.

Mr Gleason had long since stopped coming into town. His wife came instead, wheeling a pram down from Mason's Lane to Main Street and filling it with groceries and meat (they never bought vegetables, they grew their own) and wheeling it back to Mason's Lane. Sometimes you would see her standing with the pram halfway up the Gell Street hill. Just standing there, catching her breath. No one asked her about the wall. They knew she wasn't responsible for the wall and they felt sorry for her, having to bear the burden of the pram and her husband's madness. Even when she began to visit Dixon's hardware and buy plaster of paris and tins of paint and water-proofing compound, no one asked her what these things were for. She had a way of averting her eyes that indicated her terror of questions. Old Dixon carried the plaster of paris and the tins of paint out to her pram for her and watched her push them away. 'Poor woman,' he said, 'poor bloody woman.'

From the filling station where I sat dreaming in the sun, or from the enclosed office where I gazed mournfully at the rain, I would see, occasionally, Gleason entering or leaving his walled compound, a tiny figure way up on Bald Hill. And I'd think 'Gleason', but not much more.

Occasionally strangers drove up there to see what was going on, often egged on by locals who told them it was a Chinese temple or some other silly thing. Once a group of Italians had a picnic outside the walls and took photographs of each other standing in front of the closed door. God knows what they thought it was.

But for five years between my twelfth and seventeenth birthdays there was nothing to interest me in Gleason's walls. Those years seem lost to me now and I can remember very little of them. I developed a crush on Susy Markin and followed her back from the swimming pool on my bicycle. I sat behind her in the pictures and wandered past her house. Then her parents moved to another town and I sat in the sun and waited for them to come back.

We became very keen on modernisation. When coloured paints became available the whole town went berserk and brightly coloured houses blossomed overnight. But the paints were not of good quality and quickly faded and peeled, so that the town looked like a garden of dead flowers. Thinking of those years, the only real thing I recall is the soft hiss of bicycle tyres on the main street. When I think of it now it seems very peaceful, but I remember then that the sound induced in me a feeling of melancholy, a feeling somehow mixed with the early afternoons when the sun went down behind Bald Hill and the town felt as sad as an empty dance hall on a Sunday afternoon.

And then, during my seventeenth year, Mr Gleason died. We found out when we saw Mrs Gleason's pram parked out in front of Phonsey Joy's Funeral Parlour. It looked very sad, that pram, standing by itself in the windswept street. We came and looked at the pram and felt sad for Mrs Gleason. She hadn't had much of a life.

Phonsey Joy carried old Mr Gleason out to the cemetery by the Parwan Railway Station and Mrs Gleason rode behind in a taxi.

People watched the old hearse go by and thought, 'Gleason', but not much else.

And then, less than a month after Gleason had been buried out at the lonely cemetery by the Parwan Railway Station, the Chinese labourers came back. We saw them push their bicycles up the hill. I stood with my father and Phonsey Joy and wondered what was going on.

And then I saw Mrs Gleason trudging up the hill. I nearly didn't recognise her, because she didn't have her pram. She carried a black umbrella and walked slowly up Bald Hill and it wasn't until she stopped for breath and leant forward that I recognised her.

'It's Mrs Gleason,' I said, 'with the Chinese.'

But it wasn't until the next morning that it became obvious what was happening. People lined the main street in the way they do for a big funeral but, instead of gazing towards the Grant Street corner, they all looked up at Bald Hill.

All that day and all the next people gathered to watch the destruction of the walls. They saw the Chinese labourers darting to and fro, but it wasn't until they knocked down a large section of the wall facing the town that we realised there really was something inside. It was impossible to see what it was, but there was something there. People stood and wondered and pointed out Mrs Gleason to each other as she went to and fro supervising the work.

And finally, in ones and twos, on bicycles and on foot, the whole town moved up to Bald Hill. Mr Dyer closed up his butcher shop and my father got out the old Chev truck and we finally arrived up at Bald Hill with twenty people on board. They crowded into the back tray and hung on to the running boards and my father grimly steered his way through the crowds of bicycles and parked just where the dirt track gets really steep. We trudged up this last steep track, never for a moment suspecting what we would find at the top.

It was very quiet up there. The Chinese labourers worked diligently, removing the third and fourth walls and cleaning the bricks which they stacked neatly in big piles. Mrs Gleason said nothing either. She stood in the only remaining corner of the walls and looked defiantly at the townspeople who stood open-mouthed where another corner had been.

And between us and Mrs Gleason was the most incredibly beautiful thing I had ever seen in my life. For one moment I didn't recognise it. I stood open-mouthed, and breathed the surprising beauty of it. And then I realised it was our town. The buildings were two feet high and they were a little rough but very correct. I saw Mr Dyer nudge my father and whisper that Gleason had got the faded 'U' in the BUTCHER sign of his shop.

I think at that moment everyone was overcome with a feeling of simple joy. I can't remember ever having felt so uplifted and happy. It was perhaps a childish emotion but I looked up at my father and saw a smile of such warmth spread across his face that I knew he felt just as I did. Later he told me that he thought Gleason had built the model of our town just for this moment, to let us see the beauty of our own town, to make us proud of ourselves and to stop the American Dreams we were so prone to. For the rest, my father said, was not Gleason's plan and he could not have foreseen the things that happened afterwards.

I have come to think that this view of my father's is a little sentimental and also, perhaps, insulting to Gleason. I personally believe that he knew everything that would happen. One day the proof of my theory may be discovered. Certainly there are in existence some personal papers, and I firmly believe that these papers will show that Gleason knew exactly what would happen.

We had been so overcome by the model of the town that we hadn't noticed what was the most remarkable thing of all. Not only

103

had Gleason built the houses and the shops of our town, he had also peopled it. As we tip-toed into the town we suddenly found ourselves. 'Look,' I said to Mr Dyer, 'there you are.'

And there he was, standing in front of his shop in his apron. As I bent down to examine the tiny figure I was staggered by the look on its face. The modelling was crude, the paintwork was sloppy, and the face a little too white, but the expression was absolutely perfect: those pursed, quizzical lips and the eyebrows lifted high. It was Mr Dyer and no one else on earth.

And there beside Mr Dyer was my father, squatting on the footpath and gazing lovingly at Mr Dyer's bicycle's gears, his face marked with grease and hope.

And there was I, back at the filling station, leaning against a petrol pump in an American pose and talking to Brian Sparrow who was amusing me with his clownish antics.

Phonsey Joy standing beside his hearse. Mr Dixon sitting inside his hardware store. Everyone I knew was there in that tiny town. If they were not in the streets or in their backyards they were inside their houses, and it didn't take very long to discover that you could lift off the roofs and peer inside.

We tip-toed around the streets peeping into each other's windows, lifting off each other's roofs, admiring each other's gardens, and, while we did it, Mrs Gleason slipped silently away down the hill towards Mason's Lane. She spoke to nobody and nobody spoke to her.

I confess that I was the one who took the roof from Cavanagh's house. So I was the one who found Mrs Cavanagh in bed with young Craigie Evans.

I stood there for a long time, hardly knowing what I was seeing. I stared at the pair of them for a long, long time. And when I finally knew what I was seeing I felt such an incredible mixture of jealousy and guilt and wonder that I didn't know what to do with the roof.

Eventually it was Phonsey Joy who took the roof from my hands and placed it carefully back on the house, much, I imagine, as he would have placed the lid on a coffin. By then other people had seen what I had seen and the word passed around very quickly.

And then we all stood around in little groups and regarded the model town with what could only have been fear. If Gleason knew about Mrs Cavanagh and Craigie Evans (and no one else had), what other things might he know? Those who hadn't seen themselves yet in the town began to look a little nervous and were unsure of whether to look for themselves or not. We gazed silently at the roofs and felt mistrustful and guilty.

We all walked down the hill then, very quietly, the way people walk away from a funeral, listening only to the crunch of the gravel under our feet while the women had trouble with their high-heeled shoes.

The next day a special meeting of the shire council passed a motion calling on Mrs Gleason to destroy the model town on the grounds that it contravened building regulations.

It is unfortunate that this order wasn't carried out before the city newspapers found out. Before another day had gone by the government had stepped in.

The model town and its model occupants were to be preserved. The minister for tourism came in a large black car and made a speech to us in the football pavilion. We sat on the high, tiered seats eating potato chips while he stood against the fence and talked to us. We couldn't hear him very well, but we heard enough. He called the model town a work of art and we stared at him grimly. He said it would be an invaluable tourist attraction. He said tourists would come from everywhere to see the model town. We would be famous. Our businesses would flourish. There would be work for guides and interpreters and caretakers and taxi drivers and people selling soft drinks and ice creams.

The Americans would come, he said. They would visit our town in buses and in cars and on the train. They would take photographs and bring wallets bulging with dollars. American dollars.

We looked at the minister mistrustfully, wondering if he knew about Mrs Cavanagh, and he must have seen the look because he said that certain controversial items would be removed, had already been removed. We shifted in our seats, like you do when a particularly tense part of a film has come to its climax, and then we relaxed and listened to what the minister had to say. And we all began, once more, to dream our American Dreams.

We saw our big smooth cars cruising through cities with bright lights. We entered expensive night clubs and danced till dawn. We made love to women like Kim Novak and men like Rock Hudson. We drank cocktails. We gazed lazily into refrigerators filled with food and prepared ourselves lavish midnight snacks which we ate while we watched huge television sets on which we would be able to see American movies free of charge and forever.

The minister, like someone from our American Dreams, re-entered in his large black car and cruised slowly from our humble sportsground, and the newspaper men arrived and swarmed over the pavilion with their cameras and notebooks. They took photographs of us and photographs of the models up on Bald Hill. And the next day we were all over the newspapers. The photographs of the model people side by side with photographs of the real people. And our names and ages and what we did were all printed there in black and white.

They interviewed Mrs Gleason but she said nothing of interest. She said the model town had been her husband's hobby.

We all felt good now. It was very pleasant to have your photograph in the paper. And, once more, we changed our opinion of Gleason. The shire council held another meeting and named the dirt track up Bald Hill 'Gleason Avenue'. Then we all went home and waited for the Americans we had been promised.

It didn't take long for them to come, although at the time it seemed an eternity, and we spent six long months doing nothing more with our lives than waiting for the Americans.

Well, they did come. And let me tell you how it has all worked out for us.

The Americans arrive every day in buses and cars and sometimes the younger ones come on the train. There is now a small airstrip out near the Parwan cemetery and they also arrive there, in small aeroplanes. Phonsey Joy drives them to the cemetery where they look at Gleason's grave and then up to Bald Hill and then down to the town. He is doing very well from it all. It is good to see someone doing well from it. Phonsey is becoming a big man in town and is on the shire council.

On Bald Hill there are half a dozen telescopes through which the Americans can spy on the town and reassure themselves that it is the same down there as it is on Bald Hill. Herb Gravney sells them ice creams and soft drinks and extra film for their cameras. He is another one who is doing well. He bought the whole model from Mrs Gleason and charges five American dollars admission. Herb is on the council now too. He's doing very well for himself. He sells them the film so they can take photographs of the houses and the model people and so they can come down to the town with their special maps and hunt out the real people.

To tell the truth most of us are pretty sick of the game. They come looking for my father and ask him to stare at the gears of Dyer's bicycle. I watch my father cross the street slowly, his head hung low. He doesn't greet the Americans any more. He doesn't ask them questions about colour television or Washington D.C. He kneels on the footpath in front of Dyer's bike. They stand around him. Often they remember the model incorrectly and try to get my father to pose in the wrong way. Originally he argued with them, but now he argues no more. He does what they ask. They push him this way and that and worry about the expression on his face which is no longer what it was.

Then I know they will come to find me. I am next on the map. I am very popular for some reason. They come in search of me and my petrol pump as they have done for four years now. I do not await them eagerly because I know, before they reach me, that they will be disappointed.

'But this is not the boy.'

'Yes,' says Phonsey, 'this is him alright.' And he gets me to show them my certificate.

They examine the certificate suspiciously, feeling the paper as if it might be a clever forgery. 'No,' they declare. (Americans are so confident.) 'No,' they shake their heads, 'this is not the real boy. The real boy is younger.'

'He's older now. He used to be younger.' Phonsey looks weary when he tells them. He can afford to look weary.

The Americans peer at my face closely. 'It's a different boy.'

But finally they get their cameras out. I stand sullenly and try to look amused as I did once. Gleason saw me looking amused but I can no longer remember how it felt. I was looking at Brian Sparrow. But Brian is also tired. He finds it difficult to do his clownish antics and to the Americans his little act isn't funny. They prefer the model. I watch him sadly, sorry that he must perform for such an unsympathetic audience.

The Americans pay one dollar for the right to take our

photographs. Having paid the money they are worried about being cheated. They spend their time being disappointed and I spend my time feeling guilty that I have somehow let them down by growing older and sadder.

(1974)

THE BURIAL AND THE BUSKER

Gillian Mears

Part of the new highway will soon run over the remains of eighteen bodies. My best friend is under the shiniest headstone. An old section of Little Fineflour cemetery's been chosen by the Main Roads Department for resumption. My friend is only there because her grandpop said to put her next to his baby son who died of the whooping cough in 1913. The little boy's name was John George William Wyre. *Such a long name*, we said, *for such a tiny grave.* We used to hate the way the low fence marking the spot leaked rust. One Christmas holiday we tried planting pink and white Baby's Breath but somehow the weeds choked up the seedlings. My friend blamed the seed bought from Powers' Produce. She said it was probably too old to grow properly. Those dusty little packets of Yates Reliable Seed failed us after a promising germination.

The Baby's Breath is dying, we whispered, yanking out clumps of paspalum, wondering if small baby bones would be clinging in the dusty root systems. Wondering if John George William was going to emerge unexpectedly from the grey dirt.

Don't worry little man. Little Johnnie, we used soft, singsong voices. We tended the grave like a fragile baby. Thinking we were going to the river, our mothers packed picnic lunches.

Lizards went in and out of cracked cemetery cement and it would've been good to follow, just to see, we said. Would it be peaceful really in the ash-coloured soil? We were going to bring weeding forks, watering cans, but it was the middle of school holidays and the endless blue sky faded our good intentions. In the end, the river was much cooler, the willows easier to climb, than the ancient camphor laurel in the graveyard corner.

It was a big funeral but gee it was hot, her grandpop said. *She would've wanted you there y'know. Best mates and all that weren't you,* his teeth clacked. A mozzie bit my ankle. I cried on his best dark suit. My best friend's father – the ferryman – was crying too. In the corner. And he held his head as if it was about to split wide open. The superficial bullet wound was covered with a wad of gauze. *There now,* her grandpop fumbled for his pipe and pretending I was really small, said I could light it for him if I stopped crying. It felt funny, trying to balance on his knees. They'd become unsafe and suddenly too skinny. His skeleton was as easy as anything to feel, bony and old like his pipe. The ferryman cried and twisted his hair and no-one sat by him.

Nobody knew, but I was at the burial. Mum thought it best that I stay at school and handed me lunch the same as any ordinary day. It was a ten o'clock funeral. I wore my winter-uniform jumper and boiled, running the back road to the cemetery. The green wool was exactly the right colour. If anyone looked into the camphor laurel, they couldn't have seen a thing. I kept so still, even when the cars were only a glinting spiral along from the church.

Behind the cars, the town went blue and shrunken looking.

Way over the church spire to Greenwood's farm was tiny and sick too. All the paddocks dying in the drought. Someone else was early – the busker I'd seen down the street the day before. He walked right past the camphor laurel without looking up. Did he hear me scrabbling up the trunk? I recognised him straight off, though I'd only seen him once as I went past with Mum. He was playing his guitar on the footpath outside the cake shop. Mum wouldn't be persuaded to make a contribution, though there was only one lonely coin in his hat. For some unknown reason Mum was huffy about him being there at all and went right on past like he didn't even exist. I nudged her, not bearing to look in the man's direction. But instead of being generous like she normally is, even to the Trinitarian Bible Society women, she pretended to count the raisin buns she'd just bought. I went by the busker slowly, he sang so softly and his shirt was full of moons and stars and magic blue shapes. He smiled back at me as if he knew the old song he was singing was a favourite of my best friend lying somewhere round the corner, in Mr Saxton's funeral house. On that hot day I found it hard to think how cold she must be. Would she be lying next to Joy, I wondered, and hoped not.

That day before the funeral was a dry day like any other. Opposite the busker, a black labrador peed on the butcher's blackboard, half-erasing the message about Bacon Rashes and Stewing Stake on special. Embarrassing in front of a stranger – having a butcher who couldn't spell.

The stranger wasn't shy at the cemetery. From my hidden spot in the tree, I watched him twiddling guitar knobs. I thought I could see the hearse moving away from the church, yet he seemed in no hurry. He played some thin, untuned notes. They hung too high in the hot air. The cars began turning into the cemetery, making the music stop short.

The faces of people coming from church were squashed up and sad through the windscreens. Cars inched along, the way I imagine they did for the new Queen of England when she was in Sydney. The local paper had a big supplement describing the royal tour. At the burial there were local dignitaries too. The mayor of Fineflour, being a racing man, went along with his wife and wore his robes. Really though, it was hard to see who was who. The two coffins sliding from the hearse looked identical.

Everything was going too slowly; the mares' tails in the sky and the river unthreading itself from the town. A long way away, a sailing boat barely moved. Its sails were silent like the freshly dug soil, the unfinished song and the big hands of my friend's grandpop, mopping off the sweat from his face. They'd brought the ferryman from the hospital. He sat slumped in a wheelchair. He looked dead.

My cheese sandwich, neatly wrapped, slipped out of the tree. The coffins were being unloaded so I'm sure no-one heard its shuffling fall into the nightshade. Only the busker might have glanced up but I couldn't be sure. Nerdy Nadia was there with a few other girls from school. She's said I can be friends with them but they're all boy-mad. And they stared and giggled at the busker. Mum and Dad were standing with the Henrys; Dad wearing saggy black pants and stooping towards the grave as if he'd half-like to be gone himself. And Mum, holding firmly to his cardiganed elbow, as her other hand searched for Kleenex in her bra. They weren't in their element at funerals. I could see that with the January sun boring into their soft necks. Somewhere I've read how bells used to be tolled at funerals to drive off evil spirits. There were no bells at my best friend's burial – only the busker's song and the sound of the tumbling glass coming from the soft drink recycling factory.

In the drooping cardigan, my father looked sad from above. The busker stood apart from everybody else. Long ovals of sweat grew from under his magical shirt. *Interstate mourners*, Mum had mentioned that morning, *were staying with relatives or at the Standard Hotel*. He must've been one of those. I could almost smell his sweat, the only wet thing besides tears in the dry old morning. When the cars went away again, I thought I could smell it still, stronger than cat pee, through the monotonous shovelling of the grave-digger. A salty, sad smell as the dirt thudded on top of the coffins and I wondered if a few feet away there was anything left of John George William Wyre, died of the whooping cough, 1913. And who was on the bottom? My friend or her mother?

The busker left first. I couldn't believe how he walked away without waiting for me to ask the name of his song or when it was he got to know my best friend. The sun made his hair glint like metal. Maybe he was one of the Manly cousins? But the busker looked too old. When he cried lines curved like laughter down his cheeks. He walked away before the ceremony was properly finished. The mares' tails grew long and low in the sky and I felt stretched and white by the incompleteness of it all.

'Here's your drink.' Mum hands me the plastic bottle, already wrapped in a tea-towel. The fridge door thuds shut behind her.

'Thanks.' It's cold in my hands, iced overnight but it'll be lukewarm by lunchtime.

'And sandwiches. Fishpaste, your favourite, Judy, so don't go wasting them.'

'No, Mum.' Fishpaste is revolting. On white bread it looks pale pink like dog sick. I only used to ask for it because my best friend said fishpaste sandwiches made good bait. She said fish were cannibals and maybe she was right because always we got more bites than Eddie Rigglesford who used plain breadcrust.

114

The same holiday we spent mucking round the graves was also spent fishing from Kelly's jetty. For a reason I already can't remember, it was one of the years she didn't go to stay with the rellies who lived a five-minute walk from Manly beach. Normally she'd return only a week before school started back, smelling of fish and chips and sea, with even the skin under her eyebrows peeling. Her hair turned frizzy with hundreds of bleached split ends from body-surfing. Swimming in the river each day made my hair limp with a muddy feel to it. My skin went the colour of flood silt, not cracking even after six weeks. Always strange to be together after holidays but it never took long for my friend to take on the same faintly sulphuric, mud flavoured odour of all the other kids who'd stayed at home. After a few weeks back her hair seemed to get darker and her toes stopped peeling. She'd rave on for ages after about the beach though – the waves and the blond boys who were in Young Lifesavers with her cousins. My stories of catching bream and flathead on the rising river tide late at night sounded dim and tired by comparison. What had been such an exciting phenomenon – sea fish being pushed this far up the river because of the high salt levels in the water – became instantly boring. Not that she didn't try to be enthusiastic, but my fishing exploits with little Eddie Rigglesford reminded her of how Pete, a new Manly friend, caught the monster jewfish off the breakwater and even let her reel in some of the line. Or the school of whiting right under them as they waited for a decent-sized wave to catch. She had a high, excited voice that made me see the thin, silver fish, close enough to lean down and touch, runs of sunlight between them, a rippling green sea. Toasting river shrimps outside Eddie Rigglesford's toy tent was hardly worth mentioning.

—•—

'And Judy . . .' My mother plaits my wet hair swiftly, tightly so that my ears and bits of scalp poke out.

'Yeah Mum?'

'There's not much point going by the cemetery all the time. Essie mentioned to me that she often sees you there. It's been a year and no one, least of all . . .'

The screen door banging behind me blocks off her name. The Main Roads people are working in earnest now. The paper said that where the relatives of the dead can't be found, only the headstones will be moved. So the road will go right over the top of some bodies. If necessary, a new coffin will be provided so the body, or what's left, can be reburied in the new lawn cemetery between here and Fineflour. I wish my best friend could stay next to John George William Wyre. I wish just her mother would be moved but probably that's impossible. They'll be shifted together.

Since she died, my best friend's name is a silence deep inside me that can't come out. In the smooth black letters, her name looks ugly and dead. There'd been thunderstorms before I first went to view the completed grave. Dust had splashed onto the new marble. Cigarette butts were thick in the cats-eye prickles round John George's grave. This was Rose Saxelby's fault. All through the burial she chain-smoked. The round camphor laurel leaves framed her agitation. I could see the blue and white flash of the cigarette pack trembling. And she kept flicking the dead butts at John George William. While everyone else was pearled and hatted, Rose Saxelby was dressed shabbily. I thought how my friend might've laughed, because our nickname for Rose had always been Saxa and there she was looking just like a battered Saxa sea-salt box. At the burial, faces grew hot and bothered. Even though I was quite high up, I could see the black bush flies getting into people's eyes. They clustered round the white dressing of the ferryman's wounded face. A woman sprayed insect repellant in an arc, making people jump at the hiss of the can. I never knew burials were so unbearably slow. The cars squatted like overweight dogs tied out of reach of any shade. Beyond the small group below, the town went shrivelled and half-blind, squinting down on the skinny river.

This year, too, the river has gotten thin and blue without any rain. Dangerous looking. There are snakes that swim now where the secret swimming spot was. We used to drink ginger beer there after hot school days, sitting in the mud in the green shallows. Thick river weeds started choking up the water ages ago. The snakes appear out of nowhere, it seems. They move so flat along the top of the water, silent and black with little mean heads. Going past they don't even look at me in the water. Time slows down. I remember my best friend. I imagine her busker, slipping off his faded shirt to sit with me in the lukewarm shallows. I follow his smooth, beach bleached back into deeper depths, our feet treading water to a snake's quiet rhythm, until close to the bank, it slithers onto land, flash of red belly and I'm as lonely as anything with no one there to share the fright with.

The busker cried hard, standing well back from the grave. He cried so hard I couldn't keep staring at the meeting place of sky and river. Through the dim tree noises his sobbing brought back my own tears. They ran inside my mouth until I forced myself to stop watching the exact sequence of events – the rise and fall of coffins, hands, hankies and dirt – to focus again on the river fading out between bare-bellied hills. From high up, the spreading weed looked like submerged islands, thick and treacherous. In a patch of clear water the sailing boat spun toy-like and quiet. It was white and quiet like the silence in the heart of me. It was going nowhere, the boat. The river tightened in loops around it and around the withered farms.

The busker cried and cried. Mrs Dodds stopped sniffling to watch the way he leant on his guitar for support. The ferryman looked shy and shocked. Even my Dad's sunken chin popped up to sneak a glance. I noticed Nadia crying at last and how she had a way of bending her chin in to make two.

The terrible truth is, my best friend won't stay next to her grandpop's dead baby. Not really, because 1913 is such a long time ago and only John George William's headstone will get moved. Whereas when the time comes, my best friend will stay in her one-year-old coffin and be placed in a new hole with her mother. The small chunk of sandstone with John George William's details will be used in a permanent display about country town cemeteries at the local museum. Ornamental and old-fashioned words fill the oval head-stone. Because it's small, yet sturdily built, the museum is sure to want it. My friend's grandpop seems to think this something of an honour. Already his permission has been given, along with some old bits of sulky harness he thought they might be able to use. Soon John George William will be no more. The bulldozers will roll over the low iron fence, the rust of which we never could get off. What's left of him must stay forever unmarked under what, according to all predictions, will be a very busy road.

Until now, the highway has been a small hum on still summer days. I'm expecting the busker along any day now, from the direction of the hum. I have this certain feeling that one day soon, when I'm coming home from a swim, there he'll be, flicking down his black hat on the path outside the bakery. I can find out then how it is he knew my best friend and why he never finished the song. I'm hoping all the roadworks going on won't make him change his mind. In no time this town's going to be on a main road. It's something of a shock to people like old Florence Chessel to find out that cars and trucks will be whizzing past a few metres from her letterbox. She's worried that the fumes will give diseases to her roses. There's a line of Mr Lincolns behind her front fence that she's taken to fussing over more than usual.

No one can understand why the road has to go through the cemetery. Why not the other side of the hill or another hill altogether? People talk about it often. Dad thinks the bit about graves having to be moved is a small inconvenience when you realise the business the highway should bring to town. Already he has extensive expansion plans organised for his garage.

A blow against local history, was how Mr Brotherston described it on a school excursion among the gravestones. He pointed out the wealth of information contained in country cemeteries: interesting epitaphs going back to the 1920s when influenza was wiping out young people; trends in infant mortality; the dwindling populations of country areas; the craftsmanship of the old stonemasons; the differences between Catholic, Protestant and Aboriginal graves. All the time he talked, Mr Brotherston steered everyone away from the place where the road is actually going to go and away from my best friend's grave.

I saw a Jewish burial, my best friend once told me, as we sat eating hot sandwiches on top of Olive Euphemia Hamburger. Being in the Catholic section, little John George William's grave was barely visible. We always ate lunch on Olive's grave because it was shady at noon with plenty of room to sprawl.

Really weird, said my friend.

How come?

Oh, it was in Sydney when Mum was looking round for some old rellie's grave.

But why was it weird?

Because they had to put on these little crepe paper caps. It was so hot the dye ran all over the bald men so they had dirty faces. Black tears it looked like.

Do you reckon you'll be going to Sydney again next holidays? I remember asking.

I suppose so. I'm not anxiously wanting to go but it should be fun. It's just I feel terrible scabbing the money from Mum and Dad. But they reckon you should take all the opportunities you can in the country. I dunno. I still feel terrible. But worth it. Who else can you sponge out of if not your Mum?

My memory reconstructs strange conversations I think we had. They only sound vaguely authentic and more untrustworthy all the time. The truth is, it's hard to recall now how she spoke. I don't know any more. Events we shared crack like glass. The busker's song seems clearer, the dusty guitar chords. With the new road not far off, everything, even the camphor laurel tree, feels dusty. Each weekend I sit for a while in the tree, smelling the dust. These days it's possible to see the road approaching. Any time, and the graves could be relocated, I've heard my father whispering. His voice stays as soft as his favourite fawn cardigan. In the heat his voice creeps around countless cups of pale milk tea. It gives me the shivers. Like the sound of the lawn mowers pushing round dead lawns on Saturday mornings, there is a tiredness to his voice, as if any moment it will stop mid-sentence. It's a real end-of-the-year, end-of-everything, waiting feeling. There's an awful lot of fat dogs about, dragging round the town. They pant two-time, two-time as you eat ice-cream, staring up with sleepy eyes until you bite off a piece for them to eat. The slow beat goes on through the night with the sound of all the furtive sprinklers spinning on brown grass. Water restrictions began with end-of-year exams, same as any summer I can remember, but no-one cares once the sun's gone down. Like the hula hoops all Little Fineflour kids are flinging round their middles, same as they did last year, everything goes in circles. So why not the busker too? Some nights I hit the side of my head in order to make the river water drain out faster. It tickles coming out but I can't seem to hear any clearer.

My periods arrive. My first blood looks terrible in my pants: the colour of black, dead Mr Lincoln rose petals on my mother's best sideboard. Maybe I'm sick. Everyone else is. My friend's grandpop says his heart's slowed down this summer. I took his pulse for him and he's not wrong. It felt like the throb in a creek pump, weird and thumpy. The Christmas decorations he's normally in charge of aren't finished. MERRY CHRIST reads the wobbly message across the front window. You can see it as you wait to catch the ferry. He says he's still not up to spraying on the last three letters. He's not letting things get him down though, not his dicky heart nor his legs which he complains feel heavy all the day. On his dunny wall he's pinned a picture that was in the *Northern Daily News*; a photo of George Onions, turning one hundred for the local cameraman. Grandpop Wyre used to work with George a long time ago and says he'll clock in a hundred as well if George could do it so easy. Not that old George Onions' face looks easily at me when I have to go to the toilet at Wyres. The terrible black hole that's meant to be a smile is frightening. It's impossible to look at it for any length of time without feeling the strain. The cream sponge he holds, with one candle stuck in the middle, makes it all that much worse, so I end up reading the details underneath in order to avoid the face. Like a Saturday obituary, there are a few bare details: Born 24 December, last century and a resident in the nursing home for many years. A fine old local identity who dairy-farmed in the district, married a local girl and had many children, grandchildren and great-grandchildren.

It only deviates from the obituary style in the final one-sentence paragraph declaring that George is looking forward to the birthdays ahead and that good home cooking is the secret to a long life.

I've never had the heart to tell my best friend's grandpop how we met George Onions a few Fathers' Days ago when the school organised for some of the kids to present small gifts to all the old people in the men's wing of the Henford House retirement village. My best friend and I were picked as none of our relatives were kept there. I like to think it was a bad day for George Onions. He wasn't one hundred then, probably ninety-five or thereabouts. He unwrapped the small block of Bardsley's shaving soap and tried to eat it right there and then. Without any teeth he wasn't getting very far. A nurse told us not to worry too much as he was only muddling the occasion up with Easter, when free Easter eggs came from the school. She prised the soap from his mouth and left him frothing on the pillow.

The camphor laurel tree is much older than George Onions. Probably more than double his age but it won't stop the council men having it removed. And not only because of the new road. There have been complaints that the root system is lifting graves up and cracking headstones. Grandpop Wyre did some timber cutting at one stage in his life. He told me how in the old days when axes and crosscut saws were used, sap spurted from the oldest gums like blood. Is it only a matter of days before the cool smelling wood of the camphor laurel will fly out in every direction from the chainsaws? No one can tell me. Today I'm sitting higher up than ever before.

The insides of my legs are skinned and scraped from the thick bark but the climb was worth it for the elevated view. The yellow earth movers beetle back and forth not such a long way off.

Perhaps the busker will come cross-country through the blady grass paddocks, whistling the highest notes of his unfinished song. In every direction I'm waiting for him to arrive. Everything is quiet. Although it's early yet, the road workers have gathered into a small knot of tea drinkers. On the squiggle of river a sailing boat floats and floats. The aluminium dinghy tied behind winks in the sun. A man with a guitar slung over his shoulder will walk up the road. I make him appear, bright as glass in my mind, wearing his magical shirt like the Pied Piper in the fairytale, with the song ready to sing that will disrupt the silence. On the wireless I sometimes think the song is beginning – a few chords – but every time I am disappointed. The tree is expectant too, of an ending. It's possible to feel its muted protest.

Without the camphor laurel here in autumn, the rosellas won't come shattering – green blue and bright – onto the graves to eat berries. Everything gets sadder. And almost too clear. Sometimes the burial and the busker can hardly be real they are so transparent in memory. And hushed, like a calm stretch of the Fineflour on a shallow green day.

From *Fineflour* (1990)

BILLYCART HILL

Clive James

I could not build billycarts very well. Other children, most of them admittedly older than I, but some of them infuriatingly not, constructed billycarts of advanced design, with skeletal hard-wood frames and steel-jacketed ball-race wheels that screamed on the concrete footpaths like a diving Stuka. The best I could manage was a sawn-off fruit box mounted on a fence-paling spine frame, with drearily silent rubber wheels taken off an old pram. In such a creation I could go at a reasonable clip down our street and twice as fast down Sunbeam Avenue, which was much steeper at the top. But even going down Sunbeam my billycart was no great thrill compared with the ball-race models, which having a ground-clearance of about half an inch and being almost frictionless were able to attain tremendous velocities at low profile, so that to the onlooker their riders seemed to be travelling downhill sitting magically just above the ground, while to the riders themselves the sense of speed was breathtaking.

After school and at weekends boys came from all over the district to race on the Sunbeam Avenue footpaths. There would be twenty or thirty carts, two-thirds of them with ball-races. The noise was indescribable. It sounded like the Battle of Britain going on in somebody's bathroom. There would be about half an hour's racing before the police came. Residents often took the law into their own hands, hosing the grim-faced riders as they went shrieking by. Sunbeam Avenue ran parallel to Margaret Street but it started higher and lasted longer. Carts racing down the footpath on the far side had a straight run of about a quarter of a mile all the way to the park. Emitting shock-waves of sound, the ball-race carts would attain such speeds that it was impossible for the rider to get off. All he could do was to crash reasonably gently when he got to the end. Carts racing down the footpath on the near side could go only half as far, although very nearly as fast, before being faced with a right-angle turn into Irene Street. Here a pram-wheeled cart like mine could demonstrate its sole advantage. The traction of the rubber tyres made it possible to negotiate the corner in some style. I developed a histrionic lean-over of the body and slide of the back wheels which got me around the corner unscathed, leaving black smoking trails of burnt rubber. Mastery of this trick saved me from being relegated to the ranks of the little kids, than which there was no worse fate. I had come to depend on being thought of as a big kid. Luckily only the outstanding ball-race drivers could match my fancy turn into Irene Street. Others slid straight on with a yelp of metal and a shower of sparks, braining themselves on the asphalt road. One driver scalped himself under a bread van.

The Irene Street corner was made doubly perilous by Mrs Branthwaite's poppies. Mrs Branthwaite inhabited the house on the corner. She was a known witch whom we often persecuted after dark by throwing gravel on her roof. It was widely believed that she poisoned cats. Certainly she was a great ringer-up of the police. In retrospect I can see that she could hardly be blamed for this, but her behaviour seemed at the time like irrational hatred of children.

She was a renowned gardener. Her front yard was like the cover of a seed catalogue. Extending her empire, she had flower beds even in her two front strips, one on the Sunbeam Avenue side and the other on the Irene Street side – i.e., on both outside edges of the famous corner. The flower beds held the area's best collection of poppies. She had been known to phone the police if even one of these was illicitly picked.

At the time I am talking about, Mrs Branthwaite's poppies were all in bloom. It was essential to make the turn without hurting a single hair of a poppy's head, otherwise the old lady would probably drop the telephone and come out shooting. Usually, when the poppies were in bloom, nobody dared make the turn. I did – not out of courage, but because in my ponderous cart there was no real danger of going wrong. The daredevil leanings-over and the dramatic skids were just icing on the cake.

I should have left it at that, but got ambitious. One Saturday afternoon when there was a particularly large turn-out, I got sick of watching the ball-race carts howling to glory down the far side. I organised the slower carts like my own into a train. Every cart except mine was deprived of its front axle and loosely bolted to the cart in front. The whole assembly was about a dozen carts long, with a big box cart at the back. This back cart I dubbed the chuck-wagon, using terminology I had picked up from the Hopalong Cassidy serial at the pictures. I was the only one alone on his cart. Behind me there were two or even three to every cart until you got to the chuck-wagon, which was crammed full of little kids, some of them so small that they were holding toy koalas and sucking dummies.

From its very first run down the far side, my super-cart was a triumph. Even the adults who had been hosing us called their families out to marvel as we went steaming by. On the super-cart's next run there was still more to admire, since even the top-flight ball-race riders had demanded to have their vehicles built into it, thereby heightening its tone, swelling its passenger list, and multiplying its already impressive output of decibels. Once again I should have left well alone. The thing was already famous. It had everything but a dining car. Why did I ever suggest that we should transfer it to the near side and try the Irene Street turn?

With so much inertia the super-cart started slowly, but it accelerated like a piano falling out of a window. Long before we reached the turn I realised that there had been a serious miscalculation. The miscalculation was all mine, of course. Sir Isaac Newton would have got it right. It was too late to do anything except pray. Leaning into the turn, I skidded my own cart safely around in the usual way. The next few segments followed me, but with each segment describing an arc of slightly larger radius than the one in front. First gradually, then with stunning finality, the monster lashed its enormous tail.

The air was full of flying ball-bearings, bits of wood, big kids, little kids, koalas and dummies. Most disastrously of all, it was also full of poppy petals. Not a bloom escaped the scythe. Those of us who could still run scattered to the winds, dragging our wounded with us. The police spent hours visiting all the parents in the district, warning them that the billycart era was definitely over. It was a police car that took Mrs Branthwaite away. There was no point waiting for the ambulance. She could walk all right. It was just that she couldn't talk. She stared straight ahead, her mouth slightly open.

From *Unreliable Memoirs* (1980)

A DREAMER

Barbara Baynton

A swirl of wet leaves from the night-hidden trees decorating the little station beat against the closed doors of the carriages. The porter hurried along holding his blear-eyed lantern to the different windows, and calling the name of the township in language peculiar to porters. There was only one ticket to collect.

Passengers from far up-country towns have importance from their rarity. He turned his lantern full on this one, as he took her ticket. She looked at him too, and listened to the sound of his voice, as he spoke to the guard. Once she had known every hand at the station. The porter knew everyone in the district. This traveller was a stranger to him.

If her letter had been received, someone would have been waiting with a buggy. She passed through the station. She saw nothing but an ownerless dog, huddled, wet and shivering, in a corner. More for sound she turned to look up the straggling street of the township. Among the she-oaks, bordering the river she knew so well, the wind made ghostly music, unheeded by the sleeping town. There was no other sound, and she turned to the dog with a feeling of kinship. But perhaps the porter had a message! She went back to the platform. He was locking the office door, but paused as though expecting her to speak.

'Wet night!' he said at length, breaking the silence.

Her question resolved itself into a request for the time, though this she already knew. She hastily left him.

She drew her cloak tightly round her. The wind made her umbrella useless for shelter. Wind and rain and darkness lay before her on the walk of three bush miles to her mother's home. Still it was the home of her girlhood, and she knew every inch of the way.

As she passed along the sleeping street, she saw no sign of life till near the end. A light burned in a small shop, and the sound of swift tapping came to her. They work late tonight, she thought, and, remembering their gruesome task, hesitated, half-minded to ask these night workers, for whom they laboured. Was it someone she had known? The long dark walk – she could not – and hastened to lose the sound.

The zigzag course of the railway brought the train again near to her, and this wayfarer stood and watched it tunnelling in the teeth of the wind. Whoof! whoof! its steaming breath hissed at her. She saw the rain spitting viciously at its red mouth. Its speed, as it passed, made her realise the tedious difficulties of her journey, and she quickened her pace. There was the silent tenseness, that precedes a storm. From the branch of a tree overhead she heard a watchful mother-bird's warning call, and the twitter of the disturbed nestlings. The tender care of this bird-mother awoke memories of her childhood. What mattered the lonely darkness, when it led to mother. Her forebodings fled, and she faced the old track unheedingly, and ever and ever she smiled, as she foretasted their meeting.

'Daughter!'

'Mother!'

She could feel loving arms around her, and a mother's sacred kisses. She thrilled, and in her impatience ran, but the wind was angry and took her breath. Then the child near her heart stirred for the first time. The instincts of motherhood awakened in her. Her elated body quivered, she fell on her knees, lifted her hands, and turned her face to God. A vivid flash of lightning flamed above her head. It dulled her rapture. The lightning was very near.

She went on, then paused. Was she on the right track? Back, near the bird's nest, were two roads. One led to home, the other was the old bullock-dray road, that the railway had almost usurped. When she should have been careful in her choice, she had been absorbed. It was a long way back to the cross roads, and she dug in her mind for landmarks. Foremost she recalled the 'Bendy Tree', then the 'Sisters', whose entwined arms talked, when the wind was from the south. The apple trees on the creek – split flat, where the crows and calves were always to be found. The wrong track, being nearer the river, had clumps of she-oaks and groups of pines in places. An angled line of lightning illuminated everything, but the violence of the thunder distracted her.

She stood in uncertainty, near-sighted, with all the horror of the unknown that this infirmity could bring. Irresolute, she waited for another flash. It served to convince her she was wrong. Through the bush she turned.

The sky seemed to crack with the lightning; the thunder's suddenness shook her. Among some tall pines she stood awed, while the storm raged.

Then again that indefinite fear struck at her. Restlessly she pushed on till she stumbled, and, with hands outstretched, met some object that moved beneath them as she fell. The lightning showed a group of terrified cattle. Tripping and falling, she ran, she knew not where, but keeping her eyes turned towards the cattle.

Aimlessly she pushed on, and unconsciously retraced her steps.

She struck the track she was on when her first doubt came. If this were the right way, the wheel ruts would show. She groped, but the rain had levelled them. There was nothing to guide her. Suddenly she remembered that the little clump of pines, where the cattle were, lay between the two roads. She had gathered mistletoe berries there in the old days.

She believed, she hoped, she prayed, that she was right. If so, a little further on, she would come to the 'Bendy Tree'. There long ago a runaway horse had crushed its drunken rider against the bent, distorted trunk. She could recall how in her young years that tree had ever after had a weird fascination for her.

She saw its crooked body in the lightning's glare. She was on the right track, yet dreaded to go on. Her childhood's fear came back. In a transient flash she thought she saw a horseman galloping furiously towards her. She placed both her hands protectingly over her heart, and waited. In the dark interval, above the shriek of the wind, she thought she heard a cry, then crash came the thunder, drowning her call of warning. In the next flash she saw nothing but the tree. 'Oh, God, protect me!' she prayed, and diverging, with a shrinking heart passed on.

The road dipped to the creek. Louder and louder came the roar of its flooded waters. Even little Dog-trap Gully was proudly foaming itself hoarse. It emptied below where she must cross. But there were others, that swelled it above.

The noise of the rushing creek was borne to her by the wind, still fierce, though the rain had lessened. Perhaps there would be someone to meet her at the bank! Last time she had come, the night had been fine, and though she had been met at the station by a neighbour's son, mother had come to the creek with a lantern and waited for her. She looked eagerly, but there was no light.

The creek was a banker, but the track led to a plank, which, lashed to the willows on either bank, was usually above flood-level. A churning sound showed that the water was over the plank, and she must wade along it. She turned to the sullen sky. There was no gleam of light save in her resolute, white face.

Her mouth grew tender, as she thought of the husband she loved, and of their child. Must she dare! She thought of the grey-haired mother, who was waiting on the other side. This dwarfed every tie that had parted them. There was atonement in these difficulties and dangers.

Again her face turned heavenward! 'Bless, pardon, protect and guide, strengthen and comfort!' Her mother's prayer.

Steadying herself by the long willow branches, ankle-deep she began. With every step the water deepened.

Malignantly the wind fought her, driving her back, or snapping the brittle stems from her skinned hands. The water was knee-deep now, and every step more hazardous.

She held with her teeth to a thin limb, while she unfastened her hat and gave it to the greedy wind. From the cloak, a greater danger, she could not in her haste free herself; her numbed fingers had lost their cunning.

Soon the water would be deeper, and the support from the branches less secure. Even if they did reach across, she could not hope for much support from their wind-driven, fragile ends.

Still she would not go back. Though the roar of that rushing water was making her giddy, though the deafening wind fought her for every inch, she would not turn back.

Long ago she should have come to her old mother, and her heart gave a bound of savage rapture in thus giving the sweat of her body for the sin of her soul.

Midway the current strengthened. Perhaps if she, deprived of the willows, were swept down, her clothes would keep her afloat. She took firm hold and drew a deep breath to call her child-cry, 'Mother!'

The water was deeper and swifter, and from the sparsity of the branches she knew she was nearing the middle. The wind unopposed by the willows was more powerful. Strain as she would, she could reach only the tips of the opposite trees, not hold them.

Despair shook her. With one hand she gripped those that had served her so far, and cautiously drew as many as she could grasp with the other. The wind savagely snapped them, and they lashed her unprotected face. Round and round her bare neck they coiled their stripped fingers. Her mother had planted these willows, and she herself had watched them grow. How could they be so hostile to her!

The creek deepened with every moment she waited. But more dreadful than the giddying water was the distracting noise of the mighty wind, nurtured by the hollows.

The frail twigs of the opposite tree snapped again and again in her hands. She must release her hold of those behind her. If she could make two steps independently, the thicker branches would then be her stay.

'Will you?' yelled the wind. A sudden gust caught her, and, hurling her backwards, swept her down the stream with her cloak for a sail.

She battled instinctively, and her first thought was of the letter-kiss she had left for the husband she loved. Was it to be his last?

She clutched a floating branch, and was swept down with it. Vainly she fought for either bank. She opened her lips to call. The wind made a funnel of her mouth and throat, and a wave of muddy water choked her cry. She struggled desperately, but after a few mouthfuls she ceased. The weird cry from the 'Bendy Tree' pierced and conquered the deep-throated wind. Then a sweet dream voice whispered 'Little Woman!'

Soft, strong arms carried her on. Weakness aroused the melting idea that all had been a mistake, and she had been fighting with friends. The wind even crooned a lullaby. Above the angry waters her face rose untroubled.

A giant tree's fallen body said, 'Thus far!' and in vain the athletic furious water rushed and strove to throw her over the barrier. Driven back, it tried to take her with it. But a jagged arm of the tree snagged her cloak and held her.

Bruised and half-conscious she was left to her deliverer, and the back-broken water crept tamed under its old foe. The hammer of hope awoke her heart. Along the friendly back of the tree she crawled, and among its bared roots rested. But it was only to get her breath, for this was mother's side.

She breasted the rise. Then every horror was of the past and forgotten, for there in the hollow was home.

And there was the light shining its welcome to her.

She quickened her pace, but did not run – motherhood is instinct in woman. The rain had come again, and the wind buffeted her. To breathe was a battle, yet she went on swiftly, for at the sight of the light her nameless fear had left her.

She would tell mother how she had heard her call in the night, and mother would smile her grave smile and stroke her wet hair, call her 'Little woman! My little woman!' and tell her she had been dreaming, just dreaming. Ah, but mother herself was a dreamer!

The gate was swollen with rain and difficult to open. It has been opened by mother last time. But plainly her letter had not reached home. Perhaps the bad weather had delayed the mail boy.

There was the light. She was not daunted when the bark of the old dog brought no one to the door. It might not be heard inside, for there was such a torrent of water falling somewhere close. Mechanically her mind located it. The tank near the house, fed by the spout, was running over, cutting channels through the flower beds, and flooding the paths. Why had not mother diverted the spout to the other tank!

Something indefinite held her. Her mind went back to the many times long ago when she had kept alive the light while mother fixed the spout to save the water that the dry summer months made precious. It was not like mother, for such carelessness meant carrying from the creek.

Suddenly she grew cold and her heart trembled. After she had seen mother, she would come out and fix it, but just now she could not wait.

She tapped gently, and called, 'Mother!'

While she waited she tried to make friends with the dog. Her heart smote her, in that there had been so long an interval since she saw her old home, that the dog had forgotten her voice.

Her teeth chattered as she again tapped softly. The sudden light dazzled her when a stranger opened the door for her. Steadying herself by the wall, with wild eyes she looked around. Another strange woman stood by the fire, and a child slept on the couch. The child's mother raised it, and the other led the now panting creature to the child's bed. Not a word was spoken, and the movements of these women were like those who fear to awaken a sleeper.

Something warm was held to her lips, for through it all she was conscious of everything, even that the numbing horror in her eyes met answering awe in theirs.

In the light the dog knew her and gave her welcome. But she had none for him now.

When she rose one of the women lighted a candle. She noticed how, if the blazing wood cracked, the women started nervously, how the disturbed child pointed to her bruised face, and whispered softly to its mother, how she who lighted the candle did not strike the match but held it to the fire, and how the light bearer led the way so noiselessly.

She reached her mother's room. Aloft the woman held the candle and turned away her head.

The daughter parted the curtains, and the light fell on the face of the sleeper who would dream no dreams that night.

(1902)

AN AUSTRALIAN RIP VAN WINKLE

William Hay

In some states of Australia – especially in the south – there are
those curious survivals to be seen as you thread the wild ranges in
motor or coach – the roads that lead nowhere. Many will recognise the phenomenon indicated. There used to be scores of them
threading the hills and flats that rise immediately over Encounter
Bay. And it is the same today; as you flash along the fine valley
causeways, you see winding up into the uninhabited bushland
on either side, these tracks of white sand, just wide enough to
take a vehicle, and choosing one, you can sometimes trace it with
the eye before you are away – ribboning for miles over the silent
piney ranges.

Of course those neat little roads leading so persistently whereby
all human conjecture there is *nothing*, and never was anything, of
permanent consequence (appearing so startlingly in the boundless
scrub like a path in an enchanted shrubbery) have quite a steady
romantic interest for youth, and a certain family of children which
this story concerned, who sometimes took their pleasure on these
high flats over the sea, would often turn their cobby little horses into
some specially inviting road to *nowhere*, only to find it breaking off

into lesser new ones, or threading unalteringly into the unknown, beyond their courage or the daylight.

The charm of these roads may be painted in a paragraph. The soil of the uplands is almost entirely whitish sand, and as bushfires are not infrequent, there is hardly any time for undergrowth to grow, so that the pretty little piney trees, and gums, and bushes, and wild flowers grow formally as if niggardly planted here and there by the hand of man. Starting up among these green formalities are the mysterious roads, nearly always pure white, in places quite hard and scattered with white crystals, in others sprinkled with transparent, reddish gravel like a private driveway, but generally speaking simply soft, white sand, into which your horse sinks to the ankles, and in whose heaviness he frets a great deal, perspiring much and shuddering off the pleasant-sounding flies.

In the minds of the children, these roads led to more than one remarkable place of the imagination, but perhaps the more pleasing and generally accepted were that of a strange little solitary church, a Grecian temple left by the soldiers of Alexander or the lonely tomb of a great explorer, all fearfully distant and found by guess and wonderful persistence, of the kind (but for the jew-lizards and large black iguanas) just expected to be found at the end of so homely an approach. The attractions of the find varied with the hour of the discussion. If not too late in the day, the church would be conspicuous for a grove of little green peaches; if towards twilight, there were sounds of a wonderful organ. In these harmless romances, the children had something more than an amused abettor in Jake, the stockman, whose duties after the cattle in the back-scrub led to occasional meetings and homeward rides in company. In appearance, Jake was very romantic, with a head and face something resembling the portraits of R. L. Stevenson, only that he was exceedingly fair, and slightly more melancholy.

He often wore his hair quite long. When at work he always wore a white handkerchief knotted loosely round his neck. But in the evening, when he would come up to see the master, or chat with the maids, he donned a beautiful fresh suit, and a handkerchief of exquisite pink or blue silk.

Looking back, we suppose Jake was a man of quite forty. He was a beautiful rider, and carried a small stock-whip, a weapon which, like the finished swordsman of old, he would seldom use. He never varied in his dress or address. There was something soothing in his slow voice, but sometimes – very seldom – his remarks were not exactly coherent. Perhaps this was owing to his solitary life – the life of his choice. Every year – we think it was every year – he would take a month's holiday, sometimes riding off to the capital on his horse, sometimes by coach. What he did with himself on these occasions was not quite clear. On one of them he informed me he went to Tasmania to see the caves, but finding his bush dress and manners not suitable to some fine company in which he found himself, took careful pencil notes of the clothing of a member of the party, purchasing exactly similar articles as near as he could remember from necktie to hat, and restricting himself to one single ornamental cup of tea who had been used to swig from his capacious billycan. He also, he said, stopped himself in a habit he had of running down everything he saw, as it seemed to worry the party. 'For the time,' he would half sadly reflect, 'he seemed to pass comparatively well as a sort of harmless companionable joker.'

Jake seemed but absently amused at childish attempts to find romance in 'nowhere' roads or anything else, yet he would exert himself sufficiently now and then to answer a civil question about a road; and one or two specially brought to his notice of the more respectable sort were even found to possess some sort of distinction. This one led to limestone. The one yonder that fell in lumps into the valley was 'firewood'. While one approached romance and danger so far as to lead to some disused 'wells', which same were afterwards privately inspected, and found grim enough among their rushes in the grey sand, guarded by ancient railings. However, on one inspiring occasion Jake pulled them all up before a string of no less than seven mingling tracks, and pointing over these with his sunburnt hand spread out palm downwards, said 'Now, master and young misses, if you were to follow one of those roads, and knew which one to take, and knew how to keep in it and not be coaxed off among the others further on, and never grew weary of it, why, there you'd come on a peculiar thing – yes, the queerest end, right in there in the bush that you would fancy a road could come to.' Of course this was a wonderful remark for a person like Jake to make, but it was a long time before there was won from him any more about it. He would just look wonderfully superior like a sad poet and slap his hand suddenly down on his knee, making all the horses jump. All got a notion somehow (not that his face was any less calm) that it was rather serious. At last one of the children by an oblique and then a direct question discovered that this silent, quiet track led like a ghostly guide actually to a house, and that the house was empty. In the moment's awed outcry, three other facts were extracted, that it was none of your mud and whitewash places, but built of good bricks and stone, with chimneys and a staircase. So here was the strangest information, aye, deep in one of these very roads, so wild, so disused, so quiet, so suggestive of romantic ends, so eloquent with silent mystery, there was – if a person were persistent enough, were brave enough, were, alas, impossibly and Olympically skilful and crafty enough – there was to be found a building, alone and empty.

Before we go further, it is time to narrate an incident in Jake's history, of which these children were then only dimly aware.

For years without number it had been the habit of the maids to chaff Jake about a certain 'Biddy Laurence', an eccentric character, who dwelt somewhere on the road to the capital, and dealt, as the fit took her, in garden produce, though possessed of private means. Dowered with great personal strength, and capable of being roused to an awful scathing eloquence, she lived alone, associating only with those with whom she met when driving to village or capital, and certain favoured males – of whom Jake was one – who, in accordance with some tie of understanding or good feeling, undertook on occasion her ploughing and some of the heavier work. Of this strange scolding *solitary* it was not known whence she came, or what had been her history, if I fear (as is the fate of such eccentrics) they generally heard her spoken of partially in jest. Face to face, however, from her mature powers of sarcasm, and the sharp cynical, efficient expression of her eyes, she was treated with more respect. I remember seeing her (a tall, dark woman) and have never been able to forget the extraordinary power and beauty of her expression of tired scorn.

It was not quite clear in what light Jake and his sparse brotherhood of helpers should have really been looked upon in their relations with the woman – whether actually suitors for her hand, or men approved of by her difficult eye, or merely acquaintances in whom existed a sort of freemasonry of solitude – whichever it was, when we heard one day Biddy Laurence had died, there seemed some uncertainty whether Jake should be laughed at as one in a sort of mock-bereavement, or treated rather carefully as one who had really suffered a sort of loss. As a whole I think he was accepted generally as one who did not consider himself much the worse off, and this I perceive was the suggestion of his rather smirky demeanour on the subject, if as I distinctly remember he was known to be one of those named by the dead in the distribution of her belongings.

A faint interest lay in the fact that these were left to the children of a relation whose whereabouts it had been left to Jake and two visionary shepherds – his co-executors – to discover. Jake was believed to be going to look into the matter on his next visit to the capital, but there the interest lapsed.

It was not long after this that Jake was late one windy night in returning home, in fact he did not come home till the following morning, looking very ill and grey. He gave, however, no more than a trivial excuse connected with his work, and not long afterwards he was again absent all night, and at yet another time was two whole days away upon his duties, without returning. This was very unusual with him. Some one chaffed him on one of these occasions as having been 'visiting with Biddy Laurence's ghost', and though he put them off with a laugh, he looked weary and nervous. However, he soon seemed to recover himself, though he more than once repeated his absences, and we heard him chaffed most unmercifully by a certain ancient maidservant, for 'mooning like a lunatic about Biddy Laurence's place'. Perhaps they thought he was doing himself a harm. He took it always pretty well, though slowly requesting them to 'stop their nonsense'. Finally, the children gathered from various asides that silly Jake had got a scare about the belongings in the dead woman's house, and had been watching there to see if he could discover if any one was tampering with them . . . as if any one would have wanted the poor rough things!

Out of this, one day, came quite naturally to the children in private discussion the strange conclusion that the house along the secret road, of which Jake had told them, must be 'Biddy Laurence's place'. What a fancy! What a gruesome idea to think of Jake hanging about the strange place in the night!

But the story turned out stranger than this.

There occurred that terrible summer storm, still remembered

for its savagery and persistence, and Jake did not come home, and was not found for twenty-one days and nights. Searchers, having heard he had been hanging about the cottage of Biddy Laurence, went there among other places. He was, however, not found at that cottage which was padlocked on the outside (or his horse, though it had been stalled there in a shed) nor at any of the nearer houses, including those of the two lonely shepherds, his familiars, who had neither of them seen him for some while.

It might have been supposed he had taken French leave and ridden off to the capital, but that his little collie dog had come home covered with mud and matted with burrs. The animal was wild and savage with a sort of bewilderment and seemed to be trying to convey something to every one. With great difficulty it was caught and tied up in the stable in the possibility that it might lead them after the vanished bushman, but it severed the rope with its teeth and disappeared in the night.

Someone had gone off to the capital to see if Jake was there.

One evening one of the gardeners, who was milking a cow in the further paddock, heard a curious quick barking and growling, and glancing scrubward, he saw what at first looked like a horse calmly walking along and cropping the bushes with a dog 'yapping' queerly about it. But suddenly he concluded there was something amiss as something like a saddle hung under the horse's belly, and at once he perceived that the horse (bridled though matted with mud) was hung upon by an awful, tottering figure, who leant against it, clutching the reins and girths, sometimes in a sort of frightful weariness dropping his head on his hands, again slyly raising it and urging the wonderful beast forward a meander of a few cropping steps.

Jake fell when he saw the gardener running, and was picked up quite cracked in the head. He wore no hat, and his shirt and trousers were caked with mud, like the coat of the horse, and fearfully torn. His hair and beard were long and stained with earth like his face. He looked as if he had been dug up from a grave. The poor horse had been rolling and rolling till you couldn't tell his colour, till there was only a hanging remnant of the saddle ratcheted by the martingale; while his beautiful mane and tail, over which Jake had lavished so much care, were tangled up with mud and stones. The little dog, besides being extremely wild and important, had, so it was found, the remains of blood on his jaws. The children called it 'the return of Rip Van Winkle' because when Jake became more coherent he could not understand that he had been away more than a single night.

Before we relate Jake's story we must return to the children. As we shall be some time before returning to Jake, we may mention that his strange narration was at first very contradictory and hovered on the supernatural – in fact *there*, in spite of stern moments of self-correction, it has hovered ever since. There are wicked men, however, who think he was hiding with this tale a more ugly and ordinary one.

The children heard next day that Jake had been taken ill in the scrub, but they were not told how he had managed alone in his long absence. They knew of course of Jake's condition when first sighted, and two of them hurried off and examined grievsomely his tracks backward for a part of a mile. Though it had rained in the night, these were easily traceable where they now and then marred the surface of the scrub roads. Immediately after lunch, one of the children, privately retiring, rounded in and saddled his pony. He wished to see for himself what happened to Jake's tracks further back on the uplands. He intended to follow them swiftly back on the chance of their taking him to Jake's seven roads, one of which, so he said, led to the forgotten house. In short, it was his splendid thought that, given Jake's tracks led to the seven roads, and onward along one of them, surely he might take it that he knew whence his sick friend had come, surely here was the key to the puzzle and the discovery of that mysterious dwelling.

What a chance! Nor would there be any danger in following Jake's tracks to untold depths of lonely scrub, since he could find his way home again by them, enlarged by his own!

The boy got off unseen, and was soon out of sight of dwelling and sea in the higher scrub. Jake's tracks were scarred so deep every now and then upon the road or among the brush that they were followed back at a trot: though horse and swinging Jake seemed often of two minds, the former pushing instinctively for the track, the latter from all appearances making now and then an effort to pull him upon a piece of clear going. At first the road rose over patches of red gravel bright enough among the piney foliage, but presently he was led off into a white soft road, he and his pony sinking deeper between narrow shrubberies. Out of this he galloped by a strange way again into the open, and but for Jake's footsteps and a vista of the sea and its mountain was entirely upon unknown ground. At length, with a panting cry, he recognised some configuration of the trees and view which told him he was actually being led towards the place of Jake's puzzle of the seven roads. These in a few seconds opened out before him, while away into the raggedest, most unused of the seven the bushman's footsteps sauntered on beside his horse in uneven strange distortions.

Imagine the Investigator's feelings of excitement at approaching such a romantic mystery. Here were old Jake's tracks like a string leading him through this labyrinth of intersecting roads to an actual habitation, somewhere hidden among these miles and miles and miles of empty wilderness rising and falling in unbroken change before him. It was the possibility. There is such a difference between dreams and stories, and reality. It is not quite so pleasant. There is a difficulty in *doing* the thing. It is as if a person who had been making believe with you grew rather grave. A young fellow breathes hard! Along the white track, between the countless, stiff, wild shrubs, would Jake's solitary house indeed be found?

The boy pulled in an instant; and then drew off his horse, and urged it into the new road. At first it was hardly a road at all, and so much a discarded human way did it seem, and so many little bushes had grown up in the surface of it, and hemmed it close about, that it was only their bruising and the fantastic bruising of the sand by Jake that drew the explorer further. He went now at a trot, more often at a walk, and was able to observe a certain prettiness in the path. It was impossible to help reflecting how like a private driveway were some places, if only they had cleared the bushes growing in the fair red gravel. At one spot where the hard marble whiteness of the surface was powdered with little crystals, he breathlessly dismounted and pocketed one as large as 'an almond'. On either side grew the wild fuchsias, about a span high, the honey-scented bells, like the cottage-flower, only made of leather. And smaller than these, but spreading more, things covered with garnet and gold. In great numbers were the double great white everlastings on silver stalks. He disappeared entirely now into a grove of banksias with serrated leaves, and now he pushed through trailing grey bushes with soft mauve flowers. But generally speaking the forsaken way passed agedly through formal shrubs, most of them spiked and prickly, and each living, as it were, severely exclusive. There seemed something sacred in such an old road, and to ride upon it was like troubling something that was shyly dead.

Quite early Jake's footsteps had vanished from beside the horse's, so it was plain that for a time at least he was on its back. Of course there were moments when the boy was full of scepticism, not only that Jake's tracks were leading true, but that such a track would lead to anything of human solidity. How could it lead to anything more satisfying than some withered erection of its own too plentiful walls of greenery under which the sick Jake had sought to shelter himself! Then the road was now and again crossed by others, some in better use across which Jake led with a persistence barely trust-worthy, while at one point he himself waveringly forsook his own road, for one not a whit more respectable. It was difficult to retain faith with a little restive horse continually pointing out how little it had in our purpose, or any purpose at all leading that way. But to hasten our story, just sufficient will was retained to push with Jake down the long, long slope, and on over flat after flat till the gums and wattles thickened darkly about the road and down a little dip in front, half buried in sand and banksias, suddenly appeared the half of an old grey gate and chain.

As the boy pulled in, feeding his eyes on these foreign things, he heard a curious sound, like the wind in the trees but never ceasing. He felt if he should discover nothing else in the empty silent wild but a gate and chain, it would be rather peculiar. Slowly he resumed. Just a little on, a dog-leg fence poked out of the banksias, which had almost overgrown it, and two wires that had been once twisted across, were now sunken in the sand. He pushed his way along the choked old road for a few dawdling paces, when there opened in through the front leaves, just below, a little flat that had once been cleared, and showed a few cow-eaten apple-trees. Over beyond was a rise like his own, under which a creek ran with a loud constant serene sound. Just on the north of the orchard, was a bare mound, on which quite ghastily, stood a lean looking house, of two stories, fearfully plain and strong, two windows and a blind one above, two windows and a door below. *There it was*, Jake's house, but how plain from what had been imagined! At last the awed Investigator pushed down the tale of Jake's wonderful 'nowhere' road, and jigging out on the flat, saw lonely away against the scrub, eighty yards behind, a shed and barn of great logs, rudely roofed with straw held down by wires strangely suspending great stones.

Nothing could have been more motionless than the place was, or more lacking in animal life. Round the windows of the house, as he came nearer, he saw the wood had gone quite black for want of paint, while the door was just old, grey wood. If this was a little ugly, the brick-work of the house was nice and pleasant, while it was good to have the creek in there, calling all the while so loud and serene. Also the great apples on the tops of the trees were very homely, though when one was snatched and tested, it was found to be dreadfully sour. Afar – very far – in the scrub some jackasses were effusively laughing. When the mound was mounted and the house encircled at a polite distance, it was seen that two of the windows were mended with black sacking, and the old blinds, discoloured by the rain, were little more than coarse bits of stained rag. There was an enclosed plot before the front of the house, but nothing in it of human planting, not a shrub or a flower. This was just the same at the rear, where presently he arrived, not a poor bit of ivy or even a single ragged bush of geraniums. The owner had been one who had no love for flowers, or had somehow ceased to love them. What a sardonic woman! The boy wondered if this was what Jake meant when he said there was something peculiar about the house, or if there was something else. Jake's manner had not implied that there was anything awful, but only rather strange. There seemed nothing stranger than that. The back of the place was very bare. There were two lower windows, boarded up, and a door of old grey wood. There was a sphere-shaped tank half-sunk in the ground. A small shed faced the door, in which were the wheel-marks of a cart, but nothing else. A path ran down to the river, passing on its way a dairy sunk in the slope, and down below, some remnants of tree-cabbages.

The child found courage in the persistent noise of the water, and slowly sliding off his horse, tied it protesting to the shed. He thought he would go round to the front, and see if he could perceive anything through a pane of glass on one side of the door. Parting from his irreverent pony with reluctant hand, he was passing slowly round the building, when the back door drew him nearer. It hung uneven on its hinges, and there was a gap at the bottom. Surely something might be seen through the gap. When he had come close up, he found to his great surprise that the padlock was undone and hung against the post. He was surprised because he remembered when the other day Jake's searchers visited the house, that the doors were fast.

He was awed. For the instant he thought of quickly remounting. But it was wonderful how calming was the silence and that pretty creek. It occurred gradually to him that Jake must have returned here after the searchers had left, have entered the house, and then forgotten the door. He had felt too ill perhaps to fasten it. If there were anyone inside, it could only be one of Jake's two friends, with one of whom he was acquainted. Slowly his awe lessened. He could not hear the slightest sound. He took courage and knocked with his whip. If one of Jake's friends came, he would ask him if he might see inside.

There was no answer to his knock, which was so solitary it seemed to echo into the trees. He waited with a proper decency, and knocked again. If there was one thing he had no belief in it was the existence of ghosts of dead people. The house was silent. He put his hand on the old door and ventured to push it. Had he known what had happened, he would not have done so. He saw inside some nice stone flags. He pushed the door yet further, and then quite wide, so that the light crept in. This was the room where the woman had lived. Jake knew this room well of course. It smelt of incense, the smell of burned she-oak. It was quite a decent sort of place. Two black kitchen chairs with flowers along the tops; she had to have flowers somewhere; a brown cupboard made of rough boarding; a few plates in a rack, with pictures of the Rhine; a bare table under the window; a low stove in which the ashes still lay. Before the latter a heavy milking stool. The flag-stones were clean and grey. There was a bit of sacking by the table for people's feet. All was quite clean except the ashes. The stove itself was nice and black.

Against the wall there was a piebald stone, evidently for keeping the door open, and the boy pulled this before it. He took another peep about the room. Past the door there was another table, scarred with burning on which lay a penny ink-bottle, a pen, and some paper with something written upon it. Past the table, in the back wall, near the cupboard, there was a door, very rough, crossed with level beams. By this you would enter the interior of the house. To enter by this door you would have needed to mount a step. The boy began to wonder what sort of a strange look had the rest of the stern rooms. There was something strange about it, as Jake said. One peep through the door!

The door had no latch, but a bit of fretted rope hung down for a handle. He took a peep back at his pony. It was straining and snorting after a bit of grass, but the reins were strong. Advancing on tiptoe, he mounted the step and pulled at the rope. The door opened rather heavily but as easily as if it were oiled. Inside it took his breath away, it was such a change. There was a narrow old carpet along the passage, which was varnished at the sides. A narrow staircase led up above him, with polished banisters. Only a cobweb here and there. On the walls a faded wallpaper with hundreds of little black baskets of fruit, and two walnut-framed engravings, one with a great many figures of men – probably great men, for they wore frock-coats – and in the other, too, a great many figures, among which he thought he saw Wellington. There were two beautiful baskets made of 'everlastings' hanging from the dim ceiling, and there was a hatstand, in which stood a fishing rod; but he could hear no noise, only that of some flies moving to and fro.

It was not long before he thought he would go further. There was a door on either side of the front door (painted here a dusky yellow), that on the left being just open, as he could see through the banisters. The kitchen door fell behind him, pushing him in, and he advanced breathless up the carpet. The stairs, he now saw, were covered with an ivory patterned linoleum, and at the bottom, inside, hung a large cross of 'everlastings'. This reminded him that the woman was quite dead, and for a moment he fluttered in the hall like a frightened butterfly – dead as the road on which he had found his way to this lost place, along which, when Jake's footsteps were gone, he could never come again. He clung desperately to a chair of polished wood by the door that was ajar. To this presently, he reached, and gave a dreadful knock. There was nobody moving but the flies. He felt the door again and it moved like a live door from near the hinges. It allowed itself to be pushed, and he sprang up with an exclamation of amazement. The room was a pretty little sort of drawing-room, if hardly faded. A number of little chairs of dark carven wood, with cushions of a kind of green worsted covered the carpet. The light came dully through the thin blind, shining half-darkly on the faded flowers of the wallpaper, on which hung a number of interesting things, including a guitar, one string of which was broken and hung down over the dull gleam of a mirror. It was a surprisingly pretty place. There was a large engraving on the left wall which interested him greatly. It was that of a man in armour with a dark brooding face like a faithful dog, seated beside a woman who stood by a table with strange, wild, haunted eyes. What could it mean? When presently he entered the room, he several times caught the man watching what he did. It was surprisingly pretty. There was a gold clock on the mantelpiece opposite, and on either side two beautiful greyhounds carved in marble, almost as large as live dogs. On the left there was a cabinet piano, with a bit of satin on the front, and some songs on the top. Beyond the chimney, there was a faded-looking orange-coloured bookcase, with perhaps twenty books behind the glass in the top portion. But there was one little chair, as pretty a thing as anyone ever saw, covered with satin of different colours, red, and washed-out blue, and parrot green and gold. It might have been made for a child. A cruel-looking Afghan sword, without a scabbard, hung on the wall past the curtains, so long it was difficult to believe it was really meant for use. In the corner too, beyond the window, there was a large fan of peacock's feathers, the brown ones below (which you see when he flaunts his tail) and the beautiful blue ones above. He remembered superstitious people saying that peacock's feathers were unlucky except at Christmas; the eyes were rather dark. Everything was spick and span, except the broken string of the guitar, which perhaps a mouse had gnawed. Through the crack of the door, in the corner, there was a green sofa, a Chinese mat, and a round table with books on mats of green wool, besides a Swiss cottage and something else carved out of wood. Above on the wall was a coloured picture of a pretty woman with hair hanging on her shoulders, lying back, fanning herself and staring smilingly out of the frame. It would have been as startling as if you had seen somebody, if she hadn't been so sleepy. When presently he stepped right into the room to see if he was accurate about the bit of woodcarving behind the door (it was as he thought a stockwhip handle such as Jake cut with his knife and beautifully done like a snake) when he was standing examining everything, he was afraid something jumped on the wall, but it was his face in the mirror, and this wouldn't have sent him away, nor the man watching him from beneath his helmet, only suddenly, on the mantelpiece, extraordinarily faintly, he was nearly sure he heard the clock going.

He was immediately in the hall again, where he listened himself to his senses, concluding there was no sound of ticking in the room at all, and after eyeing the stairs with exceeding longing, he pushed over the hall, turned the handle of the opposite door, and took just one quick polite look. This was a pleasant dark sort of dining-room, with a great deal of grey earthenware on the tall sideboard opposite, and an engraving of Venice over the mantelpiece. This picture was an old dull friend of the child's; also a coloured picture of the Prince of Wales hunting, which he had seen in the Christmas numbers. Everything was very neat. There were some glass jugs shimmering on the tablecloth reminding a young fellow of lime juice and well water. There were some very nice brown chairs with benobbed horseshoe backs. By the fender was a yellow rocking-chair without any arms. There were some pictures over the sideboard. They seemed of dogs or of calves; and there was something in a glass case whose eyes gleamed. He was quite certain it was not the head of any one, but rather just a small wild animal or perhaps a little dead parrot. Over the table hung the usual basket of 'everlastings', round which some silent flies were swimming.

He would like to have examined everything, but thought he would not. Lingeringly closing the door, he moved to the stairs and looked up. They led straight to the back wall, and up the other side. Mounting three steps up, he eyed the stairs to the top, where they stopped before a grey-white door. Now he crept carefully up to the corner, and peeping round, perceived another door across in the left wall, like the one into the drawing-room. It was dark up here, but a glow came from somewhere. The glow he found, when he had stopped and craned just a little further up, came through the left hand door, which, like the one below, stood open a little, and from the top of which somebody had cut out a large V of wood, either for the light, or some peculiar reason. The boy presently cried out: 'Please, is there anybody here?' but he couldn't hear a sound in the house. He had mounted a little further. He would like to have seen what the bedrooms were like. It was rather a courageous thing to ascend the stair into the dark. However, he would not need to open any door, since that one was open over the drawing-room, while the jagged cut in its top had given the house a look as of nobody caring so much for it, or what any one did with it. He crept up three steep little steps and took another survey. In the dark at the back of the stairs, there was a third door. It was shut, and between the banisters and it, there was a red wooden trunk with brass nails. At the top of the stairs, where he at last breathlessly climbed, he felt a nice carpet; and ignoring the door beside him, he moved, coughing twice, across the blind window to the door which was open. A large piece seemed to have been sawn out of the top. He could not see the piece anywhere.

With a fumbling knock, he pushed the door in a little. It was a wonderful peaceful dark room. There was a green bed against the back wall, with white frills and curtains. Over on its other side was a varnished mantelpiece, on which was a clock with a gable top and a picture in the front of a trotting horse and trap. The pendulum had stopped rocking. There were numberless blue flowers on the wallpaper, like those the children call 'snake-flowers', which come out to warn you when the summer begins to blaze. In the surprise of it, it was quite possible to see some interesting and even beautiful things. On the mantelpiece there were two black wooden candlesticks, and two large yellow seashells. On one side hung a Japanese mat with pockets. On a round table by the window, there stood a workbox with mother-of-pearl in the lid, and opposite to it one of those writing-boxes which, when opened, offer the correspondent a little eminence of lavender plush from which to address her friend or her enemy. Besides these, upon the dim table, there was a basket of wax flowers of all kinds of colours which he wished rather to examine. There was yet another 'basket' of yellow and white 'everlastings'. There were such a number of things he could never remember all. On the back wall there hung a dim text, which, however, he was just able to read. It said: 'Wherefore did'st thou doubt, O ye of little faith?' On the same wall besides this, there were two small engravings in orange frames, the nearer of a man lying dead or fast asleep with his hair hanging down. The other beyond the bed seemed to be a woman kneeling. He could not be certain with so little light. There was a dressing-table beyond the bed, and some small pieces of china. Beyond the door was a chest of drawers with china handles, and beyond the window a washing-stand, with marble-top, and a curious low square basin and jug which would have been nice to wash your hands in in boiling weather. In the plain brick grate, which was clean and black, there was that kind of bitter bush they put in fireplaces.

There was just one other thing about the room that was not neat, and that was a mat at the side of the bed which was dragged up in a great fold instead of lying flat on the carpet. Like the cut in the door near his head, it made him wonder if any one cared any more what was done. It occurred to him perhaps when they lifted the dead woman from the bed to take her away, they displaced the mat without knowing it. But more likely a 'possum' had climbed down the chimney and been playing about with his little hands like the little monkeys they are. It was troublesome among those many interesting things so dimly there . . . The child drew slowly out of the memorable place, pulling the door after him. Crossing over the passage, he paused for a moment at the head of the stair beside the other door there. It would be nice, he thought, to take a look into this room before going. It would be like the other, only just so much more different to be peculiar. His hand felt for the handle, and he opened the door a fraction. It was not as he thought: it was lighter, and the flooring was uncarpeted. He hesitated and then pushed and stared his way in. It was a quite empty room, and had the pleasant, winey smell of a place where pears have been kept. There was nothing whatever in it, nor were the walls papered. It might have been a room in a ruined forsaken house. There was a hole in the blind through which considerable light entered, and there must have been a broken pane in the window glass, for into the place the sound of the river came, loud and remote, like the breathing of some serene bosom. And suddenly, all of a heap as the child stood in the bare room, he remembered that all the intimate, pretty things he had been seeing, were alone in a far away wild forest.

He stood beside the door, listening to the calm sound, and wondering about the woman. He speculated upon how she spent her Sunday evenings. It occurred to him to suppose she went to bed early and read in bed, a dangerous but pleasant habit. While thinking about her he thought of the man listening to his movements in the picture below, and this would have given him rather a grisly feeling, if it hadn't been for the sleepy woman on the wall opposite to it. He decided to go away now, while there was plenty of light for Jake's road. It would not do to be caught by twilight in such a place. The creek was nice. It would never let you think anything about it, but that it was always quite quiet. It never ceased to say it – even to the empty house.

He closed the door on the empty room, and climbed quietly in the shadow downstairs. Partly to avoid panic, and partly because he knew he would be sure to be asked by somebody or other if he was certain he was right in thinking it was *Wellington* in the engraving in the hall, he passed the open door at the bottom of the stairs and made certain it was the Duke with his cocked hat crooked as usual. In the sitting-room door as he turned back, he had a dark glimpse of the things on the wall, and the backs of chairs. He pulled himself away in a sort of panic of hurry (he was still afraid of the clock there), and passing another little door, arrived at that which led into the kitchen. This – painted russet – pulled him with a squeak into the stony room, and as he crept across the floor, he saw that there was a hole in the flags by the stove, where the solitary person had stood while she stirred at her cooking. The ghostly incense of her fires was still there . . . He found his little horse staring skittishly at something over the river (as if the quiet had bothered it) but it was quite secure. It did not seem to have had any doubt that he would ever return through the open door. As usual it would not wait till he mounted, but was moving off round the lonely house while he was still clambering. He reined it up in the orchard, and wrested another great apple from the protecting branches. It was rather better than the first, but very awful. Such as it was it must be made to content him, however, on the way home. Ah, what a burden of news and deeds he carried! How incredible! He took a last scared look at the house before he galloped out of the open. Who would have thought there were so many beautiful things in the lonely and ruined place?

—•—

How Jake's life was saved is half-revealed in the following occurrence. If we are to believe Jake he was kept alive by the dead woman.

We learn it is a fact of medical science that a person in a certain state of health, and especially in cases of bereavement, may lie in a condition of swoon without food, water or nourishment of any kind, for a space of time measured in weeks. He may return to his senses with system hardly impaired. His body may be tended by artificial nourishment, or even lie untended. Though this does not apply to Jake in that he had a different story to tell, yet remembering that he was not quite like other people, and that he may have been suffering from grief, we are helped by the point to a passable clearance of the mystery.

Before accounting for Jake's 'two days'' absence (in all two weeks and three days), and his other absences, we throw in a picture of his shepherd companions, who with himself constituted the sole society made free of her house by Biddy Laurence. Of these, his two co-executors, one was a powerful gypsy sort of creature, who might be said to live in a state of perpetual sulk. He was tall, almost black of skin, and self-possessed; most masterful and efficient in everything he cared to put his hand to; and so excellently poised in his nature, so completely at ease with his own company, that to meet and address him in the scrub alone with his gun seemed a sort of intrusion on his dark good-natured privacy. The other was a Dane, nicknamed 'the Crusader', from the air with which he approached any form of work, whether it was to clean a sty or a wine glass. He wore a red peaked beard and had an obstinate, grim expression in his small, light eyes.

To go direct from these to Jake's account of them, after the woman's death, they kept her house cleanly and decent between them, taking the singular pride of three singular men in the preservation of her pretty possessions and that each should be in the place and condition in which it was left. Each man possessed a key to the cottage, and while they met there on certain occasions to give the house a thorough overhaul, any one of them dropped in as he cared to and went through the rooms to see that all was as it should be. There were some worldly people who whispered that they met in the dead woman's hermitage to gamble, and that the natural result of such proceedings occurred. But Jake sufficiently quashed such accusers by refusing to entertain a word of evidence against the two men. His liking for the two had never allowed much beyond a sort of shrugging contempt for two more human freaks, but such as it was, it was unaltered by what happened to himself. They may have gambled and quarrelled, or they may have simply quarrelled as partners in a delicate transaction, but if they had, Jake had forgiven them extraordinarily easily. It was not easy to breed a crime out of the story, when the wounded man laughed the only reasonable plot away.

Nevertheless the web had a blackish look for one of the men as it was first spun from Jake; if against the man's denials and the victim's, there was no more to be said. It seems there had arisen a sort of troubled discussion – without a trace of heat in any of them – about a certain shifting and misplacing of sundry ornaments in the rooms, first noticed by Jake. These peculiar circumstances were rather pooh-poohed by the other two, led by the Dane, till the gypsy became half-persuaded there was something in it. At last the doubt began to grip all three, until to clear themselves in one another's eyes of the slightest suspicion of fooling with the rest, and to free themselves of the fear (less possible yet) that someone entered the locked cottage in their absence, a sort of agreement was one night come to set a trap in the house of which they should all, of course, be cognisant.

This rather gruesome suggestion again originated with Jake and was taken up scientifically by the gypsy, who was of course an adept at such things. Several suggestions, promising bodily hurt to an intruder, were discussed, though they parted undecided yet which to adopt. It spoke for the reverent care with which the men kept the rooms that the disorder agreed upon by all as most troubling to them was of a nature hardly noticeable to an outsider. In the sitting-room a string had been found broken as by a presumptuous hand in the woman's guitar. Then the pictures, especially in hall and dining-room, were constantly found crooked on the walls, not (as Jake agreed) that they hadn't each of them a different notion of what was 'straight in a picture', but these were at such a vicious angle, and often a different one on the same wall, as could hardly be dismissed as the work of earth-shock or shock of thunder. There was as well sometimes a strange smell in the rooms which it was difficult to account for, a sort of bitter, herby smell as might have come rather from an old well, or from down in a tomb, than a warmly furnished house. On top of this a pair of horseclippers, whose peculiar design all had much admired, had disappeared from a shelf in the kitchen, and no one would countenance the thought of having borrowed them.

These were some of a few objects whose disturbance seemed peculiar, but what most troubled the minds of all three, and what they had all three privately replaced and privately found disturbed again, was the disorder of the carpet in the woman's bedroom (a place, according to Jake, held with a feeling almost of veneration by them) which was constantly found drawn up in large folds about the room. It is strange how persistent had been this rather grisly untidyness, yet having quite captured the (perhaps disordered) imagination of the three watchers, it was agreed that in this composed and sleepy room some experiment in the nature of a man-trap might be made.

Jake had been previously much disturbed at the loss of the clippers and had spent one or two nights watching the clearing, without any result but a strange heaviness of mind. Not long after the 'trap' suggestion, Jake was waylaid near the clearing by a great storm, and thought he would take shelter in the house. He turned into the orchard about twilight. The lightning was the fiercest he had ever seen, almost ripping open the low canopy, while there was an awful close noise of thunder as if they were moving heavy furniture in a narrow room. Two storms were approaching beside one another, forking and banging like struggling beasts and giving little respites of wicked silence, in which the quiet creek rippled by with a dove-like sound. Jake rode to the house and let himself in at the back door. He was in the kitchen waiting for the rain to come on or the thunder to cease, when he thought he heard something drop on a floor somewhere up in the house. He opened the inner door and listened, and though he did not hear it again, he tiptoed into the passage. The storm was flashing through the blinds and fissures, and cracking loosely overhead. Inside, the house seemed to cower. He looked into the sitting-room, and came out, and went up the stairs. The last thunder-roar had made the doors rattle, and awed even Jake, whose ears were still straining after that little sound. When nearly up he thought he heard a movement in the woman's bedroom. Somewhat disordered, he struck a match, and half-dazed with the alternate clamour and silence, advanced steadily as far as her room. (When asked if he noticed in the dark, the piece cut out of the door, he said he did not notice anything of the kind, though the gypsy, who acknowledged to cutting it, said he removed it before that time.) Jake then hurled open the door and at the moment he entered it, there was a ghastly crash of thunder, and a blue light came out of the chimney and advanced over the floor towards him. He received at the same instant a sort of sickening blow at the back of the neck and fell in a swoon beside the bed.

The gypsy afterwards explained that he had removed the piece of wood from the door and taken it away, with a view to constructing the trap as agreed. It looked rather black for this man, supposing him to have entered the locked house by some private way. If you assume him to have made a murderous attack upon Jake, he might have afterwards removed the piece of wood as a blind. Some said, crediting the gypsy with panic, that the man-trap was actually in its place, being removed afterwards, and that Jake was the first to suffer from his own punishment, like the Scotch Regent of singular memory. The gypsy, however, vehemently denied that the trap was in place. Jake's story, as we have said, amusedly laughed him out of suspicion.

When Jake came to a few hours after (it is supposed he lay insensible for *days*) he could not tell where he was. There he lay in the dark, conscious of a ghastly thirst. To assuage this became a motive for movement. He had waked on his side, with a fearful stiffness in his bones; and as he groaned over on his back, his elbow struck both the roof and the side of some tomb-like place. Had he not been convinced he had been insensible only a short time, he might have supposed himself beneath the ground, though if he was buried, he knew he was not buried deep, for he could hear the thunder still pounding. He was suddenly conscious of a gentle, infinitesimal light about him. His thirst roused him to straighten out a corroded arm, and touch the side of his prison. He clutched at something which tore in his hand. It was curtaining. In the half-swooning state in which his senses swayed, he concluded he was on the floor under the poor woman's bed.

How he got under the bed he did not know, but it is possible he was there while his rescuers were about the house, and so they would hardly have found him had they entered. The Dane himself had called at the cottage two days after Jake, found the door open, gone through the house, without seeing anything, and locked it behind him. Again, by order of the stipendiary, the Dane had called in at the clearing after the searchers had been, and unlocked the cottage door. But this was over a week after the accident happened. The Dane did not go again through the house, as he did not suspect Jake of lying hid in the place all that time.

This was all lost on Jake. According to him, he came to a sort of dazed consciousness a few hours after he fell and heard the thunder thudding. Somehow he rolled and wrestled his way out on the mat beside the bed. There was a bright moonlight behind the blind, and the objects of the room were dimly shrouded. For a while he essayed to focus a weak gaze on this and that, but when he was certain of the door, and had risen to his tottering legs beside it, a nausea of giddiness seized his brain, and he swayed hoarsely in a mad dance with floor and ceiling. So wild was the fantastic frolic of the furniture that it amused him and he laughed weakly as he took a third double-somersault with the friendly door. The wall beyond the bed swayed over below him, so that the white ceiling became the wall. The grey objects of the room dived and recovered themselves like awful birds. Impatient at last, he fell like a ninepin into the passage, and with only one steady thing in his consciousness, a dream of liquid on the dried paper of his throat, found his way over to the stair railing, and crawled in a whirligig of sagging darkness to the stairs. Down these, hold by hold, he felt his way, a swooning sailor on a swinging mast, and crouched at length at the bottom, panting loudly in the faded chaos of the hall and trying strangely to steady in his mind the half-remembered position of the kitchen door. As the goblin house rocked and reeled in mischievous phantasmagoria, there was a silent 'blast' of lightning, with a tremble and report of thunder, and it seemed to the poor fellow as if all the forces of Gehenna were gathering to confuse him and shut him away from his chance of succour. He was again swaying on his uncertain feet.

His climb, however, had worse perplexed him, and he awoke in one side-room at least where the moonlight shone on some familiar furniture, and thought for one awful moment he was lost among the crazy medley of objects. So beside himself was he, that from one of the pictures in this room – an armoured man – he could not free his vision, and at last seemed to sway with the image in a mesmeric dance. Back and forth they reeled – nay, he was almost lost – when the stupidity of his extremity goading him, he drove the gibbering obsession from his eyes, and slipped and tumbled along heaving walls, and drove his way by dancing banisters, till with a dive and a quaking laugh of triumph, he fell *crash* at the foot of a heavy door, pushed it with his elbow, and knew by the step on the other side that he had won his way to the dark kitchen.

The kitchen door was open slightly, and the moon shone on the floor. Jake remarked that strange herby smell in the room. It may be thought a simple thing for the swooning man to reach the door, but he was now in a bad way, and when he had dragged himself inside, seems to have sunk for a while into a dreamy stupor, in which the shaft of moonlight danced mockingly before his eyes like a whip-poor-will. So great was his yearning for the water that he several times thought himself risen and swaying towards the door, to find the stone flags yet against his hands. It must be noted that he had reasoned the cement tank useless to him, for if he could lower the bucket within, he could never raise it to his mouth; he must go downward to the river. Upon a sudden, in his almost swooning state (so he affirmed) he distinctly felt he was aided in an effort to gain his feet, and guided *outside the house*, where he quite swooned away. This may be taken as the reader pleases. He awoke shortly after to find himself lying at the right side of the house on the mound above the orchard. He was conscious of a slight sound behind him. As he turned his head towards the back of the house, he quite clearly saw a figure in a bonnet and shawl blend with the moonshadow by the shed. He was almost startled back into clear sense. When he stared upon it fixedly the shed was empty.

So fearful was his thirst, that he immediately rose and staggered down towards the river, which he could hear and indeed almost see in the uncertain yet bright night. The poor fellow got no further, however, than a large apple-tree at the bottom of the slope, 'neath which he fell, sinking again into oblivion.

He awoke in the long weeds under the tree, still (as he had it) in that night, which the moon still lit, but which was grown calm. He was conscious of waking twice, once with his throat a torture, yet unable to move, and again in perhaps a worse condition of want, yet just able to move his head. In this latter state he discovered not far from him in the grass an old white jug lying half on its side with its lip missing. It had the earth stained look of a vessel that has been cast aside for a long period. After some time staring at it, a hunger for the liquid it had once held, led him to drag himself over to it, in the hope of finding a drop or two of rain-water lying at the bottom. When he had pulled it from the sort of nest in which it lay, he found it heavy, and three-quarters full of a rather muddy liquid. Then and there it was trembling at his mouth, but when he would have finished it at a draught, he found it fiercely tart, burning his throat, yet so satisfying to his craving, that he put the old vessel down only half emptied. It may be that some apples had dropped from the tree into the jug and mingling with some rain-water fermented into an ardent spirit. Whatever it was, a drink of such power had never before passed his lips. The effect on him was extraordinary. He felt revived, and yet he felt mysteriously elated.

His body seemed to grow firmer, and the blood to dissolve in his aching limbs, but if anything he was become more light in the head. The landscape was clearer to his vision and quiet, but as the minutes passed and he lay there in the shade as wide-awake as the mean house out in the moon he began to imagine a curious thing. He thought that he could hear the footsteps of somebody passing to and fro above him. It was done very slowly as by one looking about him as he trod, and he might have given it up as his horse, which must have broken out of the shed, but that it kept to one spot. He rose up on his elbow and screwed his head about the tree but there was nothing on the slope but a few logs and a couple of young trees with dark shadows. When he again dropped his length, after a few minutes, he heard the slow, slow pacing. Jake could not get his mind off it, but he could not see the top of the slope for the apple leaves. He gave it up and lay listening. Suddenly he smelt a strong odour of crushed hoarhound as the weed is called, followed by a *thump* in the grass behind him. When he had got round his slow, stiffened neck to its limit, he had, he was certain, another glimpse of that stooping human figure as it vanished up the orchard-side.

Soon after, as he lay there in the shade under the apple-tree, he heard the sound of voices up at the house. He insisted that he heard these voices because at first they were so ordinarily conversational that he mistook them for human ones, and tried to struggle himself up to call for help – but he began suddenly to doubt if they were human, for they began to sing the tune of a hymn, 'Though dark my path, and sad my lot', yet never singing more than the first two lines, and repeating them again until they suddenly went. Jake had the muddled thought that perhaps these were spirits who had never been able to finish the spirit of the verse in their human existence. They had only just gone when loud and weirdly a bell rang down over the river, the sort of large homely bell they ring at picnics to tell the children it is time for tea. 'Te-rang, te-rang, te-rang.' But it too was gone in jerky inconsequence almost while it summoned so insistently. This was a strange experience for the poor bushman, but somehow (whether from the elation produced from the strong drink, or the still mazed condition of his mind) hardly at all terrifying. The noises ceased as the wind changes, and here he lay alone in the moonlit orchard, with the sad crickets and the creek simmering by always so beautifully unaltered.

He was dozing off, wondering at the nonsense of his brain, when – hark! – there was a sudden great crying-out behind the house, hardly beyond the raucous echo of something happening inside. Jake was almost struggled to his knees, with 'help' in his mind (so certain was he these were horrid doings), when it seemed lost in a fearful chaffering of shrieking birds. Sharp on this, exceedingly pretty, a small silver light sprang up by the water, and was answered by another in a black window in the house. Once again arose that funny, insistent, angry old bell, *'te-rang, te-rang, te-rong, te-rong'*, dropping suddenly with an illogical clatter as if thrown on the ground. And a little after Jake was immeasurably astonished by the sound of two deep chords struck on the piano, followed by two impish trebles 'dotted', as it were, with the point of the fore-finger. These were repeated again and again, till they were gone like a startling memory, and the calm river rippled alone in the solitary place.

But to hasten to the last of these dubious experiences – so far from all human aid and sympathy – little more occurred to surprise him, excepting that once, from half a doze, he heard a stock-whip 'cracked' close over the river: once, twice quickly, and then a while after away down the water, a loud, unbearable 'crack'. After that, for a long time on, the silence of the orchard was not broken in this strange way and he was left lying there in the normal night with his thoughts.

His mind was still excited and he could not sleep, but, as the effect of the drink, perhaps, began to wear off, his spirits became sad and disturbed. It was gathered from his guarded remarks that the poor woman was heavily on his mind – that her loss and the deprivation of her presence in the world, settled on him with dim grief. Doubtless he had reviewed his life without her before, and had found it at least bereft of something unreplaceable, and now, lying with powerless limbs, in a half-swooning state, he muddled her up with these half-real things with illicit longing, even would have followed after if he could that grey figure in the bonnet, in the hope of finding in it something resembling yet the woman who had died. But with his doubtful head and tottering limbs, he was not able to hunt the clearing after that figure, in which he only half believed (the reader, doubtless, is convinced it was but one of the guilty men), or do more than lie dreadly wondering if the dead woman were still among these invisible beings about her haunted house. Here he was, quite convinced he had received help from *something*, and while he had more than the courage, if he could, to stare it in the face, was troubled at the feeling that it might be connected with this strumming on the piano and impish ringing of bells, that it might be transformed into some impish ghost, among a set of impish spirits. It was worse to him, even than that he could not pursue her, that having gone from the world that had known her voice, she might not be happy away there. Jake felt that he had rather the woman was locked in her grave, than that her particular look and character should have changed, or lost in self-respect. This new dread settled on him till he became bitter and inconsolable: filled him, poor fellow, with an uneasiness that touched the vitals of his life.

At that time the thunder was still murmuring in the south, and a hoarse noise of wind began to move sleepily in the trees.

The river rustled by before him, the very similitude of that line of the poet:

The poetry of the earth is never dead.

Its loud calm insistence reassured the bushman. Fear-stricken, he swayed up upon his hands to look upon it – to listen to it rippling by. There it was sweetly and somnolently washing the feet of its trees. It filled some of the lonely emptiness of Jake's heart to see it. His eyes followed it up till they looked once more on the house above. The tall narrow front of the building was now in shadow. His eyes went hurriedly from window to window. There was a vacant emptiness about them which seemed almost bottomless. It seemed inconceivably desolate, ruined and alone. The voice of the river was all that was left of the woman in the moonlit solitude. He cried out suddenly and fell on his side in the grass, his staring eyes caught on a log just above him on the slope. Upon it there was a figure seated. It was stiff and motionless. It wore no hat and its wild hair hung on its shoulders. Its chin was in its hand, and calm as the river in the sound of which it had died, it was looking down upon him with a scornful, half-smiling face.

— —

Jake's troubles were not over with the morning. The reader remembers how bemazed he was when found, and while absent at the clearing over a fortnight, long held to it that he was away only the one night. It must also be remembered how some said the clearing had been the scene of just a common, hushed-up brawl. But many thought differently, and to the present day, when the thunder rolls heavily over the Bald Hills, the village wives will say, 'This reminds me of the fortnight Jake was lost,' or 'This is as bad as the night Jake Lewkner saw the ghost of Biddy Laurence.'

If Jake had seen the ghost of a good spirit that night, he was confronted by something like the image of an evil one in the morning. The sun waked him, shining right under the tree, but when he tried to rise he found himself, if clear in vision, so weak and feeble he was scarcely able to move his limbs. He turned at once to the broken jug, to which he was barely able to crawl, and felt a little better after his second drink. He was lying near the jug, head on arm, when he heard two loud sounds not far off, one of which led him to get up on his arms. The first was the unmistakable thumping of hoofs, and when he had looked this way and that, he saw somewhat to his pleasure, his horse moving near under the trees, and watching uneasily while it tore at the grass. It was in a fearful condition, its coat and mane matted with creek mud, and its saddle half torn away. He called it feebly by name, and it shot up its head, and stared in his direction. The other sound was a curious dragging and rustling just in front of the tree, and now that his head was higher, he saw swaying in the yellow grass, a great, black iguana, coming fair for him with its half-waddle, half-glide. He had never seen a larger specimen of these great lizards; it must have been eight feet from forking mouth to swaying tail. It perhaps had been approaching him in the morning dusk, for it was plainly making for him, and from its alert head and shooting fork, seemed already trying to fascinate him to rigidity or somehow to be triumphantly aware that he was unable now to crawl away from it. It dragged erect and stiffly through the rustling grass. He knew that it was capable of a flashing rush. The bushman, used as he was to these ugly things, felt he was at last in a corner with one. Perhaps it had in its mind to avenge its kind for the many he had shot. Swaying there on his arms, and staring the reptile in its ruthless eyes, he considered what sort of feeble defence he might make against it. Glancing to one side after some sort of weapon, he saw not far on his right a small branch which had been torn from the apple tree. It was far too small, but better than his lethargic hands. Meanwhile the thing moved so near that he could see the sack-like pittings on its canvas skin. The horror was that it might flash upon him when it saw him move. He hoped the great thing would not get him with his hands on the ground. Just as he made a half-swooning swing towards the weapon, the beast, as if it saw through him, altered its course a little to the left, and came dashing at him with high angry head. Jake shielded his face with unwieldy hands. At the same identical instant, there was a fierce cry from beyond the tree, and down the slope came the bushman's little dog, galloping straight for the arrested reptile. A rope hung round his neck, his fangs were bare, and his jaunty little tail was cocked over his back. Fair and straight for the great thing he ran, growling shrilly, without a foot's change in his pace, while the iguana slowed towards him, forking like Satan. The dog looked a small ship to be thrown against so huge an enemy, but he seemed to know his business. As he came up, the great iguana flashed to one side, the dog jumping the other way. Then, with some unknown canine quickness, he was on the back of the flashing reptile, and had his teeth in its black neck, from which position he was whirled about, snarling awfully, and then shot off away over on his back, regaining his brave little legs and dodging round, and again getting in on the thing's back, in which something vital had been severed at the first onset, for it could no longer freely move. A third time the little animal sprang upon the creature, but this time he was not thrown off with the lashing of the other, but jumped aside and stood watchfully snarling and panting. The black skin of the reptile was terribly wounded, and it stared back at him writhing impotently, with a feeble flicker of its tongue. The little David had beaten his terrible Goliath. When the dog came warily at Jake's whisper, he still snarled, while his master somehow freed his neck of the vexing rope.

This strange rescue was near the end of Jake's adventure. He was immeasurably better for the presence of his dog and horse, and far from being incapacitated with the shock of his escape, seemed by the horrible occurrence, or that wonderful drink, to have been galvanised with a new strength. He almost immediately sat up against the tree, and began to fondly wonder if he would in a while be able to walk. Remarkably enough he experienced neither the cravings of hunger nor thirst, and had no longer any wish to reach the river where it lullabyed under the morning leaves, but he entertained a mounting hope that safety was now not beyond him. His horse had browsed nearer, and when he had been calling it awhile, it came up in the manner of these beasts and smelt his shoulder. He felt constrained to try his strength beside it and rising by the girth, the animal standing quiet, he secured and knotted the broken reins. He felt pretty well, his head steadily righting itself, and his legs promising better with use. Thus he stood collecting his strength, the beast eyeing him stealthily, and he lengthening the reins with the dog's rope. He thought that, mounting the horse, and sitting well back, with a hold on mane and girth, he might go a long way towards help . . . To hasten our conclusion, he *did* by some means or other manage to get himself upon the horse, and slowly, very slowly, left the clearing. Some said he was a night upon the journey, and this is not impossible. For certain portions of the way he clung to the martingale on his chest and face, and even, for a short ecstatic period, lay, like Mazeppa, on his back. He appeared to have twice fallen insensible in the road. On both of these occasions he was roused by the importunity of his little dog and found the horse feeding beside him. After the first interruption, he mounted the animal by the aid of some timber. But on the second, when nearer home, he was unable to mount, and with many a fall, could but cling to and move with his browsing beast.

— —

The finish of this matter of the 'nowhere roads' quite touches the poetical. It was connected with the boy explorer. If it hadn't been for his investigations, Jake would have been in a nice corner with the maids.

Just as Jake was getting well, a photograph reached the household of two children of a distant friend, whose name happened to be Laurence. The bushman became very interested in this photograph, and would examine it for long periods at a time, and even fancied that it had in the jumble of its background, a second picture of a cottage of two stories standing on a mound. In point of fact this was not only his fancy for every one could see the thing he pointed out to them – a quite common photographic phenomenon. When held in the hand it was merely the picture of two children seated on the grass of a lawn, in front of a small fountain and a glasshouse. But if looked at on a mantelpiece, or from an appreciable distance, the fountain and glasshouse had formed themselves into a narrow, tall house standing on a hillock. In many ways it was entirely unlike the house along the 'nowhere road', yet there was a distinct resemblance. Jake was rather taken with this whim of the camera, and when soon after the children came to stay in the house, he seemed much interested in them, and, as if he really was inclined to connect them with the woman, Laurence, expressed a wish to show them some pretty things in the interior of the hermit's cottage . . . Thus a party was made up of maids and children (though the maids, it must be told, were suspicious of exaggeration, and always sceptical of there being anything much worth the seeing in the woman's clearing) and one day, under Jake's guidance, two spring-drays of somewhat irreverent people jolted up into the scrub after cooking apples.

It is a point of the tale that when the boy returned from his first stolen visit, he was so frightened by the news that there had been foul play in the lonely place and one of Jake's friends was suspected of trying to do for him, that he kept secret the destination of that eventful ride, and in fear of a scolding, related his adventure, under secrecy, to two only of his play-fellows. They were as awed at their awful burden as they were for him, and if they let a hint drop in the kitchen it was only by way of expressing a belief in poor Jake and his cottage. Through various unexpected accidents and precautions, the truant had not yet confessed his escapade when enlisted for the apple-picnic, and, as they sat wedged in the carts among the apple-baskets, the three conspirators would nudge each other at some anticipatory hint of Jake's, or at the mere thought of approaching the place whose strange secret they shared.

After a pleasant journeying along the silent track (with an occasional groan as the wheels sank from the hard into the soft sand) they arrived, with cries of half-amused amazement, in the clearing. The house as they drove up was the object of some blunt criticism, and it even appeared to the child that it had a more ruinous, dilapidated look than when he first saw it, hardly a pane of glass, so it seemed, being whole in the windows. Jake eyed it rather speculatively, but he said nothing until they approached the front door, when he greeted with an exclamation of surprise, an official notice pasted upon it, threatening prosecution to trespassers. Somewhat less proudly he unlocked and threw open the door, disclosing the hall bare of carpet or furniture, the varnish scarred and colourless, the pictureless walls weather-faded and streaked with ribald drawings in red and white chalk, the only ornaments a cane chair with burst bottom, and the bare staircase. With an incredulous movement Jake turned to the door on his right, and threw it open, followed by some of the party. The room here was alike bare but for a few straws, the light streaming in through the blindless window on the blue-grey walls, the very mantelpiece having been torn away, leaving the bricks fallen outward across the littered flooring . . . Jake turned uncertainly back out of the room.

'Well, if this is your fine hall,' called one of the maids, half-mockingly, 'I don't think much of it. The staircase ain't so dusty.'

Jake attempted to reply. He began, as a man might draw palely on his imagination, to enlarge on the beauties that had been.

'Ah, goo arne! Ye're chaffing us, Jake!' (The girl was not certain there had been anything but card-playing in the place.)

Jake seemed incapable of defending himself.

At this point the Investigator stepped forward beside the helpless bushman, and stuttered out a rather excited story. He stated how he had ridden there, and seen the rooms as they once were; how it had been a 'perfectly beautiful place'; and how Jake was right in all he protested. He then, to prove his story, took them from room to room and showed them what had been here and here – here a picture, and here a beautiful chair, and here a guitar with a broken string, and here a piano with some tumbled music.

Well, everybody was *that amazed*! And Jake, followed about, taking his chaffing calmly, and listening while this or that was replaced on its legs on the varnished boards or hung for a moment on the empty nails. It gradually dawned on all that there must have been some rough play and Mr L. the magistrate had taken the valuables out of harm's way. At length the party scattered noisily among the orchard trees, or gathered laughing down beside the loud-voiced creek, and at last returned, singing, in the apple-carts.

(1921)

ACROSS THE PLAINS, OVER THE MOUNTAINS, AND DOWN TO THE SEA

Frank Moorhouse

'It was the road on which Cindy and I had driven. We drove from a long way inland on a hot day to the coast. We drove the car on to the beach and swam naked. It was that road in the dream.'

'Was this trip of special importance to the affair? What was its significance?'

'Oh yes. Yes, it was a climax. It symbolised everything. It symbolised the leaving of a hot, dusty and choking marriage for the clean, free sea.'

'I want you to describe the trip and I want you to free-associate on the dream.'

How do you describe to a psychiatrist when you are blocked by overlapping grief and jubilation. Grief from having lost perfection, and the jubilation from having had it. God, we loved then. It may have been neurotically doomed but god it felt right. I feel tears about it now. But I do not want to cry. Cindy released me. I don't mean from marriage – I had left that myself – but from a living numbness. She was coming alive out of childhood and I was coming alive out of this numbness from an anaesthetised marriage.

The marriage wasn't bad in the hostile yelling way. I've told you about the marriage. We could never admit to each other that there was anything wrong with the marriage because we were supposed to be perfectly suited and had to live out all our private proclamations about how superior our marriage was to those around us. We had to live out our marriage propaganda. And I left my wife then, not understanding why, and Cindy left me later not understanding why.

At the time of the trip Cindy and I had been together a month. We had to go inland, where a friend's book was being launched.

'You use the word "inland".'

'Yes.'

In-land. Within-land.

'Oh yes – I see.'

Well, at the launching we drank champagne, toasted, danced and cheered and sang. It was the first book by the first of our friends to publish a book. I remember holding Cindy and feeling the fire coming from her hot body. Everything was hot and delirious. It was a raging 'inland' heat during the day and like the heat of the hot coals at night.

'Tomorrow we go home. We'll drive that 360 miles straight to the sea,' I said.

'Yes. Please. Let's do that,' she said. She could be as bright-eyed as a child.

'We will rise early at daylight and drive to the sea, across the plains, over the mountains, and down to the sea. I know a road over the mountains off the highway which is shorter.'

'Yes, we'll do that. We'll swim naked.'

Drunk, we made love in the motel. I tasted the salty sea juices which came from her. I sucked them from her to my parched riverbed. Those juices left a taste that I can never swallow away. They were of the whole world.

We rose to a squinting hot sun. We had fruit juices, grilled lamb's fry and bacon, and very cold milk. We ate in bed. I saw Cindy's teeth against the milk. Very white, perfect. Then we showered together and we made love in the shower under water, standing up.

The day was very hot and we sweated as we packed the car. With bad love the packing of the car is the greatest irritation of all. For us it was the best of all games.

We drove then along the blue highway. There was a shimmer by ten. The bush had that screech of hot insects, as through burning to death. And there was a smell of scorched foliage and drying mould. Cindy looked at the shimmer of the highway and said, 'The road is dancing with us.' She said the sticking bitumen was a-kissing at our tyres.

We talked about how love was not our word. Not the word we would use. We would escape its fouled-up connotations. We wanted a new word for what we had. We celebrated our feelings by eating peanut-butter sandwiches from a country store. They tasted as no other sandwiches have ever tasted to me. And we had a can of cold beer.

We reached the mountains by two. They were cooler but still the sun was hot. They had more moisture. I supposed they were protected by the thicker growth. It was cooler because of the moisture. I drove on the winding road over the mountains. Further on I knew the shorter road which went to the coast. It was a stony and unsealed road with trees which touched overhead. The road jumped the car about because of the speed we drove over the stones – we were impatient for the sea. It is not a well-known road, no other cars passed us. It was our road. We saw the sea from the top of a rise in the stony road. Cindy squealed and pointed and hugged me. For all the driving she smelled as clean as the shower.

We drove down the last of the stony road with the dust choking up through the car. Bouncing, we came to the sealed road and the coast.

The car sang along after the stones. We drove fast to the sea, across the grass and on to the deserted beach. It was about four. We pulled the clothes off each other. Damp with sweat. Her body was just out of adolescence. Breasts only slightly larger than my own. We ran naked into the sea. Holding hands, into the cold sea. I remember the sea, cold and swirling around my penis. I felt enlivened.

It was as if the journey had been a *passing through* – 360 miles across the hot plains, over the moist mountains, through the tunnel of trees, and down the sea. We had been together a month then. It was the leaving of my stultifying marriage for the clean free sea.

But do you know something – and it is this which upset me so much since I saw you last. Cindy and I have only been separated two years. The other night I was talking to her at a party and I told her that I had dreamed of the trip. She smoked in her new careless way and said, 'What trip?' I said the trip from inland, over the mountains, and down to the sea. We made it. Remember?

'No,' she said, 'I don't remember it.'

I went out of the party and on to the balcony of the house and wept.

I'm crying now.

'That's all right. When you're ready, we'll analyse the dream.'

From *Futility and Other Animals* (1969)

TERRITORY

Tara June Winch

The truckie was heading straight to the Supercharge Raceway in Darwin. Melbourne to the Top End. He said he never usually went the coast road, but the bushfires were spread out west and this was the only way. He said that from here onwards there'd be less traffic, he said it to reassure me, but I didn't mind either way. He'd been there before, Darwin; it was where he'd met his missus. He told me about it as we drove. Diving in and out of his stories of the raceway and of a sweating community that dangles on the edge of the Arafura Sea.

A big country town, Pete said. His arms grabbed the top of the steering wheel as he arched his back, stretching. 'Yep, nice people and good pubs, and good fishing of course.' To see the ocean disappearing in the long passenger mirrors, seeing the wide blue ribs of the coast fall away beneath the ridge, let me finally breathe. I thought about us putting the girl on the train, her slumped body, out of it. I wondered if she was dead, if she'd ever wake from that sleep among the sleepers, or dream a life away.

I wondered if Billy ever would too. I wanted to forget him, his dead eyes looking through me as he shuffled the girl away, shuffling himself further from me.

On the motorway cars had rushed by me faster than ever until finally a truck dropped its gears as it passed me and waited, rumbling, further up the stretch. I ran up to the passenger side where Pete had flung open the door and smiled. Not a creepy smile at all, a fat teddy bear smile full of metal-filled cavities that made me feel safe.

In the back of the truck there were three Supercharge cars, which were to be raced that weekend. Pete said then he'd like to just rest his voice box for a while, he liked to drive in silence, said he's got four kids at home and it had been a long while since he'd had time to think, said if I didn't mind, could we just listen to music and mind our own beeswax. I told him I'd like that too, and I did.

Day eventually gave way to night, where the road and the sky faded into a mask of sparklers, scattering stars and headlight scars across the hours. We drove right through Pete's box set of country classics, and his energy drinks, right into the third repeat where I began to memorise the lyrics.

He wanted to get there by tomorrow arvo, for the fights before the races. Said it'd make it the best weekend of his life if we got there on time, said he needed to keep awake. As we passed through the long stretch from the sugar cane fields to the wheat stalks, he took the little bag of white and with his bank card against the logbook crushed it out so that it was smooth. He lined it up in skinny rows, sucked each line up his nose and grunted his way through to daylight. I lay half asleep in the cab's bunk bed, as suspension collapsed over pockets of repaired tar, counting his mutterings.

A memory slipped in between the sheets and me. Dad is there. We're at the side of our old house. He's crouching beside Mum's racer with a spanner; he's tightening the bolts on the wheel rims. With one hand he holds the bike frame above the cement and with the other spins the wheel round. The red and blue buttons slide up and down the spokes. He looks over to me, smiles. Perfect.

— —

By the time I opened my eyes against the day, the sunrise had already shifted above the top of the cab. My muscles ached, as my bones stabbed against them with the truck's sway. I felt crook, my insides abandoned, like a hulled-out apple. Just the skin to cry through, little tears welled at my pores. It was the poppies. Opium sweats, Sheepa called it, the morning after a night without them. He would boil up a pot of pineapple juice, cook it so it was warm and add some spumante to knock that shit feeling out of us. Opium bones, muscle ache and nausea. If I could make it through this, I knew I wouldn't miss that feeling again. If I could make it through.

'Mornin,' Pete said through his mercury teeth that matched his earlobe full of metal rings. His hands still rounding the steering wheel, his eyes fixed back on the moving road, the same looking road as yesterday. The only difference was maybe the dust, embracing the road a few shades redder. Heading towards the blushing Top End.

Pete said there wasn't long to go. A quick feed stop and we should be there by the arvo. He shouted me baked beans, fried eggs and bacon and a cup of hot coffee, for the road. The grease slipped out the edges of my lips before I caught it with my tongue. Meals like these could either cure the pain or feed it. I waited.

The day disappeared again in half-sleep and twanging banjos from the speakers. I asked if I could turn the sound down a bit. He said it was fine; he was getting sick of it anyway. He didn't take his eyes off my hand and forearm as I reached out for the stereo.

'You got really olive skin? Ya parents, are they European or something?'

'Na.'

'What then? Ya got something. My missus, she's Maltese. Skin like yours too.'

'My Mum was Aboriginal.'

'No shit? You don't look like an Abo.'

'My old man isn't though; his family are from the First Fleet and everything. Rich folk they were, fancy folk from England.'

'I hate Pommies,' Pete said, and back in the music and the silence, I wondered if they really were from England after all.

I couldn't wait to find Dad and ask.

— • —

Pete points at the little green shields on the side of the highway, they have a number and a letter or two above the number. He says that sign will tell me how far away we are from where we're going. The next one that I spot has the letter D and a 98 written underneath. 'How long does that take?'

'Depends if there's any towns to go through matey, but probably around an hour and a bit I reckon. But we're going to take a detour, a pit stop, kid. Local attraction – only Fridays, won't see it again. You'll love it . . .'

And soon the highway forks and we drop gears onto a skinnier road that leaves the white paint outline behind. We drive a fair while down where the trees have begun to overgrow the crumbly bitumen edges. I almost start to panic until the side of the road opens up to a field of parked four-wheel-drive utes and troop carriers. A hand-painted sign dangles from the back of a tin shed. Palm Creek Rodeo.

The truck's gears take their final dropdown, hissing and shuddering the cab, as Pete drives over to the end of the field and stops. We climb out onto the steps and fling ourselves down.

We begin to walk across the jumbled rows of cars, when the sun falls just below the tree line and a cool wind catches my nape. I loosen my jumper from where it's tied around my waist.

Pete's pink skin is camouflaged among the sea of red dirt cars as we near the side of the shed. A big wind pushes its way beneath the four-wheel-drives and beckons at my legs. The boundary of eucalypt trees cry out above clawing desert oaks, as they perch themselves on the land. A big gust flings the trees backward and then forward like the concave of lungs. The air whooshes about the trucks and whistles deep in my ears, I throw my head up to the sky's bellowing.

Grey gums inhale. Pausing breath. A slow thudding noise replaces the sky; it drives over the rodeo fence as I pull the jumper over my head, the hood crowning my face.

What I saw was not meant for my eyes.

A jawbone crunches under a slice of bare knuckles. Bloodied eyeballs throw blank expressions. Mouths fling spittle streamers about the dirt red ring. Frantic, finger-bitten punches claw tangled in the shiny skin.

I hear Pete's voice in my head, *the fights before the races.* I can't take my eyes from the horror, the osmosis of blood and blood beneath the dust-flung dusk. Bones crack under the fighter's grated ribs, his oars of the dinghy swinging – slipping to the ground. The fighter thrusts a knee in between the other fighter's lung cage. It caves him skyward like a skinny stray cat. All the men roar back. Fierce men. Black men and white men, separated by only skin, only by skin until it rips open and the red blood and red dirt become the same, same red brute. The smell chokes me, fighting, of Aunty's Tooheys Old, unwashed sheets, marinated, raw beef. The fighter who's down, half naked and pissing his pants and pleading, is taken under the armpits and dragged from the ring, leaving the short ditch of urine and blood across the ground. And as another fighter clears the fence, I notice the money-shuffling hands. The stink of bourbon leaks across the fifty-odd men and the few bleached heads of tattooed women. Leaking from belly laughter and sing-along heaving breath.

I wrench my eyes from the blood, and up to the faces, the spectators, not like I'd imagined rodeo men, more hard shiny faces and no cream creased shirts. They wear big hats though, guilty of some principled crime underneath their wide brims.

— —

Some things you never *ever* forget. The way your dead mother used to smile. The way sunrise flashes against the tabletop of the ocean. My brother's scared eyes looking up from the kitchen floor.

Some things stay with you, even if you manage to prise them out of your history, they somehow come marching back with a slung shotgun to blow away anything you've managed to build. To destroy your world, the world that's not real but you wish it was.

And I'll never ever forget that day, at the rodeo fights, and all the days that that day had brought with it. The day that I found my father. There he was, watching the men bleed faces. There he was, Dad. The day I truly faced him, at his side, not the stranger I'd wished for, or made myself imagine. He was the monster I'd tried to hide.

He had a hand like a claw, so full of engorged veins and leather red welted skin, so strong and like his face that hung mirroring the ravaged. How could I forget him? His fingers slung over the cigarette as he sucked from his lips that were pressed close against his forefinger and thumb. His neck contorted against the inhaling charred breath. He hunched over the whole habitual scene like he always had, down at the flame and across the room. That look, that exact face. That was his anger face.

I remembered now, when that anger face became his always face and the world ceased to be real, to be able to be understood, so I had left it behind. I couldn't remember the endings to the memories of him. But here they were laid bare – the bores of him that I had hidden. Exposed for the fluid truth to punch through.

He is there. We are at the side of our old house. He's crouching beside Mum's racer with a spanner; he's tightening the bolts on the wheel rims. In one hand he holds the bike frame above the cement and with the other spins the wheel round, where the red and blue buttons slide up and down the spokes. He looks over to me, smiles, because he hears the car pulling into the driveway. 'Stay here and play,' he says as he rounds the corner to the back of the house. Through the walls I hear the spanner; it thuds against a void, and then shatters the bathroom tiling, that chiming noise. And it's just a mess of skin now, slapping and slow pounding. 'You fucking bitch.'

Midnight whimpers, so faint, so light as if never of a victim. We see it through the crack of our bedroom door. Billy and me, watching Mum's head swinging into the cupboards, her crazy hair flinging into her own bloody mess. 'Don't tell me to get a fuckin' job.'

He's run out of yarndi, he heads inside the house, clearing the back steps. We hide in the corn stalks that Mum had planted. We don't huddle together, Billy and me – we are separated by the violence.

Mum is in the shower. I can see him in the kitchen; he's boiling the kettle. I see the steam rise as he rips the jug cord from the wall and disappears into the hallway. This time she screams. His aim was always perfect, like sunsets.

And Mum could grow her hair see, leave it out and let it go crazy. Let it hide melting skin. It's a shame women are so clumsy. Let her hair go crazy, like they thought she was, crazy just like he had made her.

I remember now, my mother was a beaten person. She wouldn't scream at his fist, she wasn't the type to fight his torments. She bottled all the years too; until one day all those silent screams and tears came at once. And with such force that they took her away. The screams must have been so deafening, the river of tears so overflowing that the current could only steal her. The flood breaking so high, that she had to leave us behind. We couldn't swim either.

Mum's stories changed when he left. She became paranoid and frightened of a world that existed only in her head. Who was going to beat her mind? Dad wasn't there anymore, but she still saw him, he still managed to haunt her. I remember the madness, the fear. Was he hiding under the bed, Mum? Was he in the cupboards reaching out for your wrist? Was he under the house? Is that why you dug up the backyard? Why you became blank and told us nightmares instead of dreamings?

Poor Mum.

And now, I could let him go. Because only when I remembered, could I finally forget.

I tugged on the drawstring of my hood and walked back to the truck. I waited until Pete threw himself up into the cab and rocked with the suspension.

'Bit outta control there, hey? Only in Darwin, bare-knuckle fights. Only in the Territory! Don't worry; you'll never see that again.

So, where to in Darwin, which resort are you staying at my lady?'

'I'll get out on the highway; I'll be right on the highway, Pete. Gotta go back, I forgot something.'

From *Swallow the Air* (2006)

IDYLLS OF YOUTH

Miles Franklin

I was a creature of joy in those days. Life is made up of little things. It was a small thing to have a little pocket-money to spend on anything that took my fancy – a very small thing, and yet how much pleasure it gave me. Though eating is not one of the great aims of my life, yet it was nice to have enough of any delicacy one fancied. Not that we ever went hungry at home, but when one has nothing to eat in the hot weather but bread and beef it gives them tendency to dream of fruit and cool dainties. When one thinks of the countless army of one's fellows who are daily selling their very souls for the barest necessaries of life, I suppose we – irresponsible beings – should be thankful to God for allowing us, by scratching and scraping all our lives, to keep a crust in our mouth and a rag on our back. I am not thankful, I have been guilty of what Pat would term a 'digresshion' – I started about going for the mail at Dogtrap. Harold Beecham never once missed taking me home on Thursdays, even when his shearing was in full swing and he must have been very busy. He never once uttered a word of love to me – not so much as one of the soft nothings in which young people of opposite sexes often deal without any particular significance. Whether he went to all the bother and waste of time accruing from escorting me home out of gentlemanliness alone, was a mystery to me. I desired to find out, and resolved to drive instead of ride to Dogtrap one day to see what he would say.

Grannie assented to the project. Of course I could drive for once if I didn't feel able to ride, but the horses had been spelling for a long time and were very frisky. I must take Frank with me or I might get my neck broken.

I flatly opposed the idea of Frank Hawden going with me. He would make a mull of the whole thing. It was no use arguing with Grannie and impressing upon her the fact that I was not the least nervous concerning the horses. I could take Frank with me in the buggy, ride, or stay at home. I preferred driving. Accordingly the fat horses were harnessed to the buggy, and with many injunctions to be careful and not forget the parcels, we set out. Frank Hawden's presence spoilt it all, but I determined to soon make short work of him.

There was one gate to go through, about four miles from the house. Frank Hawden got out to open it. I drove through, and while he was pushing it to, laid the whip on the horses and went off full tilt. He ran after me shouting all manner of things that I could not hear on account of the rattle of the buggy. One horse began kicking up, so, to give him no time for further pranks, I drove at a good round gallop, which quickly left the lovable jackeroo a speck in the distance. The dust rose in thick clouds, the stones rattled from the whirling wheels, the chirr! chirr! of a myriad cicadas filled the air, and the white road glistened in the dazzling sunlight. I was enjoying myself tip-top, and chuckled to think of the way I had euchred Frank Hawden. It was such a good joke that I considered it worth two of the blowings-up I was sure of getting from Grannie for my conduct.

It was not long before I fetched up at Dogtrap homestead, where, tethered to the 'six-foot' paling fence which surrounded the flower-garden, was Harold Beecham's favourite, great, black, saddle-horse, Warrigal. The vicious brute turned his beautiful head, displaying a white star on the forehead, and snorted as I approached. His master appeared on the veranda raising his soft panama hat, and remarking, 'Well I never! You're not by yourself, are you?'

'I am. Would you please tell Mrs Butler to bring out Grannie's parcels and post at once. I'm afraid to dawdle, it's getting late.'

He disappeared to execute my request and reappeared in less than a minute.

'Mr Beecham, please would you examine Barney's harness. Something must be hurting him. He has been kicking up all the way.'

Examining the harness and noticing the sweat that was dripping from the animals, panting from their run, he said:

'It looks as though you've been making the pace a cracker. There is nothing that is irritating Barney in the least. If he's putting on any airs it is because he is frisky and not safe for you to drive. How did Julius happen to let you away by yourself?'

'I'm not frightened,' I replied.

'I see you're not. You'd be game to tackle a pair of wild elephants, I know, but you must remember you're not much bigger than a sparrow sitting up there, and I won't let you go back by yourself.'

'You cannot stop me.'

'I can.'

'You can't.'

'I can.'

'You can't.'

'I can.'

'How?'

191

'I'm going with you,' he said.

'You're not.'

'I am.'

'You're not.'

'I am.'

'You ar-r-re not.'

'I am.'

'You are, ar-r-re not.'

'We'll see whether I will or not in a minute or two,' he said with amusement.

'But, Mr Beecham, I object to your company. I am quite capable of taking care of myself; besides, if you come home with me I will not be allowed out alone again – it will be altogether unpleasant for me.'

Mrs Butler now appeared with the mail and some parcels, and Harold stowed them in the buggy.

'You'd better come in an''ave a drop of tay-warter, miss, the kittle's bilin', and I have the table laid out for both of yez.'

'No, thank you, Mrs Butler. I can't possibly stay today, it's getting late. I must hurry off. Goodbye! Good afternoon, Mr Beecham.'

I turned my buggy and pair smartly round and was swooping off. Without a word Harold was at their heads and seized the reins. He seized his horse's bridle, where it was over the paling, and in a moment had him tied on the off-side of Barney, then stepping quietly into the buggy he put me away from the driver's seat as though I were a baby, quietly took the reins and whip, raised his hat to Mrs Butler, who was smiling knowingly, and drove off.

I was highly delighted with his action, as I would have despised him as a booby had he given in to me, but I did not let my satisfaction appear. I sat as far away from him as possible, and pretended to be in a great huff. For a while he was too fully occupied in making

Barney 'sit up' to notice me, but after a few minutes he looked round, smiling a most annoying and pleasant smile.

'I'd advise you to straighten out your chin. It is too round and soft to look well screwed up that way,' he said provokingly.

I tried to extinguish him with a look, but it had not the desired effect.

'Now you had better be civil, for I have got the big end of the whip,' he said.

'I reserve to myself the right of behaving as I think fit in my own uncle's buggy. You are an intruder; it is yourself that should be civil.'

I erected my parasol and held it so as to tease Harold. I put it down so that he could not see the horses. He quietly seized my wrist and held it out of his way for a time, and then loosing me said, 'Now, behave.'

I flouted it now, so that his ears and eyes were endangered, and he was forced to hold his hat on.

'I'll give you three minutes to behave, or I'll put you out,' he said with mock severity.

'Shure it's me wot's behavin' beautiful,' I replied, continuing my nonsense.

He pulled rein, seized me in one arm, and lifted me lightly to the ground.

'Now, you can walk till you promise to conduct yourself like a Christian!' he said, driving at a walk.

'If you wait till I promise anything, you'll wait till the end of the century. I'm quite capable of walking home.'

'You'll soon get tired of walking in this heat, and your feet will be blistered in a mile with those bits of paper.'

The bits of paper to which he alluded were a pair of thin-soled white canvas slippers – not at all fitted for walking the eight miles on the hard hot road ahead of me. I walked resolutely on, without deigning a glance at Harold, who had slowed down to a crawling walk.

'Aren't you ready to get up now?' he inquired presently.

I did not reply. At the end of a quarter of a mile he jumped out of the buggy, seized upon me, lifted me in, and laughed, saying, 'You're a very slashing little concern, but you are not big enough to do much damage.'

We were about halfway home when Barney gave a tremendous lurch, breaking a trace and some other straps. Mr Beecham was at the head of the plunging horse in a twinkling. The harness seemed to be scattered everywhere.

'I expect I had better walk on now,' I remarked.

'Walk, be grannied! With two fat lazy horses to draw you?' returned Mr Beecham.

Men are clumsy, stupid creatures regarding little things, but in their right place they are wonderful animals. If a buggy was smashed to smithereens, from one of their many mysterious pockets they would produce a knife and some string, and put the wreck into working order in no time.

Harold was as clever in this way as any other man with as much bushman ability as he had, so it was not long ere we were bowling along as merrily as ever.

Just before we came in sight of Caddagat he came to a standstill, jumped to the ground, untied Warrigal, and put the reins in my hand, saying –

'I think you can get home safely from here. Don't be in such a huff – I was afraid something might happen to you if alone. You needn't mention that I came with you unless you like. Goodbye.'

'Goodbye, Mr Beecham. Thank you for being so officious,' I said by way of a parting shot.

'Old Nick will run away with you for being so ungrateful,' he returned.

'Old Nick will have me anyhow,' I thought to myself as I drove home amid the shadows. The hum of the cicadas was still, and dozens of rabbits, tempted out by the cool of the twilight, scuttled across my path and hid in the ferns.

I wished the harness had not broken, as I feared it would put a clincher on my being allowed out driving alone in future.

Joe Slocombe, the man who acted as groom and rouseabout, was waiting for me at the entrance gate.

'I'm glad you come at last, Miss Sybyller. The missus has been in a dreadful stoo for fear something had happened yuz. She's been runnin' in an' out like a gurrl on the look-out fer her lover, and was torkin' of sendin' me after yuz, but she went to her tea soon as she see the buggy come in sight. I'll put all the parcels on the back veranda, and yuz can go in at woncest or yuz'll be late fer yer tea.'

'Joe, the harness broke and had to be tied up. That is what kept me so late,' I explained.

'The harness broke!' he exclaimed. 'How the doose is that! Broke here in the trace, and that strap! Well, I'll be hanged! I thought them straps couldn't break only onder a tremenjous strain. The boss is so dashed partickler too. I believe he'll sool me off the place; and I looked at that harness only yesterday. I can't make out how it come to break so simple. The boss will rise the devil of a shine, and say you might have been killed.'

This put a different complexion on things. I knew Joe Slocombe could mend the harness with little trouble, as it was because he was what Uncle Jay-Jay termed a 'handy divil' at saddlery that he was retained at Caddagat. I said carelessly:

'If you mend the harness at once, Joe, Uncle Julius need not be bothered about it. As it happened, there is no harm done, and I won't mention the matter.'

'Thank you, miss,' he said eagerly. 'I'll mend it at once.'

Now that I had that piece of business so luckily disposed of, I did not feel the least nervous about meeting grannie. I took the mail in my arms and entered the dining-room, chirping pleasantly:

'Grannie, I'm such a good mail-boy. I have heaps of letters, and did not forget one of your commissions.'

'I don't want to hear that now,' she said, drawing her dear old mouth into a straight line, which told me I was not going to palm things off as easily as I thought. 'I want a reason for your conduct this afternoon.'

'Explain what, Grannie?' I inquired.

'None of that pretence! Not only have you been most out-rageously insulting to Mr Hawden when I sent him with you, but you also deliberately and wilfully disobeyed me.'

Uncle Julius listened attentively, and Hawden looked at me with such a leer of triumph that my fingers tingled to smack his ears. Turning to my grandmother, I said distinctly and cuttingly:

'Grannie, I did not intentionally disobey you. Disobedience never entered my head. I hate that thing. His presence was detestable to me. When he got out at the gate I could not resist the impulse to drive off and leave him there. He looked such a complete jackdaw that you would have laughed yourself to see him.'

'Dear, oh dear! You wicked hussy, what will become of you!' And Grannie shook her head, trying to look stern, and hiding a smile in her serviette.

'Your manners are not improving, Sybylla. I fear you must be incorrigible,' said Aunt Helen.

When Uncle Jay-Jay heard the whole particulars of the affair, he lay back in his chair and laughed fit to kill himself.

196

'You ought to be ashamed to always encourage her in her tom-boyish ways, Julius. It grieves me to see she makes no effort to acquire a ladylike demeanour,' said grannie.

Mr Hawden had come off second-best, so he arose from his half-finished meal and stamped out, banging the door after him, and muttering something about 'a disgustingly spoilt and petted tomboy', 'a hideous barbarian', and so forth.

Uncle Jay-Jay related that story to everyone, dwelling with great delight upon the fact that Frank Hawden was forced to walk four miles in the heat and dust.

From *My Brilliant Career* (1901)

NULLARBOR HONEYMOON

Dorothy Hewett

I am running down George Street with a northerly blowing grit in my face, one and a half hours late for my wedding. I can see Chris on the corner, furious with heat and waiting.

'Where the hell have you been?'

'I walked the wrong way, towards the Quay instead of the railway.'

'For Christ's sake, how many years did you live in this city?'

'I wasn't thinking, but look, I bought a new blouse in Farmers.' And I'd almost stolen a new pair of shoes but I was too honest or too scared. I can still see them floating, high heeled, pale beige, Italian leather. I twirl in front of him.

'Get fucked,' he says and strides off through the maze of streets, rolling a little on the balls of his feet from the remembered motion of the sea.

We walk up the hill by the park on opposite sides of the road. He is wearing thongs and a crumpled yellow shirt with a frayed collar. He might have changed into something decent.

Outside the Registry Office our two witnesses are waiting, Englishmen, dressed up to the nines with white carnations in their buttonholes. The registrar is confused, his eyes searching for the bridegroom. Chris steps forward. He probably thinks I've picked up some derro in the park, I think bitterly.

Now we are in the nearest pub, one of those typical Sydney pubs, dirty green tiles, stinking of Tooheys Old. Reg is ordering half a bottle of champagne. 'I'll shout you a wedding breakfast,' he says magnanimously. 'What's on the menu?'

'Poi'n'peas,' mumbles the adenoidal barmaid. When we come out again into the glare of the streets Reg puts his arm around me. A cockney who has pulled himself up by his bootstraps in Australia, he is used to taking charge.

'Well,' he says, 'Em can come home with us . . . And Chris . . .' He leaves the sentence hanging. He doesn't care where Chris goes. Chris bristles. 'Emily's coming with me.'

Together we walk away down the hill, smiling. I have no idea where we are going.

Chris takes me to the little terrace in Redfern where he always stays with a folkie friend when he pays off a ship.

'This is my room,' he says. I look around. The walls are splotched and peeling with damp. There isn't a stick of furniture.

'But where do we sleep?'

'On the floor. I've got a blanket in my kit.'

'I will not,' I say indignantly, 'sleep on the bare floor on my wedding night.'

We buy a double mattress, pillows and unbleached sheets from Grace Bros. The day is coming to a close, so we order steak and salad in a greasy cafe on the corner of Crown and Cleveland, but the steak is off so Chris sends it back to the kitchen. The cafe owner stands belligerently by our table.

'The steak is good.'

Chris shoves a forkful of dubious meat in his face. 'You eat it then.' The Greek eats it.

When we walk back to the terrace house we are still hungry but too tired to do anything about it. The room is full of shadows. Riffling through his friend's record collection I discover a copy of *The White Haired Girl*. 'Listen to this,' I say, as the strange, heart-breaking wail fills the little room.

I am sitting with Len in a crowded Peking cinema. The only Europe-ans among the mass of Mao-suited Chinese. We are entranced by the music, the story of the tragic outcast singing on the mountainside.

'Turn that fucking caterwauling thing off.'

I stare at Chris in horror. 'But it's *The White Haired Girl!*'

'I don't care who it is. Turn it off.'

'It's a great modern Chinese opera.'

'If you don't turn it off I will!'

He lunges across the room and switches it off.

'I can't live with you! I'm going,' I say bitterly. 'You're a philis-tine – I've got nothing in common with you.'

I storm out and begin to pack up my things. I'll go back. It's been in my mind like a temptation ever since we flew into Sydney. *The White Haired Girl* has done it. It is the straw in the wind. I see myself catching the train at Central, getting off at Rockdale, lugging my case across the overpass. Will he still be there with his head full of voices, his only companion the lop-eared, brindle dog he found on the tip?

'Well, goodbye, I'm going.'

'That didn't last long,' Chris is lying full length on the sofa with his eyes half-closed. 'Would you like a cup of coffee before you go?'

'Okay.'

When he gets up to put the coffee on I catch at his sleeve.

'Chris?'

We look at each other and laugh. Nine years of life with the madman in the house above the railway cutting go up in smoke. How could I ever have imagined I could go back? No, for better or worse, I'm married now to this big man with the sleepy eyes and the sense of humour who hates *The White Haired Girl*.

Afterwards she lay beside him in the airless bedroom listening to the love cries of Redfern, the crunch of fist on bone.

'Y'knocked me down y'fucken cunt, what'd y' do that for?'

'I only pushed y'.'

Her wedding night hadn't been much of a success. She was still bleeding and Chris had a fixed primitive belief that a menstruating woman would give him the clap. The abortion had been her idea. She couldn't bear the thought of a shotgun wedding and anyway she wasn't sure that he wanted to marry her. He was one of those old-fashioned militants who believed that marriage destroyed your usefulness in the working-class struggle. Of course she wanted him to say, 'Don't worry, we'll have the baby,' but he didn't. He was always good at those fatal silences that decided so much without a word being spoken. So with her legs in stirrups and a drip in her arm she'd had a painful curette in a surgery in the Cross. The toilet was strewn with bloodstained napkins and cottonballs. She'd fainted twice in the taxi and Chris had to carry her in a fireman's lift through a roomful of people.

The abortion had made a big hole in his money.

'I'll have to ship out again,' he said.

She remembered how relieved he looked, excited even, when he told her he'd picked up for the Brisbane run sailing tomorrow. He had already left her.

She stared at him horrified. 'But you said you loved me.'

'It's all right,' he said. 'It's not the end of the world.'

'It is, it is,' she sobbed. 'I'll never see you again.'

'I'll come across to the West sometime.'

'Sometime,' she said bitterly. 'No you won't, you'll forget about me.'

He looked at her helplessly. 'Well then, we'd better get married.'

But she was worried about Chris's politics. The Party was calling him a Revisionist and had failed to reissue his Party card. Worldwide the communists were in turmoil. Kruschev had given his speech on Stalin's crimes, the Russians had destroyed the Hungarian revolution, the intellectuals had been expelled or resigned in droves. When Emily joined the Communist Party she had been told you could never resign, it was a lifetime commitment and she was still a good party girl. She made an appointment to see Eddie Maher, the Secretary of the Trade Union Committee.

'What do you want to know?' he asked her.

'Is it all right to marry him?'

He looked across his desk, smiling at the small, serious woman with the naive eyes.

'Chris is okay,' he said, 'he's like a lot of our waterfront comrades, they keep on butting their heads against a brick wall until the blood flows. They're anarchists. They never give up and they never get anywhere. But go ahead and marry him if you want to. He's a good bloke and you might tone him down a bit.'

In the Left Bookshop in Market Street the manager thrust his long furtive face across the counter.

'You've been seen around with that Chris Ryder. I'm warning you, he's in bad odour with the party.'

'Too late,' she laughed, 'I married him yesterday.'

Next morning, Chris goes off to retrieve his Matador truck. It has been driven all over Sydney while he was at sea. We are full of hope, we will confound the sceptics, we will drive back across the Nullarbor to the little city where my children are waiting and my mother's friends are darkly predicting: 'You won't see hide nor hair of her again.'

Under the tarp Chris has rigged over the roll bars we have stowed the double mattress, drums of water, a spirit stove, camp oven, kerosene tin, frying pan and billy can. Looking back on that epic journey we made, the Matador trundling along with a top speed of 85k, the tarp flapping in the wind, it seems to me like the journey of an ant crawling across the vast map of Australia. Past rivers and towns, salt lakes and farms, rumbling over cattle grids, we moved in a cloud of dust, pulled inexorably towards the magnet of the great saltbush plains. Occasionally we camped in a caravan park or a showground where we could have a cold shower, but mostly I washed in the kerosene tin, heating the water up on the spirit stove. Sometimes we ordered steak and eggs from a roadside cafe while I fumed at Chris flirting with the waitress. At night, wrapped in blankets in the back of the truck, we slept under a multitude of stars. I have stopped bleeding. I am dying for Chris to make love to me again. Parked above the beach at Port Augusta I search frantically through my port for my diaphragm but it's disappeared.

'Have you got any French letters?' But of course he hasn't.

'Couldn't you get some from the chemist?'

'What, at this hour? Have a heart. We'll fix something up in the morning.'

I sit moodily on the tail of the truck.

'You don't even care. Well, you don't do you? You never have cared.'

'Shut up and go to sleep,' he says.

Down on the beach a party of young folkies are playing their guitars, singing Australian bush ballads.

'Don't just lie there, say something.' But he only turns over and sighs while I nurse my dangerous rage.

'Okay,' I tell him. 'I've had enough of this. I'm going.'

'Going where?' he mutters.

'I'll hook a lift back to Sydney with one of the truckies.'

'Suit yourself,' he says.

Pride drives me on. I can't turn back now.

'Better take some dough then.' He gropes for his wallet.

'Half each. That's fair.'

I take the notes and pick up my port. The light from the folkies' campfire frames the ring of faces, the clink of bottles, the laughter. I walk away from the Matador towards the distant town. Only once I turn back, seeing it hunched under a great wheel of stars, the only secure signpost in all this immensity. I sit on my port on the highway, watching the semis like great lighted ships sailing down on me, shaking the earth. What am I doing here? Running away again, and what will happen to the children? *You won't see hide nor hair of her*, but there is nowhere left to run to – only the madman's house above the railway cutting and I'm finished with that kind of love, the kind that risks everything and always fails. Wandering along I am lonely, maybe I can join the folkies and sing all night around their campfire. They are drunk now, singing the most racist song in their repertoire:

O don't you remember Sweet Alice Ben Bolt,
Sweet Alice so dusky and dark,
the Warrigo gin with a straw through her nose,
and teeth like a Moreton Bay shark.

When I reach the Matador I get undressed and climb in, lying close against Chris, groping for his hand.

'Em,' he mutters, 'Em.' He turns towards me and I take him into me, so warm, the slow rolling movement like the endless enveloping motion of the sea. I can hear the Gulf water brushing against the sand.

The terrible sheepwash tobacco she smoked
in her gunya down there by the lake . . .

Huge shadows roll down the Flinders Ranges, semis shudder towards us like mirages floating on water, drawing us dangerously close in the wind of their passing.

Early morning in Ceduna, white limestone on the Bight, smell of dust and salt, last touch of civilisation, last reliable water.

Chris fills the drums in the pub yard. An Aborigine in a limp felt hat is chopping wood, his axe strokes thudding in the frosty air. Penong, low scrubby hills, and an old cowboy flogging a country and western tape. He's written a song about his dead son, killed in a Queensland rodeo.

The border, a busted tyre and an empty oil drum, WELCOME TO WESTERN AUSTRALIA; Eucla, a silent nervous woman pulling petrol among the sand dunes; a cold beer and a hot shower at Madura.

Two old photographs have survived from that time: one of Emily, desolate, dressed in black with a couple of mongrel dogs nosing around her skirts. Another, dead tired, dusty, barefoot, slumped on the running board of the Matador drinking a mug of tea.

They are out in the desert now, on a corrugated dirt road, potholed with bulldust, the carcasses of dead bush animals or a wrecked car chassis on the verge; an occasional water tank dark on the skyline, no trees, only the endless grey monotony of the saltbush plains.

Chris is singing tunelessly:

I was a canecutter but now I'm at sea,
stool it and top it and load it up high,
once cane killed Abel but it won't kill me . . .

'I'll take you to the canefields for a season,' he says. 'We can live in the cane barracks.'

Emily imagined a shed lined with single stretchers, singleted men coming in exhausted, black from the burn-off, the cane rustling outside.

'Where would we sleep?'

'We could hang up a blanket.'

'But the children. How would the children go to school?'

'You could teach them.'

'I can't, I can't. I have other things to do, books to write.'

'Or we can take a tent,' Chris says, 'and camp out in the big scrubs. It's always cool up there with the mists falling.'

That's better. She can imagine the romance of it. But what irony, to live under that great canopy while Chris cuts it down. Of course she knows what he wants. He wants her to share his wild, wandering, footloose life. But how can she when she wants him to share hers? She remembers waiting for him in Melbourne under a huge oak tree in the Botanical Gardens. He'd come straight out of the stokehold in his greasy overalls with his poems in his pocket. She'd read them, thinking, These are a bit rough but they've got something.

'Why don't you come to Western Australia?' she asked him.

'What would I do there?'

'Don't you want to learn how to write poetry?'

He stared at her amazed. He thought he knew already. When he does come, she buys a pink, candy-striped cotton dress for the occasion and watches him kissing a redhead goodbye on the interstate platform.

'We're going home, Chris,' she says. He is reciting Will Ogilvie:

> On the crimson breast of the sunset the grey selections lie,
> And their lonely grief-stained faces are turned to a pitiless
>   sky . . .

Then the generator burns out and the Matador gives up the ghost.

They could have stayed there for days but they were lucky. A few hours later a big semi gives Chris a lift into Cocklebiddy.

'Won't be long,' he tells her. 'I'll ring through to Kalgoorlie and get them to send out the new part. You'd better stay with the gear. They reckon they come in out of the desert and strip an unattended vehicle clean.'

She watches him disappear, waving, in clouds of dust. The silence rolls in. Far away on the horizon the willy-willies dance, bowing and scraping. Is this the Dead Heart, the Great Australian Loneliness?

I am a desert God. Find me if you can. Is there anything out there at all? She takes out Simone de Beauvoir's *The Mandarins* and begins to read. Later she makes herself a cup of tea. When the first streaks appear in the sky the wind springs up, the saltbush rustles and a flock of galahs screeches out of the sunset, flashing the pink underside of their wings. It will be night soon. She shivers. The abrupt changes of temperature in the desert always astonish her. The air is full of a tiny ticking she can't identify, a creep, a whir, a sudden cry. She remembers all the gruesome stories she's read about women raped and murdered in lonely places. She switches on the headlights. Don't panic, she tells herself, he'll be back soon. He won't leave me here in the dark alone.

From a long way off she picks up the sound of the approaching car coming from the wrong direction. Feeling suddenly vulnerable she switches the lights off again, but when the car pulls over there are children, a Methodist minister in a dog collar, with a thin, weary wife. Unpacking the car, spreading blankets in the scrub, the wife insists she join them for the evening meal. Grateful for the company she helps the woman lay out the plates on the white tablecloth while the children run around gathering up little sticks for the fire. The parson is on his knees praying by a patch of salt-bush. When the semi comes back from Cocklebiddy bringing Chris and the two young truckies with it, how delighted Emily is to see him – even when he tells her he hasn't been able to get through to Kalgoorlie.

'I'm Keith and this is Billy,' says the truckie with the cheeky grin. Billy, wrapped in his own morose thoughts, says nothing. He has lost his holiday pay digging the semi out of a sand-drift on the other side of Eucla.

'I'll give you a hand,' Chris says to the parson's wife.

'You're a true Christian,' she tells him.

Drinking tea round the campfire Chris recites Banjo Paterson and Billy finds his voice:

> Of all the things I'd like to be
> I'd like to be a sparrer,
> just sittin' on the Princess Bridge
> and gazin' in the Yarrer.

It's a strange little ditty he'll repeat like a homesick mantra in the days to come.

'I'm only twenty-two,' Keith says, 'but I got a wife and two kids back in Melbourne. Billy's sixteen and he's got nothin',' (he giggles), 'not even his paypacket.'

When Emily woke next morning the car had gone and Chris, having negotiated the longest tow in history, was knotting the rope to the towbar.

And so it began – those days and nights of eating red dust and diesel oil; Chris, red-eyed from lack of sleep, steering over potholes like a madman. When the towrope frayed and broke he used strands of wire twisted off the station fences. When they snapped and the semi lumbered on he leapt out of the cabin and fired a shot from his .303 to bring them back again. Then the wire broke for the umpteenth time and Keith said they'd had enough.

'You can leave the Matador and ride up front with us.'

'You can't do that,' Chris said. He stood there by the side of the road swaying like some weary giant but still dangerous. There was a long pause.

'That's cool, mate,' Keith said, whistling between his teeth, 'let's go then.'

He was interested in Emily or anything else to break the monotony. He wanted her to travel with him in the semi. 'Away,' he said, 'from all the dust and oil fumes,' but when he got her there he handed the driving over to Billy, and, pinned on the makeshift bed behind the driver's seat, she had to fight savagely for her virtue.

'Have y' got a jealous husband?' he taunted. Emily went thankfully back to Chris and the beleaguered Matador, but the sharp spermy smell of him stayed on her skin for days.

Sometimes she slept in the back and woke to see spindly gums crashing overhead as Chris fell asleep and veered off the road. Only once he gave up, handed over the wheel to Billy and crawled in with her. While the Matador swerved and bucked they lay locked together in a wild climax until he fell backwards to sleep like the dead. Emily lay awake under the gritty blanket, watching the Southern Cross slip down the sky.

So the grotesque cavalcade passed, rolling out of the desert down the wide, empty streets of Norseman, past the twisted gimlets, the ghost town of Coolgardie, the rabbit-proof fences. Why didn't they cut the wire for good, leave the Matador for repairs and catch the train in Kalgoorlie? They would never know. It was as if they were joined in some macabre marriage that could never be dissolved until the final end.

We reach the escarpment at dawn and look down on the city lying in its green bowl with the Swan River meandering through it. We are like the dust bowl Joads gazing down on the Californian orange groves. It's like a miracle, a mirage of the promised land. A few early-risers are out in the streets gazing after us open-mouthed. The semi is badly crippled, great gouts of diesel oil foul the air. The Matador, caked with oil and dust, drags in its wake like an injured insect. When we pull up outside my parents' house in their posh suburb above the river, the children, running out to greet us, stop aghast. Who are these strange inhuman monsters, painted black and red like demons, who have staggered out of the desert?

But life goes on, the stories are soon told, and we go home with my three children to live, as Chris always says, 'in the backyards of the bourgeoisie.'

It is literally true. My father has subdivided the block and built me a grace and favour residence on the old tennis court. Sometimes I still imagine I hear the soft thud thud of the balls, love thirty, deuce, advantage Emily.

My mother refuses to believe we are married until Chris triumphantly produces our marriage lines. Her friends had predicted that my life was over. With three little kids to keep I would never find another husband. Well, I have found him. And we lie wrapped together in the second bedroom fucking deliriously, with a new diaphragm. (You can buy them over the counter. Small, medium, large.) But it is too late. Willow, called after Will Ogilvie, will be born in early December.

Billy and Keith, stranded in Perth with their crippled semi, are bedded down in my study. It is the least we can do.

But things are turning sour. Keith is making a big play for my sister's young housekeeper. He has also developed a habit of sneaking up behind me while I am doing the ironing. I can feel his erection through his jeans. He wants to know when Chris will be shipping out.

The inevitable always happens. Chris picks up a ship and arrives home with an ultimatum.

'I'm shipping out in half an hour and I've ordered a cab for you in fifteen minutes.'

Keith leaves with black looks and a muttered protest about ingratitude. Billy goes out the door saying:

Of all the things I'd like to be
I'd like to be a sparrer,
just sittin' on the Princess Bridge
and gazin' in the Yarrer.

I feel a bit guilty. After all they towed us under duress for over two thousand kilometres but I know I could never handle Keith on my own.

The women in the Union Auxiliary tell me they love being married to seamen.

'Every six weeks is another honeymoon, the kids are yours, and you're your own boss in between.'

But I hate it. I try to write but I can't. I am silent with loneliness.

So after six weeks on the Darwin run Chris pays off the *Lady Isobel* and comes home, to discover that the Matador tool box is missing.

'The bastards!' he says, and I wonder if they are still driving backwards and forwards across the Nullarbor in some other semi, ghosts of a life we might have lived.

(1996)

AN INTRODUCTION TO *THE BATTLERS*

Kylie Tennant

An English reader wrote of *The Battlers*: 'All its people should, of course, be put in a lethal chamber, but somehow by the end of the book, one manages to regard them with sympathy and interest.'

That reference to the lethal chamber was a great shock to me. I felt, though, that to have chipped even a flint off such a mind was of some moment. It had never occurred to me that vagabonds, failures and criminals, about whom I habitually wrote with affection, might, to orderly and reasonable people, be candidates for extinction. This was before even more orderly and reasonable people brought to a dreadful practicality methods of removing large numbers of persons, under the excuse of wartime expediency, from a life which however miserable still gave them breath and hope.

The people who are absent from *The Battlers* are much more alarming from the human point of view than those with whom the book deals: the people who 'look on our labour and laughter as a tired man looks at flies', who consider that those who cannot pass examinations and tests for fluency in language or modern skills, should be filed away under a number in an institution. It is true that in the past century the wheels have moved so fast that there are increasing numbers of us left limping in the rear if we cannot translate the mixtures of Greek and Arabic which result in larger engineering achievements, fouler cities and a general level of dread.

Pockets of primitives, among whom I would number myself, have been abandoned by the roadside, breathless in a roar of exhausts and dust. More and more people are *battlers*, not only on the track, but in the suburbs, the factories, the automated living where to be a man or woman is no longer any claim.

I have long borne the reputation of being an observer of human behaviour, a binocular naturalist objectively recording wildlife in human form. If I have said that I sought the society of unlettered and poor people from choice, because I took pleasure in their company and gained more by it than I did from the learned, this has been laughed off as mere perversity or quaintness. How clever to select such little-used material!

The human eye records best at the pace at which one walks. In fact, to see properly one must sit still. In a fast car, attention is given not to small details but to the larger objects in the landscape. To meet the people I wished to write about, it was necessary to camp where they camped, go at their pace, learn the meanings they gave to words that were used by others in a different sense. Also I must think and feel as they did. This takes time and a large amount of common hardship.

I can remember sitting by a muddy pool in which the horses and men had been bathing and from which I had just drawn a kerosene tin full of drinking water. I was reading a letter in which friends told of a very good white wine they had drunk with ice (*ice*!) at a fashionable hotel. It made me smile ironically to think that for the price of those drinks my companions on the track could live for a week.

Laughter is one of the goods that are never rationed. Indeed, among primitive people laughter is the great protection. A famous Arctic explorer told how the Eskimos among whom he was living were so exhausted by a seal hunt that when they had drawn up their catch on an icefloe, they all went to sleep. While they slept, the icefloe broke away taking their food supply with it. The cream of the jest was – and they rocked with laughter as they related it – that the polar bears would be so glutted with the slaughtered seals, they would not come ashore and so the villagers would lose that food source also. Think of it – the polar bears, too! – they *had* to laugh. A civilised man would not see anything funny in such a situation; but then a civilised man has other defences against lack besides the ability to go hungry and grin about it.

If there is one thing I regret about the long journeys I took along the track, to live with the Battlers, it is that I did not ever come to terms with the horse that drew my van. I had never driven a horse before, and that jib mare and I regarded each other with mutual suspicion. It was not till long after that horse and I had parted for ever that I learned to know how horses think and feel, or to come to any sympathy with them. The horse was to me a burden of responsibility. I had to hobble it, feed it, track it when it wandered. After driving a car I was impatient with a living creature in place of a machine. Even its harness was complicated and strange.

The horse knew of my unhandiness and took constant advantage of this, nearly succeeding in maiming me on several occasions. After a long variance I came to a town where I bestowed the mare in a safe stable. An old drover showed me a knot which, he maintained, would hold any horse securely. Alas! in my impatience and incompetence I strangled the horse, tying it with the new knot. My version of the knot turned out to be a slip knot, and the poor mare, alone and frightened, pulled on it ever tighter and tighter until she died. To have murdered a horse by ignorance and lack of skill is a painful matter, even when the horse is by no means beloved.

I am sorry for it and have continued to be sorry for it for many years. When I hear of others who have committed nameless crimes, I remind myself that probably a good deal of ignorance and callousness were to blame as in my own case. There is, however, less excuse for strangling a fellow creature in mere hastiness and bungling than for other deeds. I would proffer that many horses are natural suicides, and even the best of them neurotic and self-centred. Although I have had enforced association with other horses, finding many of them gentle and affectionate, I have always regarded them with some reserve.

The code of the *travellers*, with whom I worked and camped, was not my code of behaviour. I do not believe, for instance, it is salutary to take a whip to your wife, although this was behaviour which was spoken of in certain cases with approval. Nor did I regard fist fights between drunks as a social diversion. If I had my reservations about my comrades, they always treated me with the kindliness and gentleness the best people show a helpless idiot. I aroused in them both pity and bewilderment and this worked very much to my advantage. Those who are accustomed to a position of bitter inferiority come fresh to the pleasures of philanthropy.

At stealing sheep I was a hopeless failure, making far too much noise; but I continued to enjoy my share of the fresh mutton. Whatever was looted in our passage, my share, although I had done nothing, was placed aside because I was 'one of the mob'. I shared with them what I had. I remember two men sitting by my campfire planning to steal an old set of harness from a 'cocky's' barn.

'Why go so far?' I asked. 'I have a new set of harness, and you could take *that* without any trouble.'

They were outraged and insulted that I should even think they were capable of it. They spoke severely, and with much bad language, of people with minds like mine. One does not steal from one's mates, for that is unforgivable. Also one tolerates in friends conduct that in unknown persons would incur censure.

I ask you to make the acquaintance of the Battlers, as worthy of friendship and requiring it, wherever you meet them, as primitive tribesmen, wanderers in cities, patients in institutions, jailbirds, and others whose acquaintance has no immediate advantage, assuring you that however burdensome the charge, you will be the better for it, unless you are superior or patronising. Humility is all.

There may come a time, and not so far distant, when all of us could be in need of the virtues of the Battlers: which boil down to a talent for survival. After twenty years, people tell me, the *travellers* are now all working industriously in an affluent society. I doubt this. Give me yet another twenty years, and I may be able to point out to you little groups of migrants and wanderers, among whom you may be one, making as best they can in circumstances they have not chosen. Even the most intelligent and superior are casting about now in their minds for boltholes. Do not pity the lean desert dweller until you have learnt to go without water.

From *The Battlers* (1941)

THE ROAD TO GUNDAGAI

Linda Jaivin

Dearest Fiona,

How's life in Darwin? Is the work with Aboriginal women going well? Let me know if you crave anything from Sydney. I can't send you the cafes of Victoria Street, or fireworks over the Opera House, but anything else your heart desires that can fit in a postpak, just let me know.

It's been an age since I've written. Can you forgive me? I've been flat out, what with exams to mark and preparing my paper on 'Like Chocolate for Water: Food and the Femme Fatale in Contemporary Cinema' for a womyn's studies conference in Canberra last week. I know I should probably tell you all about the conference, and the papers, and all that, but I can't resist jumping straight to a little adventure I had on the road.

It was funny because, just the night before, I'd been talking with Chantal, Julia and Philippa about fantasies (they all send their best, by the way), and I'd admitted that, as ideologically suspect as it may sound, I rather fancy the odd macho muscleman. But I'm getting ahead of myself.

Don't you love driving long distances by yourself? I bet you do a lot of it up there. Of course, there are times you do crave company. Like when you see that sign that says 'Injured Wildlife, phone XXXX' and you just want to turn to someone and quip, 'If they're injured, how are they going to get to the phone?' But I digress.

I left Canberra to drive back on Thursday evening, getting on the road a bit later than I'd intended. I hadn't been driving for very long when my engine started making these wretched clunking noises. Soon, steam was pouring out of the bonnet. Luckily, I was almost at Goulburn. I took the turnoff and kept going till I reached the Big Merino. You know the Big Merino – it's that huge concrete sheep that squats on a souvenir shop, one of those places selling heaps of eye-glazing generic Australiana like Akubra hats and fly-swats in the shape of the map. The merino has little red eyes that light up at night. (The locals say that once it had testicles too, but that they were sawn off – an urban, sorry, rural myth?) There's a restaurant and a service station just next door. I was praying that the service station, which is the biggest in the area, would still be open and a mechanic on duty. It wasn't. I was beginning to panic. Thinking the car was about to blow up, I pulled into the parking lot there anyway.

There was hardly anyone around. They were just shutting down the souvenir shop for the night when I got there, and the last of the staff were locking up, getting into their cars and driving off. I opened the hood and stared in despair at my smoking engine. Do you remember when we vowed that we would learn about our cars so that we would never be intimidated by male mechanics again, and we could fix them ourselves? I don't think we ever got much beyond changing the tyres. Well, I could've kicked myself for not taking it more seriously. I was trying not to panic. I was thinking, now that's the fan belt, and those are the spark plugs, and that's the carburettor – isn't that pathetic? You're probably wondering why I didn't just call the NRMA. Well, there's no logical reason at all. I just didn't think of it. I didn't get my PhD in common sense, after all, I got it in film theory. As you know, they are completely unrelated fields. I'm sure it would probably have occurred to me to call them before much more time had passed. As you'll see, fate intervened first.

A huge rig pulled into the parking lot, and began to circle me. Slowly. My heart jumped into my throat. I was thinking *Thelma and Louise*, I was thinking trouble. The driver stared out the window of his cab at me. I glared back, trying to look fierce and potentially armed.

'G'day,' he called out, in a friendly tone of voice. 'Bit of strife with the vehicle?'

I nodded cautiously, still suspicious. He asked if he could help and, before I had time to consider my answer, hopped out.

It was a warm night. He was just wearing a T-shirt and jeans. He was probably in his fifties and, as he bent over the hood, I got a good look at him. I was still thinking along the lines of how I would describe him to the police. His face was suntanned and deeply etched with lines. He had well-defined, thick eyebrows, and attractive blue eyes, from which fanned a bold network of smile lines. He had light brown hair sprinkled with grey. It was cut short and probably for just ten dollars in some country town, you know the look. He didn't seem like a bad sort. I began to relax.

He fetched his toolbox from his truck and set to work. Every so often, he'd look up at me and explain, in his deep rumbly voice and really broad Ocker accent, what he was doing. I wasn't taking in a word of it.

I was noticing how hard the muscles of his arm were, how they rippled and bulged as he fiddled with the engine. His hands were large and callused. Each fingernail was outlined in black, with dirt and engine oil. He had a tattoo on his right arm of a bunch of red roses, and there was a blue and gold oriental dragon on the left. The hair on his arms was thick and blonde, his skin browned and freckled from the sun. The back of his neck had the look of tan leather. He was solid around the waist, which only increased his very manly attractiveness. His legs appeared strong and powerful through his jeans.

There I was, PhD, lecturer in women's studies, big noisy critic of even most educated males as having questionable, not wholly reconstructed attitudes towards gender politics, sort-of wannabe lesbian (we've discussed this, haven't we? how you never quite feel accepted within the hard core of feminist circles if you're not a lesbian?) who in all my thirty-three years have never even slept with a guy who had less than a Master's, and there I was being rescued like a classic damsel in distress by this big brawny bear of a man – and absolutely wetting my pants over him at the same time.

'Thanks so much for this,' I finally managed to croak. My voice had inexplicably gone all husky.

He grinned. 'No worries.'

'See this?' He pointed to something-or-other near the, you know, big bumpy thing in the middle where the spark plugs go. 'That was where your problem was. She'll be right now.'

'Mmmm,' I replied, vagueing out. Leaning closer to him, I breathed in his pungent male odour, all sweat and motor oil. My heart was beating. Without really thinking about it, I shifted my position slightly, so that our arms touched, and it was, literally, like a jolt of electricity. A great big shiver ran down my back.

'Cold?' he asked, the hint of a smile playing around his lips.

Then, can you believe it – I still can hardly credit it myself – I replied, in my new, Mae West voice, 'No. I'm hot, actually.' Insinuating my body against his, I pressed my lips against the crinkly brown sausage of his neck. Honestly, Fiona, I've never ever done anything like this before in my life. I've hardly even had any one-night stands!

And you know I've had my eye on this very nice, sensitive and intelligent fellow in the Asian Studies department, Sam, for months now. I think he might be interested in me too, but the political correctness vibe on campus makes it very hard for anyone to make a move. It's not like either of us really fears the other would jump up and scream 'sexual harassment' or anything, I mean, I'm not his boss and he's not mine, we're just colleagues, and not even in the same department, but the mood on campus surrounding all this sort of thing has left everyone a bit edgy. Maybe it's just me. Maybe I've forgotten how to flirt. Well, I thought I'd forgotten how to flirt.

'Struth,' chuckled my truckie. 'You are hot, aren't you?' He put down his tools. He leaned over and kissed me, not at all tentatively or gently like those MAs and PhDs have always tended to do, but with a kind of rough urgency that, well, if I'm admitting everything else I can admit this too, I really liked. He grabbed my breast and squeezed my nipple hard, through my shirt. Cars whizzed past on the road. We were shielded by the hood of my car, which was still propped up. But when someone drove into the parking lot to turn around, we found ourselves suddenly bathed in the beam of headlights and jumped apart, a little self-consciously.

Glancing around, he said, 'Come on,' took my hand, and led me over to behind the Big Merino. There are some picnic tables there. He sat down on a bench and pulled me onto his lap. Fumbling with the buttons on my blouse, he finally just ripped it open. He grappled my breasts out of my bra and rubbed them and pinched the nipples. I threw my head back and closed my eyes. He nibbled and sucked, occasionally biting my nipples so hard it hurt, but I liked that too, the wild intensity of it all. I was straddling him by now, my skirt riding up high on my hips, and he was kneading my arse with those strong hands. (You should see the grease and oil stains on the blouse and the skirt – they're practically fingerprints! And half the buttons are torn off the blouse. It's funny, but I was just thinking about disposing of those old things the other day and getting some new clothes. Now I have to!) I could feel his dick straining hard against his jeans, and I was riding up and down on it.

Is this too pornographic? Are you shocked? I can't really stop here, though, can I? Besides, if it's pornographic, do you think it proves or disproves Robin Morgan's thesis that if rape is the practice, pornography is the theory? What happens when we women write the pornography? Can we rape ourselves? I've been thinking about this issue a lot lately. The other day, Philippa shared one of her erotic stories with us and asked about the latest line on pornography. I've never quite understood the difference between erotica and pornography, have you? I mean, is erotica merely porn with literary pretensions? Or is something pornography if written by a man but erotica if penned by a woman?

Anyway, there we were, writhing away. I was really digging his gamey smell. I don't think I'm going to give up on intellectuals after this by any means, but they do tend to have a bad habit of wanting to shower before going to bed, and I think I'm just not going to allow that any more.

He took my hand and placed it on his crotch. Then he unbuckled his belt and unzipped his fly, and took my hand right down into his jocks. His dick felt hard and hot under my touch and I swear I could even feel the pulsing of his veins. He squirmed around a bit so that I could pull down his trousers and his underpants. 'Hold on a tic,' he said. He wrapped my legs around his back (my arms were already around his neck) and stood up. Hobbling along (his trousers had fallen down to his ankles), he carried me over to the back wall of the Merino, his tongue down my throat the whole time.

As I slid down his body and onto my feet again, I became aware of music playing. You know those tapes they play in souvenir shops? Songs of the bush, that sort of thing? It seems when they'd locked up the shop, the attendants had forgotten to turn off the tape. Anyway, he now put one of those big paws on the back of my head and pushed me down to my knees, urging my mouth down on to his ginormous cock (certainly the biggest I've ever seen!). He leaned over sideways. I could hear the sound of leather sliding along cloth – he was slipping his belt out of his trousers. Without pulling out of my mouth he leaned over me and yanked my hands behind me and strapped them together, behind my waist, with the belt. I could tell he wasn't fastening the belt very tightly. I'm pretty sure I could have gotten my hands out if I'd wanted to. It was frightening and thrilling at the same time. He used his hands now to control the rhythm by pushing down on my head. We both responded to the muzak coming out of the store, so I ended up sucking to the beat of 'Waltzing Matilda'. After a long while – but I don't want to seem like I'm complaining because I was enjoying every minute of it – I could feel his balls begin to tighten. He groaned. Lifting my head off his knob, he unfastened the belt and helped me to my feet. My knees were raw from the pavement and my stockings were in shreds, but I didn't care.

Now, he pushed me against the wall, where the stucco strip between the windows dug into my back. He dropped to his knees, clawed down my undies and my torn pantyhose and, well, he gave as good as he got. I remember having one, oddly lucid thought, and that was of registering that directly above me was a round window exactly where the sheep's arsehole should have been. I don't remember much else except that he took me right over the edge, and then immediately did it again, and I could hardly stand by the time he finished.

He had a cheeky grin on his face as he stood up again, wiping his mouth and chin with the back of his hand, and saying, 'I love a wet woman.' He took a condom from his wallet and gave it to me. My hands were shaking, and I could hardly rip the little package open. Then I couldn't tell which end was up. Don't you hate that? Trying to roll it down and it won't go because the teat's facing in and it's upside down? Anyway I worked it out. Would you believe, and I'm not exaggerating, his dick was so big that, in fact, I actually couldn't roll on the condom – he had to show me how to stretch it out with my fingers and pull it on that way. He whirled me around now, so that my back was to him and shoved me up against the wall. I vaguely made a note to interrogate myself thoroughly – at a later, more convenient date – on why I found this rough, domi-nating sort of sex such a turn-on. It really is a worry, ideologically speaking. Anyway, it was. A turn-on, I mean. Now I was bent over, arse up, head down, hands flattened on the pane-glass to steady myself. 'The Road to Gundagai' was playing now, and he entered me in energetic thrusts perfectly timed to the music while gripping my hips with his hands. The sensation of that massive rod sliding in and filling me up was both agonising and exquisite. When he really began to slam it in, I orgasmed again while staring through the glass at rows of stuffed koala bears waving little Australian flags. He came too, with a powerful, animal grunt. We just rested there for a few minutes, his arms now wrapped around my waist, his hot, sweaty, prickly chin resting on the back of my neck. Then we straightened up and got our clothing back in order and headed to our vehicles, arms around each other's waist.

I could hardly walk.

He removed his toolbox from my engine, closed the hood, and

said, 'You shouldn't have any trouble getting that going again now.' He added that I should have it checked by a mechanic when I got back to Sydney, and said he'd wait and see that I was able to get off okay.

'By the way,' he said, in a tone that was almost paternal, 'I wouldn't let strange men tie you up like that. That was shocking. Someone could really do you harm, you know.'

Still a little unsteady on my feet, I thanked him, for everything, including the advice, and got into my car. Everything was purring, including me. I waved goodbye and got on the road. And that was that! We never even asked each other's names. My leg muscles are still sore, and everything else is tender, and all the clothes I was wearing that day are wrecked (I stopped at another petrol station outside of Mittagong to change) so I know it wasn't just a hallucination. Besides, I've still got the Wide Load condom wrapper ('maximum head room') that I picked up from the ground as we left.

I wonder what Sam would have thought of it. He'll never find out, of course, but I'd love to know whether he'd be turned on by the idea, or repulsed. Part of me would like him to be turned on, and the other part, maybe the good Catholic girl in me, would prefer it if he were horrified. As if that were somehow a guarantee that Sam was a higher life-form, more capable of caring and commitment or something. I think I'm getting in touch with my inner pagan. I must reread Camille Paglia.

I really did mean to tell you all about the conference, but maybe I'll do that in another letter.

Do tell me what you've been up to. You owe me a vicarious adventure.

Much love,
Helen

From *Eat Me* (1995)

JOURNEY TO HORSESHOE BEND

T.G.H. Strehlow

During Sunday Allan Breaden and Heinrich had spent much time in discussing Strehlow's desperate plight, and the problem of how to bring him closer to medical help. Both men were convinced that Strehlow was far too ill to continue his journey in the buggy. Only a motor vehicle could take him to the next station; and the best plan would be for the sick man to wait for Mr Wurst from Appila to come to Idracowra. The train on which Mr Wurst had arranged to bring his car had been due to reach Oodnadatta on Friday night; and even if he had not been able to leave the railhead till midday on Saturday, he should by now be well on his way north from Oodnadatta.

When Allan Breaden and Heinrich visited Strehlow in the block-house on Monday morning, both were deeply shocked to see him looking so ill. His day of rest had not improved his condition in the slightest. There was no time left for any hesitation or indecision. 'Mr Strehlow,' said Allan, 'you can't leave Idracowra in your buggy today. Your horses are knocked-up, and this hot weather knocks hell out of any man even if he's in the best o' good nick. Tell you what I'll do. I'll send two boys down to Horseshoe Bend with a letter

227

to Gus, telling him to send the car on to Idracowra as soon as it gets to The Bend. His donks will take about six hours to pull the car over the Finke and the box-gum flats for the first twelve miles. After that it's hard, solid going till the car gets here, and our donks will pull it over to the station. That'll let you have a spell here till the car comes. The old blockhouse isn't much of a place to stay in, but at least it's solid and keeps you out of the sun.'

The sick man was only too ready to accept Allan's offer. But when he was about to express his thanks, Allan quickly brushed his remarks aside. 'Look, it's nothing what I'm doing. Everyone in this country would be only too glad to do the same for you. I'm only sorry I can't do more.' And with those few words Allan strode out, told two of his stockmen to saddle up the two best riding horses in the yard, and sent them off with a letter to Horseshoe Bend.

After Allan Breaden had left him, Strehlow was able to give himself up to his self-questionings and to even deeper reflections on the problems of pain and the nature of man's relationship towards God. Now that the letter had been sent to Horseshoe Bend, there was nothing left for him to do but to wait and think. His wife remained in the room to attend to his needs, and his meals were brought to him from the station kitchen. In any case, he had little appetite for food. His upper body had been wasting away for weeks, as was becoming painfully apparent from the hollowness of his cheeks and the strange new bony appearance of his once strong and heavy hands. Loss of appetite, lack of sleep, a grossly swollen lower body, and his never-ending struggle against pain had reduced him to a state of near helplessness. But his powerful heart was still beating strongly, and his clear brain was more active than ever.

On this morning Strehlow knew that only a miracle could save him, and he knew that it was beyond his power to bring about that miracle.

— ‑ —

Except for one or two brief snatches of sleep, Strehlow spent most of the day pondering over his personal relationship towards God. The camel-mail team, returning from Hermannsburg, halted for about an hour in the lengthening shadows of the tall river-gums at the station while Jack Fountain sipped a leisurely cup of tea with Allan Breaden and Heinrich. Then Fountain resumed his journey, and soon the camels had vanished once more into the southern gum flat on the road to Horseshoe Bend. Slowly the hot sting of the sun lessened, and the scorched and weary land became covered with an intricate lacework of shadows.

At six o'clock there was a sudden commotion in the camp. A cloud of dust could be discerned rapidly approaching the station along the Horseshoe Bend road. Within minutes the shapes of horses and of four riders could be seen emerging from this cloud of dust, and by the time this horse party had reached the bank opposite the station, keen-sighted watchers had already identified the riders – they were Mrs Gus Elliot of Horseshoe Bend Station, accompanied by one of her dark stockmen and the two messengers sent out by Allan Breaden on the previous morning. The whole population of Idracowra rushed forward as the riders dismounted, and the air became filled with their shouts and greetings. Mrs Elliot dismounted with the athletic grace of an experienced horse-woman. She shook hands briefly with Allan Breaden and Heinrich, and then asked to be taken without delay to the log cabin where the sick man was anxiously awaiting her news. The shouts of the population had already informed him who she was.

One look at Strehlow told the young woman that he was close to death; but she concealed her apprehension about his condition perfectly, and smiled pleasantly at him and at his tired wife as she went straight to the point of her errand.

'Mr Strehlow,' she said in a rich low-pitched voice, 'I've come with a message for you from the Reverend Stolz. The car he and Mr Wurst were coming up in from Oodnadatta broke down in the Stevenson crossing north of the Alberga on Sunday morning. The Alberga had pretty well knocked the car out, and the Stevenson finished it off. Mr Stolz was lucky enough to catch the camel-mail from The Oodna soon after the car broke down, and he spoke to Gus, my husband, over the phone as soon as he got to Blood's Creek this morning at half-past nine. When Gus told him he'd got a message from Allan last night about your wanting to wait at Idracowra, Mr Stolz grew quite alarmed. He wants you to come down to The Bend immediately, so's you'll be on the Overland Telegraph Line. He said there's a doctor in Oodnadatta at present, and you could get medical advice from him or from the Hostel by phone once you got to The Bend. But that's not all,' she added quickly, when she noted the look of pain and deep disappointment that had come over the tired face of the sick man; 'Mr Stolz said he was arranging for a local car in Oodnadatta to come up as far as The Charlotte, to take up the doctor himself, and Gus will bring on the doctor from there to The Bend by buggy. There shouldn't be any trouble as far as The Charlotte – most of the country up there is, as you know, hard gibber country.'

'And now, Mr Strehlow,' concluded Mrs Elliot, 'here's our last suggestion. As soon as Gus heard that your horses were all knocked-up, he said to me, "Ruby, take our buggy horses and one of our boys to Idracowra and bring Mr Strehlow down." It might take us thirteen or fourteen hours to get back to The Bend; for we'll have

230

to go pretty slow over those gutters in the table mountains. There'll be no moonlight tonight – it's almost new moon, you know. But we'll be close to The Bend by the time the sun's up, and you'll be sitting under a roof next to the phone before the day turns into another scorcher.'

——

Horseshoe Bend was fully living up to its mythical reputation as a heat-creating totemic centre on that oppressive Thursday morning which awakened the two parties of tired travellers that had arrived from Idracowra on the previous day: the temperature had not gone much below the nineties during the night, and the mercury in the thermometers had quickly climbed back to the century mark by ten o'clock in the morning. At this hour hot north-westerly gusts were whirling and whipping up the sand from the dunes and the river flat on the far side of the Finke into shrieking waves of yellowish-brown dust which kept dashing against the barren, rocky expanse on which the station stood and hurling themselves in fury against the groaning metal sides and roof of the hotel building. The latter was a wood and iron structure – the roof and the outside walls had been constructed from sheets of corrugated iron, and the inside walls and the ceilings from ornamental figured tin. On a hot day the heat inside the hotel was virtually unbearable, and the only relatively cool spots for its guests were to be found under the shade of the verandas which protected all four sides of the hotel. Strehlow, who was too ill to be moved except for the most necessary purposes, was forced to sit in his chair and to endure the near bake-oven temperatures of his tin-lined room even during the hottest hours of the day.

Strehlow was much lower in point of physical strength and

mental alertness than he had been only the day before. Mercifully perhaps, his overwrought mind began to wander every now and then, and in his moments of delirium he did not seem to be conscious of those excruciating pains that had begun to rack his body most of the time. But these fits never lasted very long, and then his low moans would show how much pain the very act of taking breath was causing him. The lower portion of his body, from his chest downward, had become swollen to such an extent that he could no longer put on any clothes, and his lower limbs hence had to be covered with a sheet during the day and with a threadbare blanket at night. From the chest upward his body had wasted away till all his ribs and most of his bones were visible in clear outline. His once powerful hands had become so thin and emaciated that his wedding ring had fallen off his left hand a couple of hours after his arrival at Horseshoe Bend.

While Strehlow sat helplessly in his room, the men and women around him were sparing no efforts in their battle to save his life. The owner of Horseshoe Bend Station and the proprietor of its hotel, Gus Elliot, had made many long telephone calls on the previous day. The doctor from Marree who was staying at the Oodnadatta Hostel had been contacted several times, even though his medical advice remained of necessity singularly ineffective. There were no medicines at Horseshoe Bend that could be recommended for the patient's treatment, and the only possible measure of relief – surgically tapping the sick man's swollen body – had to be deferred till the doctor himself could reach the sick man. The telephone news about the possibility of car transport, however, had been most reassuring. The doctor had been only too willing to undertake the trip to Charlotte Waters in the event that a suitable local car and an experienced bush driver should be found. Acting on further special pleas made by Pastor Stolz by telephone from

Charlotte Waters on Wednesday midday, two hours after Strehlow's arrival at Horseshoe Bend, Joe Breaden had at last consented to take the doctor to Charlotte Waters. The twenty-four-hour delay in Breaden's final answer had been caused by the necessity for making arrangements that would ensure adequate petrol supplies for the car: there were no refuelling points located north of Oodnadatta. The doctor, too, had been compelled to make arrangements for an anticipated lengthy absence from his usual place of duty. He was the medical officer responsible for attending to the health problems of the railway employees, and was normally stationed at Marree. He visited Oodnadatta only once a fortnight, on the weekend when the fortnightly passenger train reached this northern rail terminus. However, the comforting fact remained that Stolz's final telephone call from Charlotte Waters had definitely clinched the matter of car transport, and Joe Breaden and the doctor now hoped to leave Oodnadatta on Thursday or Friday. Their car was expected to reach Charlotte Waters some time on Friday or Saturday, and the doctor had agreed to continue his journey from the telegraph station to Horseshoe Bend in Gus Elliot's buggy.

--•--

By the time of Elliot's departure Strehlow had passed through many hours of pain, delirium, and exhausting mental struggle. There was no longer even a faint flicker of hope left in his mind: to pray 'Thy will be done' now meant asking God for strength to die with the fortitude of a servant who had been loyal unto death. Thoughts of what would happen to his wife and son, whom he was leaving behind him completely unprovided for in a country that he had never regarded as his homeland, began to oppress him more and more, and his inability to give any directions for the future to the unsuspecting woman who was soon to become a helpless widow preyed ever increasingly on his mind. Yet he knew that his lips had to remain sealed in her presence. To endure her grief and her despair in addition to those torments of the body and soul through which he was now passing would have been more than he could endure. The man who had been regarded in every way as a rock was beginning to crumble under the incessant hammer-blows of excruciating pain, his resistance undermined by his own doubts and fears.

Late in the afternoon Strehlow could bear the cruel struggle no longer: he would have to shed his pride in the strength of his own self-sufficiency and confide his last requests to a sympathetic person who could be trusted both to keep them secret while he lived and to carry them out after his death. Hesitantly he turned towards his wife, trying to screw up his courage to ask her to leave the room. Mrs Strehlow was quite unaware of the struggle that was going on in her husband's mind. She had been sitting patiently opposite to him, attempting to cheer his spirits by informing him of the moves that were being made to bring a doctor to his side. 'Darling,' she said, with a ring of relief and hope in her voice, 'just think of it – the doctor should be here by Saturday afternoon. Everything will be all right after that. He will be able to give you relief immediately. And when you are stronger again, we will be able to go on, and this time in a car. Mr Wurst is merely waiting in Oodnadatta for new car parts, and then he will make the second attempt to come here to Horseshoe Bend.'

'Frieda,' the sick man suddenly interrupted her, 'please ask Mrs Elliot to come. I want to talk to her – and, please understand me, I want to talk to her alone.'

Mrs Strehlow looked at him in staggered surprise. She had never before been asked to leave her husband's room unless he had wanted to talk to someone in a purely official or clerical capacity. But surely he could have no clerical reasons at this moment for seeing Mrs Elliot? However, she rose and left without asking any questions, only too willing to humour her husband and always ready to believe that his actions were invariably prompted by the best of reasons, even if he would not give them to her. 'Mrs Elliot,' she said, when she came into the hotel kitchen, 'my husband wants to speak to you. And he wants to speak to you alone. I will wait here. Please go – he is almost too weak to talk this afternoon.'

Mrs Elliot hesitated for a moment for the thought of being alone with a dying man terrified her. Then she noted the pleading look in Mrs Strehlow's face and assented. She hurried into the sickroom. One glance at the sufferer's tortured and twitching face, red and purple from the never-ending struggle of breathing, told her that the man before her would not have many more days, or even hours, to live. 'Mr Strehlow, I believe you asked for me to come,' she said in a low voice, trying hard to conceal her shock at the obviously serious deterioration of his condition. 'Is there anything I can do to help you?'

'Please do sit down,' Strehlow replied. 'Yes, Mrs Elliot, I want to ask you to help me, please. There are several things I want to talk to you about.'

Mrs Elliot pulled up a chair and sat down close to him so that he did not have to raise his voice much above a whisper. His breath was coming in half-choked gasps, and she wished to save him any unnecessary physical strain.

'I must be brief,' Strehlow explained. 'My strength has almost gone.' She nodded sympathetically.

He paused for a moment, summoning up his courage to give his final confidences to a young woman who had been a virtual stranger to him before she had come to take him away from Idracowra.

Always self-reliant in the extreme, he had never fully put his trust in any man, still less in a woman, but always only in God. Mrs Elliot, however, had been different. Though she still looked only a charming young girl, she had proved herself to be a spirited woman whose strength of purpose and physical stamina were beautifully matched by her deep compassion for him and by her kindness to everyone who needed her help. Strehlow felt that, of all the people present at Horseshoe Bend, she was the only person who could now be told the full truth about his condition and given the last directions for assisting his loved ones after his death.

'Mrs Elliot,' he began hesitatingly, 'I am dying. I have not many more hours to live . . .'

— · —

An ominous, leaden Friday morning dawned after an oppressively hot night. It had been a night when the thermometer had not fallen below ninety degrees; a night when sleepers had tossed off all blankets and spent most of the snail-paced hours perspiring lightly even when lying on top of their bed sheets or camp sheets; a night when the easing of the hot north-west gale that had roared, raged, and rampaged during the day had served only to increase the breathless closeness of the overheated and stifling atmosphere; a night when even those sleepers who had moved their beds into the illusory freedom of the open air had still felt oppressed by a sky that seemed to shut in as with a blanket the heat reflected against it during the day by the sun-scorched ground; a night in which sleepers had tossed, turned, complained, groaned, sworn, and cursed loudly, debilitated by the almost intolerable and completely enervating discomfort.

As the hours slowly dragged on in the sickroom at Horseshoe

Bend, Strehlow was coming to dread more and more that he, too, was going to be one of those men whose rock-like faith in God was going to be put to the final, crushing trial. Or that, like steel wire stretched taut in a laboratory testing device, it would have weight upon weight added to it until it snapped. While the corrugated iron building around him groaned and creaked in the fierce sun, he was fighting for his very breath, as his life was being slowly choked out of him, gasp by strangled gasp. He felt as though the clutch of giant hands was crushing his chest till his lungs could no longer take in sufficient quantities of life-giving air.

At four o'clock, as a last desperate measure, he was given a draught of medicine prepared by a chemist in Quorn for the relief of 'asthma due to a dropsical condition'. It had been procured by Stolz to alleviate Strehlow's breathing troubles. No one knew what the medicine consisted of, and no one had much faith in its efficacy. Unfortunately, this drug did not lessen Strehlow's breathing difficulties: if anything, his gasps grew even worse, till the last reserves of his strength were being consumed in the effort of getting air into his choked lungs. When Pastor Stolz left the room, after watching the tortured victim writhing in his chair for almost an hour, Mrs Strehlow, who had been sitting nearby in helpless fear, moved closer to her husband. To comfort him, she began to sing one of his old favourite hymns that gave expression to a believer's trust in God in situations like the present. It was the hymn *Sollt es gleich bisweilen scheinen*, whose first two stanzas ran as follows:

> Should dark doubts sometimes awaken
> That God's folk are left forsaken,
> Then in faith I know for sure:
> God helps those who long endure.
> Help He has today suspended

> He has not forever ended
> Though at times in vain we plead,
> Help He gives in deepest need.

At this point the sick man interrupted his wife's singing. 'Don't sing that hymn any more, Frieda,' he begged, in a strangely dull and strangled voice: 'God doesn't help!'

'O darling, please don't talk like that,' she pleaded tearfully, slipping down on her knees before him. 'God will help when His time has come. You have always said so. Perhaps His hour has come now.'

The sick man did not reply. His body shook, his lips quivered, the swollen veins in his purple face pulsed heavily, but he remained silent. He had, at long last, spoken what he knew to be the full truth – that his hour of death was at hand and that any further pleas to God were futile. God had said a final 'no' to all prayers – the communication line between God and the two people in the sickroom had been severed inexorably.

The clock in the next room struck five. Mrs Strehlow persisted bravely in pouring out her words of comfort, but it was doubtful whether the sick man was even capable of listening to them any longer. He had clearly come to the end of his strength. After some minutes he closed his eyes, still without uttering a word, and Mrs Strehlow rose to her feet and sat down on the chair opposite, patiently watching him. Stolz came in quietly for a few moments, and then went out on tiptoe so as not to disturb the sick man's rest, for he seemed to have fallen asleep at last.

It was as though Strehlow's final remark had greatly helped to ease his mind. He had ceased pretending to his wife that even a rock-like faith could sway the Almighty. What he had said represented, in a way, a free version of the psalmist's despairing cry, 'My

God, my God, why hast Thou forsaken me?' He had been completely honest at last with himself, with the wife who still believed
that he would live, and with God. And now his restlessness slowly
disappeared. His breathing, too, became less strained and more
regular, as though great physical relief had come to him at last.

Strehlow slept for a little longer than half an hour, during which
time his wife watched him with lessening anxiety. Then he suddenly
gave a gasp, followed by a deep sigh. His breathing stopped for a few
moments. Mrs Strehlow sat up, startled and suddenly apprehensive.
There was a second deep sigh. After that the sleeper's body slumped
against the back of the chair, and lay there motionless. The great
swollen veins that had stood out so clearly in the wasted throat
pulsed convulsively a few times. Then all movements stopped in
the body, and a bluish tinge began to spread over the face.

It was a quarter to six in the evening.

With a cry of cold fear Mrs Strehlow leapt from her chair. 'O
my God, he's dead!' she sobbed wildly and collapsed before the
moveless body that lay before her, slumped in the high-backed
easy-chair.

Soft swift footsteps behind her made her turn her head back.
It was Mrs Elliot, who had been standing outside the door, whispering with Pastor Stolz about the sick man. 'O Mrs Elliot,' she
sobbed, 'he's dead – my Carl is dead. And I didn't even know he
was dying . . .' She broke down in a spasm of convulsive sobs. The
young woman put her arms around her and raised her to her feet.
'Dear Mrs Strehlow,' she said in a voice almost choked by tears,
'your husband doesn't have to suffer any more. He is at peace at
last. You must come away from her with me. I've got a new room
ready for you tonight.'

Mrs Strehlow stopped sobbing. 'But I don't want to leave my
Carl yet,' she whispered. 'He has always been so good to me. Oh,

what will I do without him? Please let me stay with him a little longer!'

'Please, my dear, you must come with me now,' insisted Mrs Elliot, gently but firmly. 'There are lots of things that still have to be done for your husband. We must get him out of the chair onto the bed and wash his body before it grows rigid. But there are others who'll help me – it's better that you shouldn't be there when we do these things. You'd only be upset, and you're completely worn out already. You've nursed him all on your own for two months already, and you need a break. Please do come with me now – you can look at him again, once everything is over and he is lying on the bed.'

Mrs Strehlow offered no further resistance, and Mrs Elliot took her into the adjoining room, where two beds had already been made up. 'The second bed is for [your son] Theo,' Mrs Elliot explained. 'I thought you might like to have somebody to talk to tonight in case you can't go to sleep in this heat.'

As Mrs Elliot turned to leave the room, Pastor Stolz entered. 'Sister Strehlow,' he said in a low-pitched yet resonant voice, 'I have come to express to you my deepest sympathy. In this grave hour I can do no more than commit you to the care of the Lord, Who has promised to be the protector of the widows and the orphans. He will comfort you and care for you.'

'Pastor Stolz,' replied Mrs Strehlow, bravely trying to speak coherently in spite of her tears, 'I just cannot understand it. I did not know that my Carl was dying. It was just as though my eyes were being held shut so that I could not see anything. And now he has gone – and I did not even get to tell him before he went how much I loved him. The last words I said to him were spoken when I was so very upset, and he did not reply to me.'

She broke down and buried her face in her hands.

Stolz's voice was calm as he comforted her. 'Sister Strehlow, you have done the impossible for your husband for many weeks. Don't blame yourself now for anything that you didn't do. I am sure that God Himself in His mercy shut your eyes so that you could carry on as you did till this very hour.'

When Mrs Strehlow had calmed down a little, Stolz continued. 'And now let me tell you what Mrs Elliot and I were whispering about just outside the door as your husband died. She had received only a few moments earlier a telephone call from Charlotte Waters, telling her that Breaden's car which was to bring the doctor up from Oodnadatta had been held up by an unexpected flood in the Alberga. It could not hope to get through for several days, perhaps even for a week, depending on how quickly the Alberga went down. Gus had rung to ask her about your husband's condition. He wanted to know, should he wait at Charlotte Waters for that time or not. When Mrs Elliot told me this, I knew it was God's wish to call unto Himself the soul of His weary servant and to give him his reward for his faithfulness unto death. That was why all our little human efforts to intervene had to fail. What has happened has been the will of the Lord of life and death. The Lord gave, and the Lord hath taken away; blessed be the name of the Lord!'

From *Journey to Horseshoe Bend* (abridged) (1969)

ST VALENTINE'S DAY

Peter Rose

On 14 February 1974 – St Valentine's Day – Mum and I drove to Wangaratta. We were on our own except for the dachshund, Sammy, which travelled in the back, staring disapprovingly at haystacks and livestock. Being an innate nostalgist, I always wanted to hear about our original move to Wangaratta, back in 1955. I couldn't remember it, having been an infant at the time. Vague memories of putrid swaggies trudging along the Hume Highway were probably seeded much later, or dreamt. My mother, driving in her cautious way, reminisced. She told me she had dreaded the prospect of leaving Melbourne. Having left Tongala, with its ambiguous childhood memories, she probably disliked the thought of going back to the country. An astute woman, all too familiar with the intrigue and acrimony that beset football clubs, she must have known what awaited them in the recently polarised town, half of whose inhabitants duly shunned their sports store, funded as it was by the interlopers, the Wang Rovers.

Mum was also a creature of the city. Postwar Melbourne was a vibrant place for someone like Elsie. As a young woman she had performed in countless theatres and moved in a large, stimulating circle. During the day she worked as a stenographer near the Victoria Market. Then she married into a gregarious sporting milieu. She frequented the legendary Rivoli and Mario's Restaurant. The last thing she desired was the claustrophobia of a small town, with a co-op for fashions and biannual visits from the Elizabethan Theatre Trust to look forward to ('*Rigoletto* in Myrtleford', as the old joke went).

But one thing solaced Mum as she set off for Wangaratta in 1955. She loved radio, then in its halcyon days. Radio was universal and inviolable. Even in Wangaratta she would be able to listen to her beloved 'Nicky' and his sidekick, Graham Kennedy. When she began to miss her old world she would be able to listen to a concert or serial or news broadcast. Elsie, whom I later dubbed 'Reuters' Rose, was addicted to the news. An hour without a bulletin was hollow, unfulfilled.

The first thing Mum did when she reached Wangaratta was to unpack the 'wireless' and switch it on. Silence and static greeted her. She had forgotten about the Great Dividing Range. There were no Melbourne radio stations: no 'Nicky', no Graham, no Jack Davey. The only station she could pick up was 3NE, the local one. It had just acquired a copy of 'The Black Hills of Dakota' to go with its other Doris Day records. It played them all day.

My mother sat on the kitchen floor and wept.

— · —

When we reached Wangaratta on St Valentine's Day, listening to the radio of course, we went straight to the Challmans' house. Uncle Hughie, discharged from hospital, seemed cheerful, if weak. We sat in the kitchen drinking tea and eating Auntie Chall's immemorial Melting Moments. I always loved returning to Wangaratta.

I loved being back in Auntie Chall's kitchen where the Roses and the Challmans had spent so many evenings together. I loved hearing about old friends, including a passing reference to a boy called Ross, the first boy I ever kissed. I loved the familiar dark cool of the Challmans' house, with its floral carpet and porcelain figurines and seductive Sammy Davis Junior and Judy Garland records, which Marie had added. I wished that she and Barbara were with us.

Throughout the day old friends kept arriving to say hello. I didn't recognise all of them. They knew me, though, and teased me about my height. They asked fondly about Dad and my brother Robert. Within a few days some of them would be writing to us, using a different tone: those old, refractory phrases. We discussed a recent murder near Wangaratta. Murders are always gripping in country towns. This one was too stupid, too gratuitous, to be forgotten. It had happened a few summers ago. A fourteen-year-old girl – Ella was her name – was walking her Alsatian beside the Hume Highway one morning. Her family had stopped for a drink on their way north. Ella was mature for her age, blonde, leggy and attractive. A local, driving along the highway, spotted her, was 'reminded' of his estranged wife and shot her with his rifle. She died beside the road.

Mum and I remembered it well. We knew Ella. Her family, recent immigrants from Scandinavia, had lived near us in Lemana Crescent. I recalled the police arriving on Christmas morning to ask Dad a few questions. I had met Ella once or twice. Not long before her murder she had knocked on our door and politely warned my parents that she was organising a Christmas party. I was far too awed by Ella's beauty to speak to her. I was similarly dazzled by her handsome brother, Erik, and by the way his name was spelt. Both of them had the sort of classic good looks that always rendered me speechless with shyness. After the murder the family remained secluded, but now and then, around dusk, I saw Erik walking the Alsatian, profoundly sombre.

The insanity of Ella's murder riveted us in the cakey kitchen. Later Mum and I asked about friends, shopkeepers, the Wang Rovers. I kept looking at the high, exposed cabinet. Installed by some local carpenter, this rose to the ceiling and was full of Auntie Chall's impressive collection of teasets and dinner services – one for every occasion. It was like a mini-museum, florid and frangible. The cabinet was leaning over as mesmerisingly as ever. Ever since I was a boy I had been privately waiting for it to collapse. No one else commented on its Pisan tilt, so I said nothing. It was the slowest disaster in history.

Gingerly I removed some plates from the perilous tower. I have no idea what we ate for dinner, but Uncle Hughie no doubt spurned dessert and called for The Tasty Cheese. This aromatic rite had always fascinated me as a child, inured to processed cheddar. I thought Uncle Hughie sophisticated to the point of tetchiness.

Evidently people were tired and we all went to bed at about eleven.

— • —

Sammy woke me around two in the morning, wanting to be let in. Sammy was a highly intuitive dog, with a pedigree as long as a Remington ribbon, as Henry James said of his dachshund. Soon after – I didn't hear the telephone ring – Auntie Chall came into the room and said, 'Peter, you've got to get up. Robert's had an accident. You've got to go home.' Her voice was grave. She had never sounded like that before. I felt sure Robert was dead. It had happened, after all, the horror we are always half expecting in life. Now we had to hurry to its side.

Instantly there was terrible activity in the dark house. My mother was already up, dressing. She too had been awake when the call came. Perhaps it was the heat that woke her. But she had felt an odd premonition before leaving Melbourne. She had gone into Robert's old bedroom and looked at some mementoes. It occurred to her that if anything happened to me she would have ample memorabilia – all my silly cards and poems – but that if Robert were to die she wouldn't have anything to remember him by.

We packed our things, not speaking to each other. Weirdly, I washed my face. Mum told me to hurry up and we went out into the night. There was no light in the small garage at the end of the drive and Mum became frightened. I didn't know how to drive then (and would delay learning for another decade because of what happened), so Elsie, a nervous motorist at the best of times, had to drive back to Melbourne. We squeezed into Dad's big powerful lime-green Ford. Reversing down the narrow drive we hit the wall twice. Uncle Hughie, in his dressing gown, had to scamper out of the way. Then we had to get out and clean the windscreen, which was encrusted with insects. We all moved around in silence, saying nothing. Finally, jerkily, Mum and I set off.

It was still hot. Locusts were everywhere. All night they rushed at us, smothering us. My mouth was dry. Mum wept occasionally but mostly we talked about the surprising volume of traffic on the Hume Highway and the suicidal locusts. Tacitly, we knew we had to maintain some sort of conversation. Mum sensed that I was nervous about her driving. Knowing that Robert might already be dead, she said to me, 'It's all right, I won't lose another son.'

We ticked off the familiar towns along the way: Glenrowan, Benalla, Euroa, Seymour. The bypasses we all take for granted hadn't been built yet, so we drove down the empty, flickering main streets. Away from the towns, the semitrailer drivers, as if knowing we were in a hurry, kept indicating to my mother when it was safe to overtake. Elsie had rarely overtaken anyone in her life. On the few occasions when she had, after much deliberation, overtaken a slowcoach, Robert and I, sitting in the back, would congratulate her and we would all breathe a sigh of relief.

My mother had been told to go straight to the Austin Hospital in Heidelberg. I was too callow to know what that might signify, though I did wonder why Robert had been moved from Bacchus Marsh, where the accident had happened, to the Austin. But Elsie knew where she was going, and why.

It was 4.30 a.m. when we arrived. As we neared the ugly hospital on the hill I decided that if Robert was dead I wanted to deliver the eulogy, possibly a strange wish for a young brother.

We left Sammy, oddly quiet, in the car and went to Casualty, where a pleasant nurse directed us further up the hill to Ward Seven. When we reached the waiting room Uncle Kevin was there to greet us. Terry or someone must have rung him, in Dad's absence. I was relieved by Kevin's facial expression. I knew immediately that Robert was still alive. But Kevin looked startled when the doctor, duly alerted, came out and spoke to us. Kevin's prominent jaw was quivering. He was obviously deeply shocked. The doctor introduced himself as David Burke, head of the spinal injuries unit. I seemed to be having trouble hearing or comprehending what was being said. Then my mother broke down and the doctor began consoling her. Kevin, a pragmatic man just like my father, said, 'He's all right *in himself*' – a phrase that would always fascinate me, one for the philosophers. Kevin told us that Robert had taken the news exceptionally bravely. Then I heard the words that Robert would never walk again, and I too started crying. I slumped on a bench away from the others. Mum remembers me sliding along the bench and cowering in a corner with my face averted. Fat unavailing tears fell on the polished floor.

But then my mother shocked me. 'It would have been better if he'd died,' she said. For the first time in my life I snapped at her. 'That's a terrible thing to say,' I reprimanded her. She looked at me benignly and said nothing. I was eighteen. I had no sons of my own. I had never nursed anyone. I had never been nursed. I had no idea what quadriplegia meant. I couldn't even spell it.

We never mentioned it again.

— - —

In the years that followed we all wished they had broken the news to us differently. Mum, as we would learn, had reason to. If only they had had more time or better resources. If only they had prepared us a little, sat us down, taken us into a private room, given us a drink after the journey. Mum had been driving all night. Almost forgotten in the crisis was the fact that she had had major surgery six weeks earlier and was still recovering.

Yet there were reasons for Dr Burke's sense of urgency and candour, however confronting. Apart from the fact that his main responsibility was not our equilibrium but keeping my brother alive (for Robert's survival was by no means assured that night), Dr Burke and many of his peers believed that directness was preferable to evasions or euphemisms. The relatively new director of the spinal injuries unit, then in his mid-thirties, had trained in Britain with a pioneering surgeon in the field who insisted on being frank with patients and their families, even at the outset. Dr Burke had previously worked in America where he was disturbed by the misleading promises made by some neurosurgeons, and by the dismay of quadriplegics and their families months later when they failed to regain the use of their limbs. He thought this deeply irresponsible. So Dr Burke was frank with Robert when he was admitted to the Austin, just as he was forthright with us.

When I visited Dr Burke in July 2000, he admitted that this policy was not without its critics. 'It's a bit controversial still,' he told me.

We were sitting in a small office near the reception desk at Ivanhoe Manor in Melbourne, where he helps road accident victims cope with quadriplegia and head injuries. I had sat outside for a few minutes, waiting to renew my acquaintance with Dr Burke, whom I hadn't seen since 1974 and by whom I had always been somewhat intimidated. The reception desk was clearly the busiest part of the hospital. It was almost five in the afternoon, always a hectic time in a hospital. Dinner was being served and patients put to bed. I watched a boy of eighteen or nineteen trying to use a public telephone, assisted by an aide, all his movements twisted, uncontrollable. I kept thinking about him during my interview with Dr Burke as sounds of laughter, coins being changed, patients chided or placated, penetrated the thin walls. I thought of Robert, who had spent more than half his life in institutions of this kind: frenetic, rackety, always vaguely hysterical.

Dr Burke elaborated: 'There are people who feel you shouldn't give people that sort of bad news straight off. I always believed, and it was taught to me by my predecessor, that it was more important to be honest with patients and with the relatives right from the start. Tell them the truth, as much as you can, but deliver it in a kind way, without being too blunt. But don't give them false hopes.'

I presumed that Robert, being the sort of laconic person he was, would have welcomed the truth. Dr Burke generalised in response: 'You don't necessarily give them the whole story first up. You've got to tailor it to suit individuals a bit. With some relatives you just know they're not ready to hear anything very much that first time. But you don't tell them untruths, you don't make false promises, and you don't tell them something you know is just not true – because you'll get found out and then you lose them forever.'

Cautiously I said that those interviews – imparting the terrible news to patients once or twice a week – must have been difficult, notwithstanding professional experience and exigencies. He must have done it hundreds, even thousands, of times. I wondered where Dr Burke was when he got the news in February 1974. He too must have been rung up that night, called away from dinner or the theatre or the *Lancet*, to be confronted by 'just another of our crashes', more maimed promise in the sixty-second bed, never empty for long. The director of the unit was always notified first.

Dr Burke agreed that it was a distressing role. He said it was one of the reasons why he had moved away from spinal cord injuries ten years after Robert's accident. 'I just felt that I was saying the same thing to the same people, the same families, time after time, and that it was time for a change. It gets to you after a while, even though it is a very important part of your work.'

He reminisced about his subsequent work in Armenia after the 1989 earthquake. This left many people with severe spinal cord injuries, but with few local specialists to treat them. Dr Burke was one of countless western doctors who volunteered. He spent three months in Armenia. ('Talk about a return to the good old days of spinal injuries! I mean, the sort of facilities we used to have at the Austin well before Robert's time – and even then the facilities were pretty basic.') Because none of the medicos spoke Armenian or Russian, they had to recruit university students to translate for them when they spoke to the victims and their families. The students, many in their teens, none au fait with quadriplegia, were the ones who had to tell the truth ('the talk I gave your family'), thus breaking people's hearts. Dr Burke was full of admiration for the way the students coped. Many wept after the first interview, 'but they were right from there on'.

I asked Dr Burke if he remembered how Robert reacted to the news. He doesn't recall anything unusual. He told Robert that he had sustained a serious injury to his spinal cord. He had broken a bone in his neck. His spinal cord was badly damaged, which was why he was paralysed. There was no feeling, no movement, and there was a real possibility that this might be permanent and that he might not walk again. He told him that if any recovery was going to take place it would happen during the next few weeks. He didn't go into further detail. As Dr Burke told me, 'It would have been something fairly straightforward, pretty much from the shoulder, but delivered in a friendly kind of way.'

My conversation with Dr Burke lasted for an hour. It was amicable, unreserved, at times gently rueful. When I told him about Robert's final illness he fell silent, clearly distressed and surprised that it had gone on as long as it did. He hadn't heard the details before. He asked about my work as a publisher at Oxford University Press and told me he was reading the book about James Murray and the mad American who helped him compile the *OED*. I thanked him and left him to his emergencies. As I passed the reception desk a fire alarm began to wail. Those patients able to walk and their visitors – haunted, exhausted mothers and sisters – poked their heads into the corridor, variously concerned or amused, wondering if they should evacuate the building, wondering if they could be bothered. A beleaguered nurse hurried along the corridor reassuring people that there was no need to worry, that it was only a false alarm, but the fire alarm continued to wail. It was still going when I reached my car. Fire engines pulled into the street as I reached the intersection.

251

I thought about that old dream of mine – the one with cemeteries and infernos – in which I belatedly recognised my young guide.

— • —

Mum and I, still in the waiting room, asked if we could see Robert. Dr Burke said we could as long as we composed ourselves. We did. We walked down a corridor, past tiny offices with nurses filling out graphs and rosters. Then we entered Ward Seven for the first of many times. It was in darkness, except for a space around Robert's bed. The newcomers usually arrive during the night, after their car or diving accidents. Some of the other patients in the long, crowded room must have been aware what was going on, but they said nothing. Nurses were leaning over Robert's bed, whispering. They were still working on him. I wondered why the bed had to be so high. It was like a bier.

Robert was lying on his back, looking rather beautiful. His head was shaved. They had already drilled holes in his skull and inserted calipers attached to eight-pound weights. Robert's head was pulled back, immovable. There was a tube in his mouth. Mum kissed him. His first words to her were, 'I'm in trouble'. Then he let out a profound sigh. She can hear it still. I too kissed Robert, the last time I would do so for twenty-four years. His brow was sweaty, feverish, but alive. Stupid or stupefied by now, I asked him how he was, how he was feeling. Then I think I said, 'I love you'. He smiled at us, quite calm. There were no howls, no complaints. When he spoke his voice was brave but unusually high-pitched and uneven. Later, remembering my Conrad, I wrote in my journal, 'There was a storm in it. He was brave, braver than I would be, but there was destruction of terror in his voice.'

Robert was clearly tiring. The nurses had sedated him. Reluctantly, we said goodbye and left. I thought about the terror Robert must have felt as they cut him from the car and drove him to Melbourne in the ambulance. I was unhappy about leaving him there alone, with the doctor's cruel words ringing in his ears, despite the drugs and devices.

We rejoined Uncle Kevin in the waiting room. He had just rung my father in Las Vegas and broken the news to him. Now Dad was hurrying to the airport. We decided that Kevin and I should convey the news to my maternal grandmother while Mum drove home on her own. It was light outside – bright, indifferent day. I didn't trust it any more. Kevin and I set off in one of his business vans. I was keen to speak to Nan as soon as possible. She, like her daughter, was a devotee of the wireless and an early riser. We didn't want her to hear about it on the news.

We drove to Prahran in silence. At one point Kevin ran over an unlucky dove. Normally squeamish about such things, I watched it happen without flinching, too numb to react.

When we got to Nan's flat she was sitting on the edge of her bed, as if waiting for someone.

My mother was right, of course. I didn't know it then, but I would learn. Whatever the consolations, and they were profound, she was right. No one deserves to suffer as Robert did.

From *Rose Boys* (2001)

THE MILK RUN

Christina Stead

Lydham Hill was the name of the knoll and of the cottage, too; it was painted on the stone pillars where the iron carriage gates closed the now unused drive. The cottage stood on the crest of a high ridge overlooking Botany Bay, some eight miles distant and was built foursquare, east-west, so that they could look from the veranda straight between the headlands, Cape Banks and Cape Solander, to the Pacific.

They could see from the attic windows the obelisk standing where Captain Cook first landed with his botanists, Banks and Solander, and they could see on stormy days the little launch they called *The Peanut* tossing between the heads as it went towards Kurnell. The cottage was built of rough-hewn sandstone blocks cut in the quarry down the hill and hauled up in the old days. The trees round the house, Norfolk Island and other pines, pittosporum, camphor laurel, were seventy and more years old and the pines had seeded in the old neglected orchard where the seedlings grew higher every year, faster than the children. The knoll itself was ironstone capped and penetrated by heavy, thick and almost pure clay, gamboge yellow, stained red where the ironstone stuck out its nodules.

It was almost country still; few houses, large pastures, unpaved streets of sand or clay, foul and grassy gutters. The short street Lydham Avenue, which went over the hump before the house, westward, was a hazard, almost impassable in wet weather. Cartwheels, horseshoes, boots, umbrella ferrules were sucked in by the clay. In the hot sun the clay soon turned to dough and then to pottery. A messenger boy, the young postman, the women and children of Lydham Hill, had to cross the clay to get to the tram or the shops and might lose a handkerchief, a parasol, a shoe, a parcel; and after poking at it gingerly, afraid to fall in the muck, would abandon it and struggle to the clay bank and look back just as if the thing had been carried out to sea. The postman's prints, first of a sandshoe which he lost as he crossed to Lydham and then of his naked foot, and a copy of the *St George Call*, which he had dropped while trying to get his shoe back, remained week after week. The footprints and tracks remained and even at the next big rain they did not disappear, but only formed little foot-shaped puddles and long canals.

The Council occasionally sent men with a cart and shovels to scrape off the surface; and with it, they gleaned the lost articles and went away with the cart, leaving behind an identical clay surface, but with the banks higher now, until the people in Lydham Hill had to cut steps in the bank, yellow clay steps.

It was warm, October, summer just beginning. October is the month of the roof-raising equinoctial gales, which shouting, bring down trees and capsize sheds. It was a Saturday. The day and night before there had been gales; rain in the morning – in the evening, a sunset the colour of the saffron tearose at the gate. Matthew, going for milk on Friday had lost a sandshoe. 'Clumsy ape,' said his father, goodnaturedly, flipping his cheek with the nails of his left hand and at the same time explaining that he and Matthew were lefthanded; and he went on to explain how very difficult this made things for his neighbours, a lady say, at public dinners; and that Matthew later on, would find it awkward, too. Matthew was seven. Then his father, going barefoot, had squelched happily out into the mud and got the shoe back. It needed soaking and cleaning. Said his father, 'From now on you go to Dappeto barefooted; it's good for the feet anyway.' Dappeto was his grandfather's place, where he got the milk.

All the week, in the evenings, his father with his elder brother Jimmy-James, had been lopping the lower boughs off the Norfolk pines down the horse-paddock side. They called it the horse-paddock because it was rented to a brown horse for one pound a week, a lonely horse that could be seen streets away on their slope and which people thought was their horse; but they were not allowed to speak to it.

With the cut branches the three of them built a gunyah, an Aboriginal shelter, placing the tall boughs against a goodsized trunk, lacing them together with small branches. It made an odorous half-tent, green, dark, with a floor of old brown pine-needles, nine inches to a foot thick, so that even now it was dry and warm, on the slope.

Matthew had dragged some of the other boughs to the bottom of the white paddock, a pony's paddock, so called because it had a white railing. In it they kept two fullgrown emus named Dinawan (a native word for emu) and Dibiyu (a native word for the whistling duck because this emu whistled). Dinawan and Dibiyu had come to them newly hatched chicks, striped and about the size of fowls. Beyond this fence at the bottom Matt had built this gunyah to share with his friend Lyall Lowrie, also seven years old, a boy who lived in one of the new brick cottages downhill. There was building all around them, fascinating for the boys.

Matt and Lyall were sitting in the gunyah close together, talking in low interested voices. It was quite warm, though the sun was striking higher at the trees as it westered. Matt, though he did not say so, was hiding from the house. The boys had torn away the rough pine-needles and were poking in the soft blackish felted earth. They had found some small red ants.

'That's the beginning of an ants' street,' said Matthew.

'I know, one street on top of the other,' said Lyall.

'Like a city of the future,' said Matthew.

A whistling began. Matthew peered through the pine-branches. A woman's voice came down the hill. Matthew said,

'I have to go for the milk. Do you want to come?'

'Where is it? The dairy?'

'It's my grandmother's place: about a mile.'

But Lyall had to go home. He climbed a branch, reached out for the fencetop, dropped down, shouted, 'I'll see you tomorrow.'

'If I don't have to work,' said Matthew.

Matthew toiled up the orchard path, made of pebbles stuck in clay. At the south end of the house was a lattice, with one panel sagging from the gale. His father was repairing it. A tall strong fair man, burnt red by the sun, he stood in the opening leading to the brick yard, a courtyard almost entirely enclosed by domestic build-ings in sandstone, a shelter from the hilltop wind.

'Milk-oh!' said his father.

'I made a gunyah,' said Matthew.

'Good-oh. And now skedaddle.'

Matthew was a fair sturdy boy who closely resembled his father. His sunbleached hair was whiter; he had a thick down over his temples joining his pale eyebrows, and it ran over the sides of his cheeks where his beard would be.

As soon as he came in sight of his father, his eyes became fixed on the man's face, he smiled with an unconscious faint rapture and, his head turning, his glances followed his father, a restless, energetic man, never still.

'Do you love your Dad?' said his father, smiling with coquettish cunning at the child.

The boy burst out laughing, 'Yes, Dad!'

His worship of his father was a family joke, a public joke and something that irritated his mother. They talked about him when they thought he was not listening. He was always listening idly, his head turned away, while he played with ants, bees, wasps; and mooned, as they said. The ants, bees, wasps did not sting him; they would hang resting on his hand. His idling, playing was not a ruse. In his dreamy pastimes, he liked to be a part of what he heard, the snatches and inconsequence of their talk, part of the wasps, the rush of wind, an entire life, vague but delicious. He could sit in the sun watching the ant-trails for hours; he never hurt the ants. His father told him they were ant-engineers, ant-architects, ant-soldiers, ant-nurses, ant-scouts; but he scarcely thought of it. 'Perhaps another Darwin,' said his father; and he said the same when it turned out that Matthew was slow in school. Darwin was slow in school. But at other times, Matthew galloped about shouting; no one knew what he shouted. His father was pretending to block the way. Matthew could get very angry. His father was curious about it and teased him. With a rough push, the boy got past and went to the kitchen. The milkcan stood on the table, a workman's billycan of grey flecked enamel with a tin top that served as a cup. He set off. His feet were bare. They were solid well-formed feet, with the skin grown thick and horny on the soles and blackened underneath, dark grey with dirt you could not get out, yellow-splashed at the sides, with deep cracks on the soles right down to the red flesh. He was used to having sore feet and dug deep into the soft mud, soothed.

He went down the grass slope outside the iron gates, where they were now laying the foundations to build. The men had gone and he picked up a few bright nails from between the floor joists for his father. The men liked him and let him take nails anyway.

At Wollongong Road he scanned the dairy farm opposite. Then he crossed the road and walked along by the two-rail fence. The farm buildings of whitewashed planks lay slightly below the swell of the meadow, towards Stoney Creek gully. Matt trotted down the deeply rutted tussocky footway. He had not gone far, before the boy he feared came out from the brick wall of the old house where he had been waiting, with a mad scowl, his features jumping as if on red and black wires, his teeth showing. He rushed to the fence and swung his greenhide thong on to Matthew's shoulder and face. He did not say a word but with a fierce grin of hatred jerked and swung.

'Don't,' said Matthew. He hurried along, the milkcan swinging wildly on its wire handle. His enemy followed him to the next panel and the next, but did not get through the fence on to the footway. The greenhide bat, about fifteen inches long and three or four inches wide, slapped down on Matthew's left side. He started to cry and ran along the ruts, the milkcan insensately hopping up and down and doing somersaults. But the boy, having caused terror, ceased after a few more panels and walked diagonally towards the milking sheds, turning round to make a face. The cows were coming up from the gullyside and gathering at the door of the shed. The milkman's son was a thin muscular boy of about ten, with dark hair and regular features; but when Matthew saw him, he was always snarling, scowling, grinning in fury.

Matthew reached the next block, all small red-roofed houses; but it was some time before he saw the ochre-coloured picket fence of Dappeto. Until a fortnight before, it had been his sister Emily, a clumsy girl of eleven, always in the wars, as they said, who had gone for the milk to Dappeto, every evening after school. Then one day, almost home, she fell in the clay and sent the can flying. She came home dirty, her long fair hair wet and dark-streaked over her red cheeks, with no milk for the baby and the story, 'a boy beat me'. 'What boy?' 'I don't know.' Though Matthew knew the boy, their unbelief made him think it was a lie, too.

Now, though they did not believe her and he was smaller, it had become his job to go for the milk. Even his mother had made no protest.

Here was his grandfather's house, Dappeto. Inside the fence grew all kinds of trees, camphor laurel, pittosporum, swamp box, eucalypts, wattles. He went down the lane to the side where was a big gate for the buggy. He dug his toes into the asphalt softened by the day's sun. There was the old camphor laurel with the broad low arms good for climbing and hiding, there the giant Araucaria Bidwilli, with shining dark green stabbing leaves. There was the man Tom Grove, called The Man, in the cow paddock at the salt-lick. Matthew went in under the archway where were the feed bins and up into the second kitchen. No one was there. Up a step into the kitchen. Mary the maid sat at the window knitting.

'I saw you coming. How's your mother?'

'All right.'

'What dirty feet! Where are your shoes?'

'I lost one.'

He went up another step, on to the veranda, turned right; there was the double pantry: preserves beyond in a dark room; here on the shelf three large shallow pans of milk for skimming. Mary came and poured milk into his can.

The parrot sitting on his perch on the veranda, put down his head engagingly, said 'Cocky want a bit of bread and sugar?' Mary dipped a crust in milk and sugar and gave it to the boy.

'Give it to Joe.'

'No, no,' he said, flushing. The parrot had a cunning eye and heavy beak.

'Emus have bigger beaks,' said Mary. She was a country woman from Hay ('Hay, Hell and Booligal', he knew) and saw no sense in keeping emus.

'Emus don't bite,' said Matt.

Mary, in her long flowing skirt, stepped along the veranda and handed the parrot his crust. He was a handsome Mexican said to be forty years old, as old as Mary herself.

'Go and see your grandmother; I'll get some butter for your mother.'

Up another slate step into the house, where right beside the door there was a little room called the housekeeper's room, where his grandmother liked to sit.

'Is that you, Mattie?' called a voice very like the parrot's voice.

A large solid neat old woman, with white hair strained back into a little bun, in a black dress with white trimmings, a housekeeper's dress, sat in an armchair stuck between the table and the wall. She could look out through two windows in the angle, one towards Wollongong Road, one towards the greenhouses. She smiled fondly but did not stop revolving her thumbs in her clasped bloated hands.

'Look at the dirty feet! Doesn't your mother give you shoes to wear?'

'I have sandshoes.'

'Where are they?'

'It's healthy to go without shoes.'

'Come and kiss Old Mum. How's your brother?'

'Jamstealer is all right. He's playing football this afternoon.'

The grandmother said suddenly, 'Jamstealer is not a nice name to call your brother.'

'It doesn't mean jamstealer: it's a name. Daddy calls him that.'

'It's not a nice name for your father to call his son.' Matthew frowned. The old woman rose and took his hand.

'Come and I'll get you some flowers for your mother. How is she?'

'Mother's lying down.'

She plucked flowers from the beds along the cracked asphalt drive. Her flat monk's shoes slid off the grassy verge.

'I nearly fell down on my bum,' she said, began to laugh, opening her mouth wide in her creased floury face. She kept her eyes on the little boy, 'What would your father say to that?' Matthew was shocked but said nothing. 'Milking we had a stool called a bumstool,' she said. She had come from a dairying family on the South Coast. He eyed her straight. They came back to the kitchen.

'Tell your mother to come and see her mother one of these days.'

Mary handed him the butter in a bag and the flowers and the milk.

'Scratch Cocky,' said the parrot. He lowered his head and ruffled the feathers, showing grey skin.

'Beat the gong,' begged Matthew.

Mary picked up the chamois-headed stick which hung on the gong beside the back door. Joey shifted his feet in a slow respectable dance. Mary hit the gong twice: Joey screeched,

'Stephen! Walter! Edward! Anthony! John! Arthur! Matthew! Robert! Frederick! Albert! William! Leah! Rachel! Pitti!'

It was a country woman's screech.

No air-thin boys and girls came gambolling from the paddocks and orchard, from the gardens and bowling green, hungry for dinner; though in years long gone they had come racing, in flesh and blood. Those were his uncles and aunts and Pitti was his mother, the youngest, 'Pretty'.

Matthew went back up the asphalt drive, the homemade butter in one hand, the flowers and the quart milkcan jostling in the other. When he came back to the dairy on Wollongong Road, he hesitated. He could cross towards Forest Road, heading round a triangle of land just being fenced in and invisible to the dairy boy. But he was a little afraid of the new route. He crossed and came along the other side of the Wollongong Road, along a tall apricot-coloured fence of new hairy boards. At the farther point of that triangular plot, too, was an interesting wooden post, very old and grey and eaten inside by termites. It had been smouldering for weeks, set alight by the sun, not extinguished by the rain. The sun was on the horizon. Shafts of red touched him across the dairy. He reached the end of the new fence and Lydham Hill could be seen with its great head of trees. He stumbled on a big tussock and fell. Though he kept hold of the things, the milk spilled. He got up quickly and righted the can, but there was very little milk left. He tried with the lid to catch some milk from the ground, but it had soaked away into the sand, leaving a light stain. Just a few of the grass blades held a dew of milk. When he shook them, the dew fell. He did not know what to do. He was too tired to go back to Dappeto. At home, they might beat him, worse, shout and deplore. As he still poked stupidly about looking for milk, he saw a gold coin, a sovereign, under the tussock. He knew it, for his father brought home his pay on Saturdays, spread the coins on the table, gold sovereigns and half sovereigns, silver and let them finger it. He was proud of it, what he earned.

Matthew picked up the gold coin and hurried home up the yellow clay, past the saffron tearose, the 'Chinaman's Finger Tree', a tree with yellow bell flowers, so called because they put the flowers on their fingers and rushed at each other, shrieking, 'I'm a Chinaman.'

He had his statement ready, 'I fell over the grass and spilled the milk.'

His mother was in the kitchen in her grey silk dressing-gown, with the silver and gold dragons on it, at the bottom gold water-waves and a gold tower. She had a baby's white shawl round her head, a sign of neuralgia.

'I was tired,' he complained.

'Barely a cupful,' she said contemptuously. 'Open the condensed milk, Eva. What's that?'

'Butter and some flowers and Old Mum says to go and see her.'

'I'll go and see Mother tomorrow. I wish I could leave this darn windy barn. And the emus walked in this evening and ate your father's cat's-eye waistcoat buttons that were lying on the kitchen windowsill.'

'I found this,' said Matthew, 'it's a sovereign.'

Until he had shown it, he had not been quite sure about it; was it really there?

The two women came close. 'Yes, so it is,' said his mother; 'some poor brute of a workman lost his wages and is getting a tongue-banging this minute, I know.'

'Can I keep it, Mother?'

'I don't suppose so. We'll ask your father.'

But his father said, 'It's no use crying over spilt milk,' and he said Matthew could keep the sovereign. 'You can start a savings account at school on Monday.'

Matthew turned up his fair flushed face radiant and looked at his father's face: it seemed to him all pure love. He exclaimed, 'Tommy Small whaled me; with a greenhide bat.'

They drew back, inspecting him curiously.

'Where?'

He pulled up his sleeve and there, to his surprise, there really

264

was a broad bruise. He now expected his father to break into shouts of indignation. His mother stood in doubt; his father also stood away with a strange expression, a queasy, almost greedy expression, yet shy and frightened, too. Matthew felt that they would do nothing about it.

'It's a dirty dairy,' said his father.

'Must I go for the milk tomorrow?'

'Of course, gee-up, milk-oh!'

His mother said, 'You must be a man, my son.'

They did not believe him. They thought he was copying Emily. He did not go further. Muteness crowded his mouth: his throat closed. He saw they had abandoned him, and expected nothing. On Sunday he went with his mother for the milk. 'It isn't half a mile,' she said. After that he never saw Tommy Small again. This too was something he did not comprehend; he began to feel that perhaps he was a liar, like Emily. But then the gold coin was inexplicable; and what astonished him most, in secret, was that it was he who had found it. He knew he was not clever or lucky. A thought grew inside him, evolving out of doubt and fluff, 'Perhaps later I will have just one big piece of luck;' and the gold coin remained shining in the soft animal darkness of his mind.

When the new houses were finished and he could no longer go there for nails for his father, people came to live and presently a new dairy sent round a cart. He would rush out when the milkman came, glorying in the spurting foaming quarts that they took in, in two big jugs they had bought. He stood on the brick landing outside the kitchen and watched, his tongue at his teeth. 'Two quarts, please,' his mother always said, standing in her long pink dressing-gown, her black hair fluffed out. Oh, the milk! The flowing milk.

(1972)

THE BODYSURFERS

Robert Drewe

The murders took the gloss off it. Crossing over the Hawkesbury, David began thinking of them, anticipating the bridge over Mooney Mooney Creek they would soon cross, the picnic area below where, he had read in the papers, the lovers had apparently been forced from their car two nights before, ordered to strip and then struck and run over repeatedly by the murderer's car. When David finally drove over the bridge and the station wagon rounded the bend past the murder site, he nudged Lydia and pointed it out but said nothing because of the younger kids. He thought he could see deep savage skid marks in the gravel. They were heading this Friday evening for the weekend shack David had just bought at Pearl Beach; he, Lydia, and his children Paul, Helena and Tim. Having turned over the house at Mosman to his wife since their separation, David now lived nearer town in a flat with a green view of Cooper Park. He missed the water in his windows, however, the dependable harbour glimpses framed by the voluptuous pink branches of his own plump gum tree, as well as the early morning bird calls, the barbecue, the irresistible nationalistic combination of bush and water, so he decided that at last he would buy a weekend shack on the coast.

'I see no reason why we can't get what we want,' he had remarked to Lydia, his new lover, as romantic in these matters as himself. He knew exactly what he was looking for. It must be the genuine article. It had to put the city at a respectable distance but be close enough for comfortable weekend commuting. However, locale was only part of it. Anyone of his generation would know what he wanted. No transplanted bourgeois suburban brick-and-tile villa would do. The spirit of the shack had to be right, its character set preferably somewhere in the 1950s. It would need a properly casual, even run-down, beach air. It should have a veranda to sleep weekend guests, a working septic system, an open fireplace and somewhere to hang a dartboard. A glimpse at least of the Pacific through the trees was mandatory.

In his head David carried a clear picture of weekends in his shack. For a start there would be no television. He and Lydia would surf and make love in the afternoon to Rolling Stones tapes and read best-sellers and play Scrabble. On the veranda he and his children would strengthen bonds with quoits and table-tennis. Under his gum trees friends would drink in their swimming costumes and eat grilled fish caught at dawn.

On a sunny spring day with a high swell running from the ocean straight into Broken Bay he had eventually found the shack he wanted on the central coast at Pearl Beach. It was built of weatherboard and fibro-cement, painted the colour of pale clay, and it settled on the hillside sheltered from the southerly wind and facing north along the beach. Its ceiling contained a possum's nest or two, and three mature gums, and a jacaranda in bloom filtered the gleam off the sea. The Recession was forcing the owners, a writer and her husband, to rapidly consolidate their assets and their price was reasonable. Apologetically they pointed out an old ceiling stain of possum urine. David laughed. He liked their honesty about the possum pee, the view of the surf from the wooden balcony and the lizards warming on the railing, and, in his new mood of independence and self-assertion, made them an offer. The nostalgic boom of waves had punctuated their negotiations.

An anticipatory air had overlain this weekend. David was looking forward to showing the shack to the children. This was also their first meeting with Lydia and he hoped the shack would break the ice. Along the Newcastle Expressway things looked optimistic. They sang along with the radio and Helena chattered happily to Lydia. Just beyond the Gosford exit warm spring whiffs of eucalypt pollen and the fecund muddy combustion of subtropical undergrowth suddenly filled the car with the scents of holidays.

'Not long to summer,' he pronounced.

'That's a funny name,' Helena said, pointing. 'Mooney Mooney Creek.'

'Mooney Mooney loony,' Tim burbled.

The police hadn't caught the killer, or killers, and according to the news were completely mystified. Both victims had been married to other people, but the spouses had been unaware of the affair and were not under suspicion. *Thrill Killing?* the tabloids wondered. The lovers, both in their thirties, had driven all the way from Sydney's western suburbs for their tryst by the creek. Oyster farmers on the Hawkesbury had seen their car burning at five a.m. Later people remembered hearing the high-pitched revving of an engine and perhaps some human cries.

'I hope there's some good surf,' Paul said. His board was strapped to the roof-rack. As usual lately he was alternately amiable and taciturn, in the sixteen-year-old-fashion, but did not give the impression as he often did that this was a duty weekend.

Lydia was anxious to please and turned back to smile at him, 'I'm sure there will be.'

It was dark when they reached Pearl Beach. For five minutes David rumbled about in the oleander and hibiscus bushes which scraped against the walls, searching for the fuse box where the old owners had left the key. As he stamped around the periphery lighting matches something rustled in a tree above him and a gumnut dropped with a clatter on the tin roof and rolled into the guttering. Possum, he told himself. A mosquito landed noisily on his cheek. From the black shrubbery Helena gave one of the high indignant screams she had affected since her parents separated. Lately she needed soothing and coddling for every slight and injury, real and imaginary. Meanwhile each cry and sulk, no matter how exaggerated, struck him with a hopelessness, produced a hollow despair in him which made him want to simultaneously embrace and shake her and yell, 'I'm sorry my darling, I love you, and my wounds sting too.'

He found the fuse box and the key and opened the front door. Helena burst inside, her sandals clopping on the wooden floor, crying, 'Paul punched me on the arm!'

'Jesus!' Paul said, sidling in with his sleeping bag. 'I just brushed past her. I wouldn't touch her bloody poxy arm.'

'Easy, you two,' their father said.

Lydia struggled in with a carton of groceries. 'Isn't it cute?' she announced.

'Have you seen it already?' Helena asked suspiciously. 'When did you see it?'

Some mosquitoes had followed them inside and soon had Helena whining. Lydia lit a mosquito coil and hunted up a tube of Stop-Itch. The previous owners had left them a bottle of Chablis in the fridge with a note saying 'Welcome to Marsupial Manor!' David uncorked it immediately and they swigged wine from coffee mugs while he unloaded the car and they settled in.

'What a terrific gesture,' Lydia said.

Making his final trip from the car carrying the Scrabble set, Lydia's handbag and Helena's pillow shaped like a rhinoceros, David saw the others' faces pass across the bright uncurtained windows and he stopped on the path, surprised at how earnest they all appeared, even the younger children, how foreign and intense in their tasks. They were all frowning. He could hear their feet thudding on the bare boards. He heard a low murmur from Paul and then Lydia's face over the sink lit up and she gave a laugh. She put a paper bag on her head like a chef's cap. Tim giggled.

David went inside to join them. From the balcony the night sea was as slick and black as grease in the new-moon light, and fruit bats flapped against the stars.

In the middle of the night David awoke and instantly regretted the cute rusticity of the lavatory and its position some ten metres outside in the bushes. A breezy brick cubicle, it had no electricity and a reasonable prospect of spiders in the darkness. He would have to set something up with extension cords. He took a couple of steps out the back door and pissed into the hibiscus. Back in bed, he was unable to sleep again; these nights if he woke up he always had trouble falling back to sleep. Anxieties churned in his mind until exhaustion eventually took over at dawn.

Funny, the more numerous and wilder his wakeful thoughts, the less imaginative his dreams. Since the breakup his dreams had been uniformly mundane – of buying a loaf of Vogel's sandwich bread, catching the 387 bus into town, reading the television guide – sexless, fact-filled visions in which each action or transaction was conducted with the utmost solemnity and realism. Perhaps, he told himself, they were subliminal exhortations to live a moderate, conservative life. Whatever, they were so boring and accurate in their triviality that he allowed his bladder to wake him.

And then, back in bed, the sleepless turmoil began.

Why hadn't the lovers run away? His heart pounded in sympathy. The killers must have had a weapon to force them out of their car, to make them remove their clothes, to wound or threaten them sufficiently that they didn't try to escape. Perhaps they did try. Were they chased all over the picnic area?

Was she raped? He presumed so but the papers didn't say. Did their bodies have bullet holes? No idea. Were the bodies too flattened and battered to tell? Considering these horrors, David rolled over on the doughy mattress, his hip bumping against Lydia's warm bottom with a sudden heat and pressure that surprised them both. She murmured in her sleep and turned over.

Their clothes had been found lying unburned a distance from the gutted car, so they'd been dressed when first harassed, not nakedly fornicating such as to inflame the crazy passions of murdering yokels. The killers were likely from these parts. Maybe he had stood alongside them tonight in the hotel bottle shop buying his Dimple Haig. Sandy-haired yobbos with a big gas guzzler throbbing in the car park. He had visions of headlights bearing down on Lydia and him, of them being mesmerised like possums struck by the beam of a torch.

Thump, brake and reverse, wheels spinning crazily in the gravel. Skin and hair on the bumpers.

He told himself the shack was meant to be an antidote to all this.

Amazingly on cue, screams, grunts and thuddings, eerie gurgles and whispers erupted just outside the bedroom window. His scalp prickled, Lydia sat up in terror.

'Just a possum fight,' he calmed her, his chest pounding. He got out of bed again and made them cups of warm milk. Like children they whispered in the foreign room. Her upper lip corners wore a small milky moustache. Stroking each other with an urgent solicitude, they made love aware of daily jeopardy and thin walls.

Father and daughter rose first and early on Saturday morning, murmuring and tiptoeing conspiratorially and taking their orange juice out onto the balcony. A flock of parrots exploded from one of their gum trees. The sun rising out of the Pacific slanted obliquely over their domain and brought a new arrangement of parallel shimmers to the surface of the water below. Instantly David saw he had made one mistake – there was no surf and there would rarely be. Freak conditions had no doubt prevailed the day he inspected the shack, a strange pure easterly perhaps instead of the usual southerly or nor'easter or even westerly. Why hadn't it occurred to him that Box Head would block the nor'easters, Lion Island the southerlies? It didn't matter that their beach faced the open Pacific; there would be no surfing; they would have to drive several kilometres north to swim in the surf. His personal stretch of sea was quiescent, bland as bathwater, nice for fishing, sailboarding and swimming up and down. He felt vaguely sick.

As a boy his happiness had been bound up in the ocean, the regular rising and curling of waves over sandbanks and reefs, the baking sun, the cronies lounging against the promenade, the bunches of girls gossiping and flirting on the sand, the violent contrasting physical pleasures of bodysurfing. In his twenties and early thirties he had still never tired of watching the surf. Like flames it had the capacity to induce a calming trance. It held in store everything from a happy domestic weekend, healthy dawn exercise, to a snappy hangover cure. But over the past few years, through work and travel and the particular, strangely inevitable manner in which his marriage had frayed, then unravelled, he'd lost the habit of those peculiarly satiating Australian days.

He'd liked sharing them and Angela had lost interest; or perhaps among their other discarded mutual interests they had just forgotten them.

Lydia was a bodysurfer.

Lydia had become a keen bodysurfer since knowing him. She had a history as an initiator of extreme physical incidents, as an experimenter and a changer of circumstances. She had already tried abseiling, hang-gliding, show-jumping, scuba-diving and their sexual counterparts. From his watchful position ten years further along the track he could detect in her a vulnerability to danger and a risky wilfulness with the potential to carry her, and others, over the edge. But they matched each other perfectly, blended harmoniously, gripped and floated. In the surf her recklessness made him laugh, the way she launched herself into definite dumpers, surfacing shakily in the foam with a breast out of her bathers, her hair in her eyes and a fist raised in mock victory.

Sitting yawning with his ten-year-old daughter in the quiet early sunlight he tried to pin down the exact sensation of those old ocean days. It was a combination of the exhilarating charge of the surf, the plunge on a wave, the currents pummelling and streaming along the body, the skin stretched salty and taut across the shoulders, the pungent sweetness of suntan oil, the sensual anticipation of future summer days and nights. Certainly he had never been as happy since. Therefore he could hardly be blamed for trying for that feeling again – the harmony and boundless optimism. And he had got it only half right.

Helena snuggled up to him in their warm patch in the treetops. Birds squabbled around them but they seemed the only humans awake anywhere. The world of sea and bush was comatose. He thought of Lydia buried in the valley of the saggy double bed; Paul in his sleeping bag, mouth open, hair awry; Tim flushed and cupid-lipped on the night-and-day. And Angela in her shared Mosman bed under the Amish hand-sewn quilt he had bought her in Penn-sylvania. In white stitching the old Amish lady had signed her quilt 'Mrs B. Yoder'. They didn't believe in cosmetics, cars or radios but Mrs Yoder took American Express. He did not want Helena and Timmy snuggling under the quilt for early morning cuddles with the occupants. He did not want the quilt *involved*.

Kissing the crown of Helena's head, he inhaled her parting. 'Want a swim before breakfast, my sweet?' he asked.

She was delighted. 'A secret swim,' he told her. Somehow he wanted to bind her in a conspiracy. He wanted to serve her up private sooth-ing information about their present and future. Holding hands they padded barefoot down the road to the beach. Cool clay squashed under their toes as the sun began to slant over their path. Crows and currawongs fluttered clumsily in the bushes. Under the cliff face the sea baths were like glass. Helena was the bolder. Without hesitating she ran to the deep end and dived in. The coldness shocked him when he joined her; he had to swim three lengths of the pool before his circulation adjusted to the temperature. His daughter's body gave no hint of the cold. She had been having swimming coaching and he was surprised at her new neat prowess, the precise arm strokes slicing into the pool, the efficient three-stroke breathing. When they climbed out she flicked water at him, giggling coquettishly, wiggling her chubby backside and smoothing back her wet hair in parody of a hundred women in shampoo com-mercials. He noticed her breasts were just starting to grow and she flapped her hands over them while she jigged about. It jolted him that she would cease being a child. It was only the other day she'd been born, a month overdue, in the end chemically induced. She hadn't wanted to join the world then. If only he could warn her, 'Stop now while there's still time. You don't want to get into this can of worms.'

As they left the beach he was still phrasing what he wanted to say to her, at the same time hoping that his message was somehow being telepathically understood, absorbed through the pores.

Finally he said, 'I love you, my sweet,' brushing sand from his feet.

'Me too,' she said. 'Daddy, can I play the Space Invaders?'

At the beach store she played a video game while he bought milk and the papers. The picnic ground murders were still page one of the local paper. Tests were proceeding on the woman's body to determine whether she had been 'assaulted' prior to her death. The extent of the 'injuries' made this difficult. Police asked citizens to immediately report any vehicle with suspicious dents or bloodstains.

Hand in hand they walked back to the shack. 'Can I have my ears pierced, Daddy?' she asked.

'Perhaps when you're older. It doesn't look nice on little girls.'

She was still whining as they walked inside. 'I don't want to hear any more about it,' he said.

Their mid-morning procession to the beach gave the impression of a cartoon jungle safari. Balancing his surfboard on his head, Paul amiably led the single file, followed by a talkative Helena with her flippers and swimming goggles, Lydia carrying her big bag of beach paraphernalia – towels, suntan cream, insect repellent, baby oil and magazines; Tim, the youngest, travelling light and scot-free as usual, dragging a stick in the clay, and David, bringing the Esky of sandwiches and drinks. They had decided on a picnic lunch. 'Bonga, bonga,' boomed the father, imitating native drums. 'Bonga, bonga,' repeated Helena and Tim all the way down to the sand.

Now the beach was warm, and in its most populated section near the baths, relatively noisy. Children splashed in the baths and shrieked in the shallows. Small wavelets plopped on the shore. Paul had already observed from the balcony the sorry state of the waves but had perversely brought his board anyway, as if to indicate to this soft elderly crowd that this was by no means his element. They dropped their things on the sand and the younger children raced into the water. With a superior grin at the sea Paul flopped down in the sand. 'Top waves, Dad.'

'Give us a break,' his father said, collapsing too.

Next to him Lydia was arranging her towel on a level patch of sand, ironing away lumps and wrinkles and placing her beach appurtenances within reach. Then she removed her bikini top and, her breasts quivering, the nipples wide and brown in the sun, she sat down. Reaching for the suntan cream from her bag, she rubbed some briskly into her breasts with a studious circular motion, paying attention to the nipples. More cream was squeezed onto the stomach and legs, even the tops of the feet.

David was slightly unnerved, as usual, by the act of public revelation (there always seemed to be some sort of statement underlying their sudden exposure among other people), but he had never realised how much her naked breasts actually *moved*. They had three definite motions – they were simultaneously bouncing, swinging and shivering. From the prim, diligent way she pursed her lips while she applied the cream she seemed to be either terribly solicitous of them or disapproving of their independent lives.

David avoided looking at them too openly. Ogling was out of the question. He did, however, glance surreptitiously at his elder son, but Paul, though hardly able to miss them, was staring coolly seawards.

Completing this display, still with a frown of concentration, Lydia flicked a grain of sand from one glistening aureole, spread more cream deftly over her face, and then lay back on her towel with a sigh of contentment. 'I wonder what the poor people are doing,' she said.

I wonder if women know what they're doing, David wondered. How did those tits which had been used to sexually tempt him at three a.m. suddenly at 11.30 become as neutral as elbows? Who's kidding who? He was too far gone at thirty-eight, especially after the past couple of years, to read the fine print any more, much less try to keep up with the constant changes in the rules. They were amazing, leave it at that. He was awestruck by the grey areas, the skating-over, the 180-degree turns that women made these days. The breakup and his new status, or lack of status, had made him hypersensitive to the female dichotomies – fashion versus politics, the desperate clash between ideals and glands – and their magical sleight of hand which not only hid it all and kept the audience clapping but left you with a coin up your nose or an egg in your ear.

Lying back under the sun he had to smile at the way Lydia pretended she had no exhibitionist's flair, that she didn't love to flaunt what she had, come on strong. He remembered the actual broad-daylight fuck precipitated by those exposed breasts not long ago on Scarborough Beach down south during their search for the perfect shack. They were sunbaking like this after a surf. A nipple brushed his arm accidentally, then insistently. Then began a sly stroking of his thigh, feathery touches over his groin. The sun, the ocean, the whole salty, teasing, teenage delight of it all! They'd got up without a word and strolled determinedly to the end of the beach and, behind a low cairn of rocks barely higher than their horizontal bodies, momentarily hidden from at least fifty beach fishermen, surfers and swimmers, had a most satisfying quickie in the sand.

Their single-mindedness had surprised and amused him later. 'I thought that might work,' she'd said, grinning as they sauntered back to their belongings. 'Was that like your adolescent days? I must say you were very neat – not a drop of sand in me.'

Tim and Helena ran up from the shore, sandy and squabbling.

'He's using bottom words again,' Helena complained. 'He's saying poo and bum and vagina all the time and he keeps throwing sand,'

'I didn't say vagina, I said Virginia.'

'You said vagina!' Abruptly she began to cry, turning away from them and sobbing despairingly.

'I didn't,' Tim screamed. 'You're a liar!' Overcome with rage and emotion, he fell on the sand and kicked and threshed, his yells turning to shrill cries as he kicked sand in his eyes.

'My God!' shouted David, jumping to his feet. 'What's got into you both? Do you want a hiding?'

'Shee-it,' Paul said. 'He does that all the time lately. What that kid needs is some discipline. Come here, stupid, and I'll get the sand out.'

Lydia had her arms round Helena. 'No one will play with us,' Helena sobbed. 'It's boring here.'

Lydia said, 'I feel like a swim. Let's go.'

The father sank back on the sand. Leaning back on his elbows, breathing deeply, he watched the trio race each other down to the water, Tim stopping sharply at the edge, hanging back and then wading in gingerly, the others plunging in recklessly. Lydia and Helena surfaced and pushed back their hair and jumped and splashed like any ten-year-olds. They shared unselfconsciousness; if anything Lydia seemed the wilder and giddier, standing on her hands, somersaulting and gambolling, and all the time her breasts swung and fluttered in the sun and water.

Tim was beginning to grizzle at being excluded. Sighing loudly, Paul sauntered down to him, hoisted him up in his arms and strode into the water, joining the splashing females. Paul tossed his little brother around like a beach-ball while Tim shrieked with excitement.

Squinting against the glare, David was relieved and gladdened to see his children and Lydia frolicking together in the sea. It wasn't a familiar scene from his marriage, more like one from his own early childhood, a link to it, a summer holiday at the seaside, a rare time when adults dropped their guard and pretensions and acted the goat. He was aware of the sting of the sun on his neck and this too made him happy; the clean buff-coloured sand, the fringe of gum trees, the dusty blue labiate hills, the turquoise vista of the Pacific all uplifted him. Buoyant, he looked over his shoulder and through the jacaranda picked out the balcony of the shack where his and Helena's red and blue towels were drying on the railing. A warm haze gave the shack's roof an uncertain wavy outline, and parrots still screeched in his trees.

Oddly drawn to this setting, attracted to it but, perhaps because of its newness, detached from it, he half-expected to see his children, Lydia, even himself, stroll out on to the balcony and wave a jaunty towel. But they were playing in the sea. He was lounging on the sand. Paul was lifting Tim on his shoulders. Paul's tanned back and shoulder muscles were suddenly sharply defined by the weight, and patterns of sinews moved in his arms and shoulders. Among the shrill giggles his deeper laughter rang out. Lydia was similarly hoisting Helena on to her shoulders – with difficulty – and the action threw back her shoulders and pushed out her chest and almost collapsed her in splashes and giggles.

David watched the couples face each other – grinning, dripping knights on horseback – and heard the yells of encouragement, the snorts and laughter, and saw the infection of excitability strike them. He sat in the sun with a cold constriction in his throat as the riders wrestled and the horses alternately collided and retreated, striking and sliding against each other in the shallows, softness against muscle.

If David could have spoken satisfactorily to Lydia next morning he might have described his dream that night thus:

It began with me driving an Avis car fast and north through scrubby country on a hot, dry day. The highway was clear, the airconditioning cool, and on the radio old favourites kept my fingers tapping on the wheel. Bugs smeared themselves on the windscreen, but I obliterated them with automatic spray and wipers, the wipers stroking as elegantly as conductors' batons. The car's tyres made a satisfying drumming sound on the tarred joins in the highway paving, a repetitive noise of power and resolve. All this registered on me strongly – the sense of purpose was heightened because the car had been freshly cleaned and the hygienic vinyl scent of the upholstery was high in my head.

I drove for a time, for what seemed like an hour, and from the changing vegetation – the trees were becoming even more stunted and sparse, the wild oats and veldt grass fringing the highway ever dryer and barely covering the sandy ground – I gathered that I was nearing the coast. An arrowed sign said *Aurora – 10 km* and I followed it, turning left off the highway.

A wind sprang up as the car left the protection of the hills and it whipped sand drifts across the road. The road cut through sand dunes spread patchily with pigface and tumbleweeds and led obliquely to the sea – every now and then I saw a slice of blue between the white dunes before it disappeared again. Another, bigger sign said *Aurora – 5 km* below a logotype of a leaping dolphin against the sun, and I followed it, the car planing occasionally through the sand drifts.

Soon I came to an indication of habitation: a gold dome-shaped building, a sort of civic centre, flying a flag carrying the dolphin-and-sun logo. Before its entrance was a statue carved out of limestone, apparently of King Neptune. Surrounding the gold dome was a flat grassy field, which was kept green and free of the sand drifts, I presumed, from the parallel lines of sprinklers and the presence of five or six heavy rollers, only with great municipal perseverance. As I pulled up two children came over one of the adjacent dunes and slid down it on sleds until they came to rest on the grass. I called out to them, wanting to ask further directions, but they grabbed up their sleds and climbed back up the dune as fast as they could struggle in the sand. I tried the gold building next. From a sharp cloudless sky the sun struck its gleaming surface with such a dazzling glare it was impossible to approach it without squinting. Anyway, the front doors were closed – presumably it was some sort of public holiday here – and the only other sign of life was a nervously hissing bobtail goanna which displayed its blue tongue at me from a clump of pigface by the entrance. A thin pungent smell of decaying seaweed was carried to me on the breeze.

The road circled the gold building and continued, so I drove on, still travelling slantingly towards the ocean, and around the next sandhill I saw the first rotary clothes hoist sticking up in the dunes like a lone palm in the desert, and then more of them, some skeletal, others blooming with washing, and, behind them, facing the sea, a scattering of suburban houses straight from the middle-class outskirts of any western city in the world. In this moonscape the range of architectural styles was unusually extreme, even impressive, in its randomness and unfittingness to the arid environment and climate: mock-Tudor nestled hard up against Mediterranean villa, then came three or four bleak, windswept blocks dotted with FOR SALE signs, a Cape Cod or two, some ranch-modern experiments and an Australian-Romanesque edifice. They did, however, have some features in common: two shiny cars and a cabin cruiser on a trailer sat in every driveway. A sprinkler whirred in each front garden; there were no fences but walls had been cleverly erected to shield the grass and the cars from the sea breeze. The backyards had no shelter and, while the sprinklers whirred in the front, the clothes hoists, with a steady grating hum, spun like catherine wheels in the wind. It was easy to see which way it blew – the clothes hoists all leaned like cypresses from the sou' westerly.

Suddenly the sledding children returned: they were Max and Paul. This was no surprise, the appearance together of my brother and my son, both now the same age – about eight or nine – and similarly skinny, brown-skinned and with their freckled and peeling noses and cheeks coated in zinc cream.

'In there, you nong,' Max said, pointing out a pink-brick home with a 1950s skillion roof. Max was right in that it *was* my mother who came to the door in a Liberty print brunch coat over a swimming costume, gave me an amiable kiss on the cheek and led me inside.

I know I must have seemed exasperated. 'God, I've been searching for ages,' I complained. I was actually immensely relieved. Relief flooded over me and intervening time was abruptly concertinaed into days, hours. 'You made it a bit difficult.'

My mother smiled, a little embarrassed, holding her mouth in a constrained way, like the time she had her teeth capped. 'I know, Davey. It took me a while to make adjustments.' There seemed some strain to the left side of her face, a tautness in the skin that she was shy about. Otherwise she looked very well, and I said so.

'Getting there,' she smiled. 'The dolphins keep me young.'

'They would,' I agreed. 'What do you hear from Dad?'

'Ask him yourself,' she said. 'Let's go down to the boatel.'

We drove off down the road, Amphitrite Avenue, I noticed, with me asking inane questions about her new Volvo – was she happy with the safety features, et cetera? – and presently she indicated another limestone statue of King Neptune, with trident, this one about thirty feet high, rising out of the dunes.

'I like it,' she declared firmly. 'Rex thinks it's vulgar, but I like it. The boatel's near here, in Poseidon Place.'

Was this a delicate situation? Separate living quarters? I kept my questions to myself, however, as we drew up to the Triton Boatel, a dun-coloured limestone structure built right on the edge of the ocean like a Moorish fort. Radiating out from it was a long limestone breakwater sheltering hundreds of pleasure craft, their stays and moorings rattling and tinkling in the wind – yachts, launches and power boats of all sizes and varieties, even a Chinese junk – though their owners, or any people at all, were not to be seen.

We sauntered along a sort of fake gangplank into the boatel lobby, Mum tripping very brightly through the foyer, I thought. She had discarded her brunch coat and looked very tanned and fit in her green Lastex swimsuit, just like the old Jantzen girl trademark.

Dad was behind the counter in his neat summer seersucker. He waved off my enthusiastic greeting, smiling apologetically. 'It's the off-season,' he said. 'We're still settling in, David. The last chap ran the place down. An Iraqi or something.'

'It's very presentable,' I told him. He looked a bit fidgety, though happy enough.

'The boatel business has got to expand,' he asserted stoutly. 'I couldn't wait to get here, I can tell you. Best decision I ever made, running my own show.'

'It's certainly an interesting proposition, Dad.' For some reason he was a little skittish in my company.

'All units right on the ocean, waterbeds in every room, colour TV, fully equipped kitchen, mid-week linen change where applicable. It's got to go like a bomb.'

We left Dad adjusting his Diners Club brochures in their little display stand. My mother was anxious to show me over the marine park. 'Don't worry about him,' she said. 'He's really as keen as I am about the whole Aurora concept.'

It was surprisingly not beyond my comprehension to learn that my mother was leading a new life as a vivacious dolphin communicator. She certainly looked the part as she proudly swept me in to the Aurora Marine Park, the sun catching the blonde streaks in her hair and highlighting her brown, slender limbs. She tossed a silver whistle briskly from hand to hand.

'Activity. Activity-plus is the message humming through Aurora,' she said.

What was new to me was my parents' sudden boundless punchy optimism. I felt slack and middle-aged by comparison; pale, short of wind.

Mum knifed into the pool then, and surfaced balanced on the backs of two dolphins, smiling fit for television. Her charges were just as energetic, jumping and squeaking and snorting through those holes in their heads. She had names for them, unapt modern children's names like Jasmine and Trent and Jason and Bree, and conducted some sort of affectionate dialogue using her whistle while they squirmed self-congratulatingly out of the water and bumped up a ramp towards us like sleek blow-up toys, their grey tongues waggling disgustingly at her.

'Do you speak dolphin, David?' she asked me out of the side of her mouth.

'No, I never learned.'

'I'm particularly fascinated in people exploring the intricacies of the dolphin language,' she went on. 'It's taught in the school here, you know.' She gestured vaguely. 'Humans learn it too.' And then she began speaking warmly to Bree, Trent and company in fractured schoolgirl French. They replied similarly, their beaks actually quite well formed for the nasalities and their accents rather better than my mother's. Fishy vowels hung in the air.

'Think you could hack it here?' Mum asked me suddenly, an arm each around Jason and Trent. '*Je t'aime*,' she murmured to Jason, unnecessarily I thought, raking her inch-long red nails down his tongue. He crooned appreciatively.

'I don't know,' I said. Her jargon jolted, also her recently acquired fondness for animals. She didn't even allow us to have a dog.

'You could be an aquarist,' she suggested, 'helping Damian with the makos and hammerheads.'

'What about Dad at the boatel?'

'If you prefer. *Allez!*' she exclaimed suddenly and blew a blast on her whistle. The dolphins bounced back into the pool. 'You know something?' my mother said to me conversationally, and the sunlight on the sheen of her swimsuit was so glaring it hurt my eyes, 'It may be perpetual summer here but I'm against adultery.'

'Who isn't, Mum?' I said.

'So put that in your pipe and smoke it,' she said.

In the Sunday papers there was nothing about the picnic ground murders. David thought it looked as if the police had put the case in their too-hard basket. He spent most of the day reading alone while the others swam or played Scrabble or, in the children's case, the video games at the store. Mid-afternoon he got them packed up and moving early, he said, to avoid the traffic back to the city. Driving fast to get home, and in deep thought, he crossed Mooney Mooney Creek without noticing.

(1983)

THE SHIRALEE

D'Arcy Niland

About three o'clock that afternoon Macauley was getting his things together and rolling his swag while Buster was absent with Bella. Suddenly the door opened and she came skipping in. She drew up short, and looked all round the room frowning. He kept on being guiltily active.

'Are we going?' she asked.

'We're not,' he said, truthfully.

'What are you doing that for then?'

'What?'

'All that.' She made an all-encompassing gesture. Suspiciously she walked to the chest of drawers and pulled out the bottom drawer. She looked up at him with her head on one side. 'What about my clothes?' she demanded in a tone chiding him for his oversight.

'Look,' Macauley said, 'I'm just doing a bit of sorting out. Run down and talk to Mrs Sweeney. I'm busy.'

He pushed her out the door and shut it. He sat on the bed and shook his head. Then a decisive, stern expression settled on his face, and he continued with his packing. He strapped his swag and threw it on the bed. He opened the door, and saw Buster slouched against the wall, looking like a puzzled dog.

He ignored her and walked on down the veranda. She followed him. She never let him out of her sight for the rest of the afternoon. It began to get on his nerves. Putting off the moment of telling her didn't help any. He wondered why the hell he couldn't come out with it and be done with it. He was never a man to fiddle about. What was the matter with him now?

The four of them, as usual, ate together when the rest of the boarders had finished, and at the tea-table Macauley tried to appear unconcerned, giving the impression that he would be there for years to come. To some extent he seemed to allay Buster's suspicions. She ate her food hungrily and with relish, her head down. Now and then she looked up under her eyebrows to see if he was still there. Macauley continued to strengthen her gullibility without being blatant about it. Luke Sweeney didn't help him. Neither did Bella. When he looked at her he got the impression that she was enjoying herself.

While Sweeney washed the dishes and Macauley dried up, Bella took Buster upstairs and put her to bed. Buster didn't demur. She went quietly. This was her usual bedtime and every night Bella tucked her in.

Macauley left it for an hour. Then he went up, stealthily entered the room, and took his swag off the bed. He held it in one hand, standing still for a moment. Then he bent over her bed to see if she was asleep. She was on her back, calm. He came down to within three inches of her face before he saw her eyes, big and accusing. It was as though she had been waiting to catch him red-handed.

'Where are you going?' she cried in a tone of censure and uncertainty.

He felt a surge of anger. 'You should be asleep.'

She propped herself on one elbow. 'You going away?'

'Listen,' he said, impulsively seizing the opportunity, 'it'll only be for a little while—'

'No!'

'Just a little while.' He hurried out the words against his panic to persuade her before she had a chance to get worked up. 'I'll come back later for you.'

'I'm coming, too,' she cried.

'Mrs Sweeney—'

'No!'

'. . . will look after you. You—'

'No, I want to go!'

'. . . like Mrs Sweeney.'

She was crying with alarm and consternation and desperate imploration, drowning his wheedling words in a torrent of mumbling and hurling sounds of opposition. He was surprised at the definiteness of her antagonism. Her demented unreasonableness enraged him.

He stood up. 'Listen,' he shouted. 'I don't want any shindy about this. You'll stay here, and do what you're told.'

He moved to the door with the swag on his shoulder. She sprang out of bed and tried to drag him back. He dropped the swag, and in a burst of temper took her up and smacked her backside hard. He put her roughly back into the bed and ripped the blankets up over her head.

'Now stay there,' he said.

He whipped the door open, and slammed it after him, and walked on with the rage still high in him.

Half a mile out along the road he began to feel remorseful. He felt churned up as though his guts had been puddled and put through a mangle. His hand still tingled. He argued with himself.

He didn't have to hit that hard. He didn't want to leave her like that, anyway. But there was no help for it. It had to be done. There was no other way out. Yet it was a sneak's way out, and when the hell had he started being a sneak? He was never a sneak in his life. If he wanted something he took it no matter who was looking. If he wanted to do a thing he did it, and damn everything else. He had intended to tell her. Well, why didn't he? Skulking out like that, deceiving her, leaving her to wake in the morning and find him gone and throwing the onus on others to explain and pacify. She knew he had intended to go that way, too, or did she? Could a kid fathom that? The hurt, the disbelief of knowing it seemed to be in her voice. Or was he only imagining that? Sneaking out. What did he have to sneak out for? If he had to sneak out there must be a reason, there must be something he was ashamed of. And if there was something he was ashamed of . . . ?

Still, it was the only way to handle a kid like that. And it didn't kill, it didn't maim her. It was for her own good. She couldn't be expected to understand. But she would. And she'd get over it.

He hadn't gone much farther when he heard her calling him. For a moment he thought it was in his mind. Then he looked back along the dark road towards the lights of the town. He fancied he could see a spectral figure, darkness shaped of darkness, moving towards him. He heard the scuff of feet – the slap-slap-slap of walking and the skip-skip-skip of running.

He sat down on his swag just off the road behind a tree.

He heard the panicky feet. He saw the child come into view and pass him. She slowed down, stopped, listened. He saw her run. He picked up his swag and started off. He heard her ahead of him crying a sort of rhythmic daddy, daddy.

He caught up with her a half a mile farther on. She was sitting in a huddle on the road. She launched herself at the fortress of his strength and protection, refusing to be spurned, trying to convince him that she would never be cast out from the citadel where she belonged and was safe.

She thrust herself up against his solidity and silence. He saw that she had Gooby snuggled under one arm and a bundle of her clothes under the other. She dropped them and clasped his legs.

'For God's sake!' he said. The unnatural noise in the stillness was unnerving. He shook her away. She clasped his legs tighter.

'What the hell are you doing here? Didn't I tell you to stay with Mrs Sweeney?'

'I want to come with you.'

The tears of shock and hysteria were vanishing; relief and pleading were taking their place.

'Listen to me, stop that bawling. You hear?' He waited for a minute.

'Stop it!' he shouted.

'All right.'

His voice frightened her. She feared a hiding. But she thought if she cried hard enough it would be a weapon against that. Now she sensed the annoyance and rage in him and realised that further crying would only provoke him to hit her.

He felt helpless.

'Didn't Mrs Sweeney feed you?'

'Yes, all right.'

'Didn't you have a good bed to lie in?' He was talking to her as to a grown-up. 'Didn't you have a cat to play with?'

'Yes.'

'She treated you like you've never been treated in your life before. You had the best of everything. Well, didn't you?'

'Yes.'

'Well, what more do you want? What more can I give you?'

'I want to come with you.'

He sighed, beaten, angry at his impotence. He softened his voice. 'Listen, don't you understand? I'm not leaving you. I'm only going to get a job, and when I start work I'll send for you.'

'No!'

'You'll only be with Mrs Sweeney for a little while.'

'No, no, no, no, no, no!' she raged implacably.

He gave up. 'Strike me dead, I don't know. I ought to wring your little neck and chuck you in the bushes there.'

She started to cry again. He listened for a while, letting his anger burn itself out.

'All right, all right,' he snapped, exasperated. 'Shut up your snivelling.'

He watched her gouging her eyes dry with the backs of her hands. Her convulsive sniffles jerked her body like an attack of hiccups. He had to decide what to do: whether to return and tell the Sweeneys what had happened or rely on their savvy to realise what had happened. He had decided to go back when he saw the lights of a car coming along the road from the town.

He stood on the side of the road to let it pass, but it stopped as it reached him. It was a utility, and a man who seemed to be all hat was driving it. Then a body leaned across him and Luke Sweeney called, 'Hey, Mac, have you got the kid?'

As soon as she recognised the voice Buster ran behind Macauley and clutched the seat of his pants like a crab. From this rampart of defence she shouted, 'Go away, funny old bugger. Go away, my Lukey.' She said it as though it was one word or else the name of a Chinaman.

Macauley walked over to the truck, and Buster went with him like a parasitic body.

'Bel saw her going down the street like a bat out of hell. I had to go and get hold of Andy here, and then he couldn't get his jalopy started. We scoured the town.'

'I don't want to go with you,' Buster screeched.

'Shut up!' Macauley said.

He walked round to the offside of the truck. 'Looks like it won't work out, Luke,' he said.

'We can take her back,' Luke Sweeney said. 'She'll tame down after a few days.'

'I'll run away again,' Buster threatened savagely.

'Well, what's it to be, Mac?'

Macauley thought for a moment, appearing to be undecided, but actually not wishing to show the weakness of backing down too quickly. Then he said, 'I reckon I'll have to make out somehow. Sorry you've had all this bother.'

'Aw, no bother,' Sweeney said. He chuckled. Macauley could see the devilment on his gaunt face. 'Told you a lie, Mac. We didn't scour the town. Bel said she knew where Buster was making. She only sent me along to see if the kid reached you all right.' He gave a yelp of laughter. 'O.K., Andy.' He nudged his mate and gave Macauley a tap on the cheek. 'So long, you big softy. Come and see us again before I fill me coffin. Don't let the undertaker be the last to let me down.'

Macauley watched the red tail dwindling, and he could see Sweeney in the truck wiping his eyes and saying the bit about a man must have his little joke: Sweeney the dead man full of live men's bones, the satellite of a great sun who piped off his energy and consumed him and who yet, if he was lost to her, would burn to an ember and go out.

'He's gone now,' Buster said irrelevantly.

Macauley looked down at her. 'God, you make a man wild.' He

heaved a great sigh. 'I don't know what I'm going to do with you, dinkum.'

Her eyes were full of malevolent reproof. She said with the utmost indignation, 'You shouldn't have left me.'

They walked on for another two miles, neither of them speaking. Macauley because he was thinking, Buster because she wasn't quite certain what her fate was to be: should he suddenly turn round and decide to go back to Walgett she was ready to rebel.

Then Macauley told himself there was not much point in walking farther. They might as well wait for the daylight and a lift through. It was the easiest way with her.

He made the bed, one blanket under, one over. It was only an overnight doss. Buster seemed more assured. She snuggled into him.

'Dad?'

'Don't talk to me,' he said. 'I'm disgusted with you.'

'What would happen if the sky fell on you?'

'Who cares?'

'All the stars would go bang, wouldn't they, and there'd be big bonfires and the fire brigade would come.'

'Shut up and get to sleep.'

She was like a warm dog against his back. She started to hum a little tune to herself, a tune full of broken bars. Then she muttered the words, getting them right, but flat here and there on the melody.

> 'With a swing of the left foot
> A swing of the right . . .
> Oh, what a dancer,
> Oh, what a skite . . .
> Oh, what a dancer, oh, what a skite.'

It was an old bush ballad Bella Sweeney must have taught her.

'Stop that racket,' Macauley said, and she obeyed.

In the morning when he woke he turned over. She was asleep, her face streaked with dirty tears. For a long time he looked at the tangled silky hair, the lay of the eyelids on the cheeks, the sooty eyelashes, the small pink mouth: and there was a great sense of her tininess, loyalty, and defencelessness in him. And he was moved. He felt disturbed and hostile against unknown threats.

Along the road Buster let it be understood that she still hadn't quite forgiven him for his treachery. That he could actually go off and leave her to fend for herself against the world – when he was her father, the very centre of her existence, and beloved of her – passed her comprehension. It shocked her to the soul.

Prompted by the hurt, she suddenly glared at him and told him he was a mean old nasty old father.

'That's what you think,' he said.

Her look was fiercely reproachful. 'Don't you do that any more. See!'

Her savage resoluteness amused him. He was tempted to hedge with her.

'Why? What'll you do?'

'I'll run away.'

'You mightn't find me.'

She thought for a moment. Then she said quickly, slurring the words, 'I'll walk along the road, and all the roads, and keep going on the roads 'cos I know you always walk on the roads and I'd find you.'

'I heard you say something last night I didn't like.'

'What?'

'You called Mr Sweeney a bugger. You mustn't say that.'

'Why?'

'It's — just don't say it, that's all.'

'Mrs Sweeney says it. You say it, too.'

'Yes, but I'm big.'

'Can only big people say it?'

'Girls don't say it,' Macauley explained, sorry he had mentioned the subject. 'It's not a nice word.'

'Why?'

'I don't know. It just isn't.'

'Can I say it when I'm big?'

From *The Shiralee* (1955)

SEVENTEENTH BIRTHDAY

Roberta Sykes

I've never been much of a singer, but in Townsville I'd put together a few songs I could have a go with; ones which didn't require a range of notes. I could pull out a note and sit on it, whether it be soprano or alto, but found it impossible to guide my voice from one note to another. Consequently, my repertoire consisted of one-note songs such as 'Johnny Be Good' and 'Bony Marony', which needed a good memory rather than vocal skills.

Josie and I were very excited when the Institute dance organisers announced a talent quest, with prizes of tickets to appear in some capacity on Brian Henderson's 'Bandstand'. We rehearsed so much I'm sure the other people in the house got tired of us, but not one of them said so. Instead, they'd sing along and clap, and watch us preening and selecting postures and gestures with which to win the competition.

On the big night, the hall was filled with strange men in suits, beautifully groomed, and a whole host of people, would-be performers who, we thought, had never set foot inside the Institute before. Musical instruments and several sets of drum kits blocked off a fair bit of the dance floor, and the casual and fun atmosphere we were used to had been replaced with an air of severe competition and judgement.

We were wearing our best dance clothes, which we had spent an agonising week selecting. I had on a pair of black trousers with a silver thread through the fabric, loose for movement but pegged in at the ankle, a pure white, long-sleeve poloneck sweater, which I thought made me appear 'elfin' – even though it was far too hot to wear comfortably under stage lights, flat, black patent-leather shoes, all the better to dance in, and fluorescent socks which were all the rage, and the better to be noticed in. Josie was similarly attired in her own version of the very latest 'look'.

We were almost put off by the change in the feeling of the place, and if I'd been alone, I doubt very much that I'd have mustered the nerve to go ahead with the registration. Josie, however, said she'd register us both, so I stood against the wall watching musicians and technical people rush around the stage completing their preparations. When she returned, she passed me a ticket with a number on it and said I'd be first.

'First! I'm first?' My stomach did a full loop in dread.

'No, silly. First out of you 'n' me.' My relief was tangible.

We didn't want to get our gear soiled by perspiration before our turn on stage, so we picked a good spot just to watch. As the night wore on, Josie and I kept each other's nerves steady and our enthusiasm high by giggling and earnestly, though dismissively, discussing everyone else's performance. In the breaks we stepped outside to escape the heat which built up under all those lights.

Suddenly, we heard my number being called. I pranced up on stage, shoved onto it with a good-luck push from Josie. One of the regular back-up groups had already agreed that they would play for me, so it took no time at all for me to be up there behind the microphone. Nervous? I would have been if I'd actually looked at anyone in the audience. Instead, I pinned my gaze on some spot at the back of the hall in the 'true Hollywood' style we'd rehearsed, and belted out 'Johnny Be Good'. At the first short vocal break which was filled by the musicians, I even remembered to shake my legs, stamp around and shimmy a bit to encourage the audience into the mood of the piece.

It was all over in a flash. I took my bow to enthusiastic applause, and was surprised on my way to the steps to be called back to do another number. I grinned out at Josie who was waving her arms in the air with joy. We'd rehearsed for just such an event and I slid quickly into 'Bony Marony'.

I was back in Josie's arms – she was hugging me so tight – and the next act was on stage, before I realised that it was supposed to be Josie's turn. The minute I realised, she knew it, and placing her hands on my shoulders she admitted that she hadn't put her own name in at all. But her elation at how well I had been received swept away any pangs of disappointment almost before I had time to feel them.

It was late now as the more professional acts had played earlier in the evening. The air was charged with tension while we waited to learn the results of the competition. Some of the guys in suits from the television station had already departed, leaving their instructions with the minions who had to wait until the end.

Josie and I were over the moon when my name was amongst those called to the stage to collect Participant Tickets to 'Bandstand'. I was handed two large, crisp white cardboard tickets, and I quickly shoved one at Josie. With such a coup, we knew we were too excited just to get on a tram and go quietly home to sleep, so I was more than agreeable when Josie suggested we go to a midnight movie at a city theatre.

When we arrived, it was a bit disappointing because there was only a thin crowd. I'd expected midnight shows in Brisbane to attract the same large crowds as the very occasional midnight screenings did in Townsville. Josie, at least, knew by sight a couple of the other patrons and she gave them a wave as we made our way towards the front of the theatre. I noticed everyone else in the theatre was white, but this had no great significance because almost every theatre around the country drew white or predominantly white audiences.

The film was engrossing, and I was transported into the essence of the story until my concentration was interrupted by a young man, who came to sit beside Josie and spoke to her in urgent, hushed tones. I couldn't hear what they were saying, so I was concentrating on the film when Josie shook my arm and asked me to give her all the cash I had on me. Her boyfriend had been arrested and had sent his friend out to scout up bail. This was all a bit of a mystery to me, as Josie hadn't mentioned having a steady boyfriend in all the weeks I'd known her. As I passed her my money she told me she was going to bail him out and that she'd be back before the film was over so that the four of us, including the man who was with her now, would go back to Chermside as he had offered us a lift.

I was unhappy about being left alone in the theatre. Glancing around nervously, I noticed that, as she left, Josie stopped at the group of people to whom she had waved earlier. They seemed to be contributing to the bail fund. I watched the film but without the intent concentration of before as I kept feeling the minutes tick by without Josie reappearing. I thought this was a letdown when we were supposed to be celebrating.

When the lights came up at the film's end, I looked about anxiously to see if Josie had returned, but this was wishful thinking.

I followed the small crowd outside and by the time I reached the footpath most of them had disappeared into the night. I stood around for a short while, despairing of Josie's promised return, sorting through my options. Without cash, I couldn't jump into a taxi, and even if I'd still had the few pounds I'd so trustingly given away, they wouldn't have been enough for a cab fare all the way to Chermside. It was so late that there were no trams running and the early morning trams wouldn't begin for hours. The idea of sitting alone on a tramstop during the wee hours was frightening. And the thought of walking through the city, across the bridge and over to Aunty Glad's house was also scary, not to mention having to rouse her when she wasn't even expecting me. And Josie – I didn't have a clue which police station she'd gone to or what her boyfriend's name was, and I wasn't keen to wander around the streets from one station to another looking for her. The truth was – I was stuck.

I was grateful to see that a few of the people Josie had spoken to were still hanging about, perhaps also hoping that she'd return to make some arrangement about returning the money they'd put up for bail. They looked reasonably well-dressed and quiet, so I saw no good reason to be afraid when one of them walked over and spoke to me.

'She didn't come back, eh? D'you know where she went?' His voice was polite, friendly, and he didn't come across as if he was trying to chat me up or anything.

'Sort of, but I don't know if she's still there. She's been gone a very long time.'

'These things take time, they can keep you hanging around for hours. D'you want a lift home?'

I was concerned about accepting a lift from a stranger, but there were girls standing with the group, so I supposed there would be at least two cars, or maybe we were all to go in a couple of taxis.

'Which way are you going?' I asked.

'There's a few of us, so we'll have to go all over. We'll drop you wherever you have to go.'

'Well, thanks very much. I was beginning to wonder how I was going to get home.'

A car drew up slowly on the other side of the street and as it did so, the man said, 'There's our car now. Let's go.' He was smiling, and his face looked pleasant.

As we crossed the street, some of the other people in the group peeled off and walked towards the next corner. When we reached the car I noticed that there was a man behind the wheel, and the man who'd offered me the lift opened the back kerbside door for me to get in. He got in the back as well, and then two other men broke away from the few people who remained on the footpath. One sat in the front seat and the other in the back alongside the man who was sitting next to me. The car started up immediately without a word being said, and for a moment I was filled with panic and apprehension.

'Where to, ma'am?' came a voice from the front.

'Chermside. I'm going to Chermside.' We were approaching the first corner on the main street through Brisbane, so I added, 'We turn to the right here.'

The car quickly turned to the left and I looked through the back window, stunned. 'We're going the wrong way. Oh, please put me down here. We're going the wrong way.'

No one seemed to take any notice, they acted as if they were deaf or I hadn't spoken at all. I was glad to be sitting on the kerbside door, and even though the car was gathering speed, I grabbed the handle to jump out.

I saw the shoulder of the dark-haired man sitting in the front passenger seat swivel, and the next thing I knew, his closed fist flew through the air and landed on the side of my face. My brain rocked in my head and I tried to shake it to clear the fuzziness. As my eyes began to regain focus I could see his fist coming again but it was travelling too fast. I saw what was coming but was unable to move out of its path.

When I came to, I was slumped in the seat and the car was speeding through the night. No one spoke. I lay still for a moment while I collected my thoughts, my eyes barely open so that no one would notice my consciousness. A very occasional street light shone briefly into the car, so I figured we were somewhere on the outskirts of the city, but where, I had no idea. It seemed to me it was now or never, even though the car was moving quickly, so I snaked out my hand to the door, yanked the handle up and slid myself across the seat all in one movement.

The man who had offered me the lift grabbed at me, stopping my movement, and the one in the front turned and thumped my head once more.

My next recall was of the car travelling more slowly, moving across very bumpy ground, and hitting potholes along the way. My mind was awake at last, but I couldn't get my body to respond, to make any movement at all. Then headlights from a car behind us played across the inside roof of the car, and I hoped beyond hope that it was the police, that they'd noticed this car and were follow- ing it. Still no one spoke.

Just as suddenly, it seemed, we'd stopped. Car doors were opened, the door beside me clicked open, and I was dragged out by rough hands on my good white sweater.

I was pushed around the rear of the vehicle, and I noticed that there was not one, but two, other cars parked there with their doors open and men pouring out of them.

I was pushed up against a timber wall, then the rough hands let me go. The dark-haired man who'd been sitting in the passenger seat stood directly in front of me. He had cold eyes and his face looked very grim.

'Are you going to give it up?' he asked.

'What? Give what up?' I was confused and I didn't know what he was asking me.

He reached out his hand at waist level and ripped at the top of my trousers. The fabric, reinforced with silver thread, was strong and resisted his effort to tear it. He was standing very close, so I brought up my leg and delivered him a direct blow to his testicles. He bent over in pain but uttered not one sound.

I looked around in desperation. I was surrounded by what appeared to be a sea of white male faces. Some stood in the back, with brown bottles in their hands, and I realised they were drinking beer. A very tall, blond man, strikingly handsome, stood near the front, and I could make out his features very clearly. He walked towards me, stood to the right of the man doubled over in front of me and, foolishly, I thought he was coming to save me.

'Here, don't panic. Give me your hands.' I mistook his expression for kindness, or maybe I was so desperate that my mind only saw what it wanted to see. I held out my hands to him. He took them, one in each of his large hands, and wrenched them up, pinning them to the wall on either side of me. The man who was doubled over stood up, and I realised that the tall man was holding me still so that this dark-haired monster could punch me again. His angry face and fist were the last things I saw.

I came to lying on the ground in the dark, inside a shed, and there seemed to be men moving all around. A sharp stone was digging into my back but I was unable to lift myself off it. A voice said, 'Wait,' and in the moment before I passed out again, I felt a bristled face brush roughly against my lower stomach and strong sharp teeth bite a piece out of my flesh. The pain was so severe that for a second I thought I was being stabbed, and then blackness overtook me.

I was in the middle of a nightmare. I could feel someone dragging me along the ground by one foot. My other leg became twisted beneath me until someone else pulled it free. My head was bouncing over dirt and stones. I heard a moan escape from my lips.

'Christ,' said a voice, and I looked up and saw in the moonlight shining brightly through the open doorway, that the man I'd kicked in the groin was standing at the door. I knew immediately that it was his voice. 'She's still alive.'

The sharp sound of his boots on the ground assailed my ears. When I opened my eyes again, I saw his thick boot, his kick, coming directly towards my eyes, and there wasn't a damned thing I could do to move out of its way.

I awoke to silence. My entire body felt pain, but there was no single source of it. I was naked and cold, chilled. I crawled around on the ground and my hand struck, thank the heavens, my black trousers. I pulled them on. Then I saw the outline of my sweater in a corner as my eyes became accustomed to the dark. Moonlight still streamed through an opening in the wall where perhaps there'd once been a window. My bra and white T-shirt were with my sweater, and nearby I found my shoes. I pulled them all on. I patted around in the dark, hoping to find my underpants and socks. The cold and damp were making me feel clammy. I walked out of the shed and examined everything I had in my pockets, taking stock of what little had been left with me. I had a slim wallet, empty but for coins, and a few other small bits and pieces. I'd been carrying nothing of much value, and now I had even less. Moonlight bounced off a large white card as I pulled it from my pocket. In big letters I read 'Invitation' and 'Bandstand'. It felt as though I was handling something from years ago, not just a few short hours earlier.

I looked around. The shed was in a large field. I followed the car tracks in the moonlight and came to a fence, which I walked through to where the track joined another, more frequently used, roadway. I was unsure of which direction to take. A long way off in the distance I saw a pair of carlights pass at right angles to the track on which I was standing, I set off in that direction.

I passed a driveway, just a break in a fence, and could see the silhouette of a homestead in the distance. Then I could hear dogs barking, they had probably heard me stumbling along or picked up my scent on the wind. I was too afraid of them to chance walking up the driveway to get help.

The track stopped at a T-junction where it met a narrow bitumen strip. No other car had passed, and I had no idea in which direction Brisbane lay. I was feeling very sick in my stomach, and while walking I'd become aware of a severe pain in my abdomen. I sat down beside the road to wait for more car lights to appear, but I lapsed once more into unconsciousness.

A droning sound woke me and I realised a car was coming, but it was still a long way off. I remembered the pain and slid my hand down the front of my pants. My fingers touched a gaping wound and when I pulled them out they were covered in blood. The car, when it came close enough, was a small milk van. I staggered onto the road and it stopped. I asked the driver which way was the road to Brisbane. He told me it was in the direction he was faced, but that he was turning off the road at the next corner and was unable to give me a lift. He was making his deliveries. Another car, he said, should be along very soon, and it would be better for me to try my luck with that one.

I sat back down beside the road. After a while I thought the world was moving, the trees seemed to be going up and down, and then I realised that it was me, I was swaying even while sitting down.

I had no watch, no idea of the time, but, in shock, I had no sense of urgency. Utter tiredness overwhelmed me. When more headlights appeared I stood up again and walked onto the road. The driver either didn't see until late or he was afraid to stop, because he started to veer around me. Then he drew to a halt. I asked if he was going to Brisbane, and he said, yes, named a suburb I'd never heard of, and I asked him if he'd give me a lift.

I climbed into the cabin and sat huddled near the door. The warm air from his heater began to thaw my frozen limbs. I could feel localised sore spots on my legs and body. I touched my fingers to my head and found my entire face swollen. I sobbed quietly in the dark so as not to alarm the driver.

He drove slowly, and the sun was coming up when he pulled up at the vegetable farm which was his home. We were somewhere high up, but still in the town. He swung out of the truck and said if I waited a while, he'd give me a lift to a railway station. He spoke with an accent, European, perhaps Italian or Greek, I thought.

The truck was parked in front of a very large shed or storehouse. When he'd gone back up the walkway to the house on the block, some workers came out of the shed and peered at me sitting in the cabin. Eventually, one of them came over and asked me if I'd have sex with him for money. He indicated the bunch of workers who stood, eager and hopeful, in the doorway of the building. I was too exhausted even to be shocked. When he'd gone back, no doubt to relay my unwilling response, I slid across the seat and looked at my face in the rear-vision mirror. I couldn't look as bad as I felt, I thought, if these men don't notice how beaten up I am. A crust of dried blood lay across the top of my swollen nose, and my eyes were clotted. Every inch of my head and hair was covered in a film of dirt. Tracks from my tears had created a sort of pattern in the dark shadows beneath my eyes. I looked down at my clothes. My good white sweater was filthy. It looked as if I'd been rolling in mud.

The owner returned and said he would drive me to wherever I wanted to go. When I said Chermside he just nodded and we set off. The sun was well up now and I noticed on his clock that the time was moving towards 8 a.m. I thanked him without much enthusiasm when he flopped me right outside the house where I was living.

When I walked in I went straight to the bed, and stared up at the ceiling. One of the other girls with whom I shared the room jumped up and ran out to fetch the woman of the house. She came in and very kindly and gently asked me what had happened, and was upset when I could only shake my head.

She had another girl run a bath for me and helped me to take my clothes off and climb into it. She was very distressed by the dark bruises that seemed to cover my body and by the places on my abdomen where, she thought, I'd been bitten by some sort of animal. How right she was!

When I was alone, soaking in the bath, tears again overwhelmed me, turning into great sobs. I could sense anxiety in the house over my grief and my appearance. I didn't see Josie and I hadn't asked if she was home. There seemed no point, no point in asking or saying anything.

From *Snake Cradle* (1997)

THE HORSE YOU DON'T SEE NOW

Rolf Boldrewood

Many years ago I was summoned to attend the couch of a dear relative believed to be *in extremis*. The messenger arrived at my club with a buggy, drawn by a dark bay horse. The distance to be driven to Toorak was under four miles – the road good. I have a dislike to being driven. Those who have handled the reins much in their time will understand the feeling. Taking them mechanically from the man, I drew the whip across the bay horse. The light touch sent him down Collins Street East, over Prince's Bridge, and through the toll-bar gate at an exceptionally rapid pace. This I did not remark at the time, being absorbed in sorrowful anticipation.

During the anxious week which followed I drove about the turn-out – a hired one – daily; now for this or that doctor, anon for nurse or attendant. Then the beloved sufferer commenced to amend, to recover; so that, without impropriety, my thoughts became imperceptibly disengaged from her, to concentrate themselves upon the dark bay horse. For that he was no ordinary livery-stable hack was evident to a judge. *Imprimis*, very fast. Had I not passed everything on the road, except a professional trotter, that had not, indeed, so much the best of it? Quiet, too. He would stand unwatched, though naturally impatient. He never tripped, never seemed to 'give' on the hard, blue metal; was staunch up-hill and steady down. Needed no whip, yet took it kindly, neither switching his tail angrily nor making as if ready to smash all and sundry, like ill-mannered horses. Utterly faultless did he seem. But experience in matters equine leads to distrust. Hired out per day from a livery-stable keeper, I could hardly believe *that* to be the case.

All the same I felt strongly moved to buy him on the chance of belonging to the select tribe of exceptional performers, not to be passed over by so dear a lover of horse-flesh as myself. Moreover, I possessed, curious to relate, a 'dead match' for him – another bay horse of equally lavish action, high courage, and recent accidental introduction. The temptation was great.

'I will buy him,' said I to myself, 'if he is for sale, and also if —' here I pulled up, got down in the road, and carefully looked him over from head to tail. He stepped quietly. I can see him now, moving his impatient head gently back and forward like a horse 'weaving' – a trick he had under all circumstances. Years afterwards he performed similarly to the astonishment of a bushranger in Riverina, whose revolver was pointed at the writer's head the while, less anxious indeed for his personal safety than that old Steamer – such was his appropriate name – should march on, and, having a nervous running mate, smash the buggy.

To return, however. This was the result of my inspection. Item, one broken knee; item, seven years old – within mark decidedly; legs sound and clean, but just beginning to 'knuckle' above the pasterns.

There was a conflict of opinions. Says Prudence, 'What! buy a screw? Brilliant, of course, but sure to crack soon. Been had that way before. I'm ashamed of you.'

Said Hope, 'I don't know so much about that. Knee probably an accident: dark night – heap of stones – anything. Goes like a bird. Grand shoulder. *Can't* fall. Legs come right with rest. Barely seven – quite a babe. Cheap at anything under fifty. Chance him.'

'I'll buy him – d – dashed if I don't.' I got in again, and drove thoughtfully to the stables of Mr Washington, a large-sized gentleman of colour, hailing from the States.

'He's de favouritest animile in my stable, boss,' he made answer to me as I guardedly introduced the subject of purchase. 'All de young women's dead sot on him – donow's I cud do athout him, noways.'

Every word of this was true, as it turned out; but how was I to know? The world of currycombs and dandy-brushes is full of insincerities. *Caveat emptor!* I continued airily, 'You won't charge extra for this broken knee? What's the figure?' Here I touched the too yielding ankle-joint with my boot.

That may have decided him – much hung in the balance. Many a year of splendid service – a child's life saved – a grand night-exploit in a flooded river, with distressed damsels nearly overborne by a raging torrent – all these lay in the future.

'You gimme thirty pound, boss,' he gulped out. 'You'll never be sorry for it.'

'Lend me a saddle,' quoth I. 'I'll write the cheque now. Take him out; I can ride him away.'

I did so. Never did I – never did another man – make a better bargain.

I had partly purchased and wholly christened him to match another bay celebrity named Railway, of whom I had become possessed after this fashion. Wanting a harness horse at short notice a few months before, I betook myself to the coach depot of Cobb and Co. situated in Lonsdale Street. Mr Beck was then the manager, and to him I addressed myself. He ordered out several likely animals – from his point of view – for my inspection. But I was not satisfied with any of them. At length, 'Bring out the Railway horse,' said the man in authority. And out came, as I thought, rather a 'peacocky' bay, with head and tail up. A great shoulder certainly, but rather light-waisted – hem – possessed of four capital legs. Very fine in the skin – yes; still I mistrusted him as a 'Sunday horse'. Never was there a greater mistake.

'Like to see him go?' I nodded assent. In a minute and a half we were spinning up Lonsdale Street in an Abbot buggy, across William and down Collins Street, then pretty crowded, at the rate of fourteen miles an hour; Mr Beck holding a broad red rein in either hand, and threading the ranks of vehicles with graceful ease.

'He can go,' I observed.

'He's a tarnation fine traveller, I tell you,' was the answer – a statement which I found, by after-experience, to be strictly in accordance with fact.

The price required was forty pounds. The which promptly paying (this was in 1860), I drove my new purchase out to Heidelberg that night. One of those horses that required of one nothing but to sit still and hold him; fast, game, wiry and enduring.

When I became possessed of Steamer, I had such a pair as few people were privileged to sit behind. For four years I enjoyed as much happiness as can be absorbed by mortal horse-owner in connection with an unsurpassable pair of harness horses. They were simply perfect as to style, speed and action. I never was passed, never even challenged, on the road by any other pair. Railway, the slower horse of the two, had done, by measurement, eight miles in half an hour. So at their best, both horses at speed, it may be guessed how they made a buggy spin behind them. Then they were a true match; one a little darker than the other, but so much alike in form, colour, and courage, that strangers never knew them apart.

They became attached readily, and would leave other horses and feed about together, when turned into a paddock or the bush.

A check, however, was given to exultation during the first days of my proprietorship. Both horses when bought were low in flesh – in hard condition, certainly, but showing a good deal of bone. A month's stabling and gentle exercise caused them to look very different. The new buggy came home – the new harness. They were put together for the first time. Full of joyful anticipation I mounted the driving seat, and told the groom to let go their heads. Horror of horrors! 'The divil a stir', as he remarked, could be got out of them. Collar-proud from ease and good living, they declined to tighten the traces. An indiscreet touch or two with the whip caused one horse to plunge, the other to hold back. In half-and-half condition I had seen both draw like working bullocks. Now 'they wouldn't pull the hat off your head', my Australian Mickey Free affirmed.

By patience and persuasion I prevailed upon them at length to move off. Then it *was* a luxury of a very high order to sit behind them. How they caused the strong but light-running trap to whirl and spin! – an express train with the steam omitted. Mile after mile might one sit when roads were good, careful only to keep the pace at twelve miles an hour; by no means to alter the pull on the reins lest they should translate it into an order for full speed. With heads held high at the same angle, with legs rising from the ground at the same second of time, alike their extravagant action, their eager courage. As mile after mile was cast behind, the exclamation of 'Perfection, absolute perfection!' rose involuntarily to one's lips.

In this 'Wale', where deceitful dealers and plausible horses abound, how rare to experience so full-flavoured a satisfaction! None of us, however, are perfect all round. Flawless might be their action, but both Steamer and his friend Railway had 'a little temper', the differing expressions of which took me years to circumvent.

Curiously, neither exhibited the least forwardness in *single* harness. Railway was by temperament dignified, undemonstrative, proud. If touched sharply with the whip he turned his head and gazed at you. He did not offer to kick or stop; such vulgar tricks were beneath him. But he calmly gave you to understand that he would not accelerate his movements, or start when unwilling, if you flogged him to death. No whip did he need, I trow. The most constant horse in the world, he kept going through the longest day with the tireless regularity of an engine.

They never became quite free from certain peculiarities at starting, after a spell or when in high condition. Years passed in experiments before I wrote myself conqueror. I tried the whip more than once – I record it contritely – with signal ill-success. It was truly wonderful why they declined to start on the first day of a journey. Once off they would pull staunchly wherever horses could stand. Never was the day too long, the pace too fast, the road too deep. What, then, was the hidden cause, the *premier pas*, which cost so much trouble to achieve?

Nervous excitability seemed to be the drawback. The fact of being attached to a trap in *double* harness appeared to over-excite their sensitive, highly-strung organisations. Was it not worthwhile, then, to take thought and care for a pair which could travel fifty or sixty miles a day – in front of a family vehicle filled with children and luggage – for a week together, that didn't cost a shilling a year for whip-cord, and that had *never* been passed by a pair on the road since I had possessed them? Were they not worth a little extra trouble?

Many trials and experiments demonstrated that there was but one solution. Success meant patience, with a dash of forethought. A little saddle-exercise for a day or two before the start. Then to begin early on the morning of the eventful day; to have everything packed – passengers and all – in the buggy – coach fashion – before any hint of putting to. Both horses to be fed and watered at least an hour before. Then at the last moment to bring them out of the stable, heedfully and respectfully, avoiding 'rude speech or jesting rough'. Railway especially resented being 'lugged' awkwardly by the rein. If all things were done decently and in order, this would be the usual programme.

Steamer, more excitable but more amiable, would be entrusted to a groom. Silently and quickly they would be poled up, the reins buckled, and Railway's traces attached. All concerned had been drilled, down to the youngest child, to be discreetly silent. It was forbidden, on pain of death, to offer suggestion, much less to 't-c-h-i-c-k'. The reins were taken in one hand by paterfamilias, who with the other drew back Steamer's traces, oppressed with an awful sense of responsibility, as of one igniting a fuse or connecting a torpedo wire, and as the outer trace was attached, stepped lightly on to the front seat. The groom and helper stole backward like shadows. Steamer made a plunging snatch at his collar; Railway followed up with a steady rush; and we were off – off for good and all – for one hundred, two hundred, five hundred miles. Distance made no difference to *them*. The last stage was even as the first. They only wanted holding. Not that they pulled disagreeably, or unreasonably either. I lost my whip once, and drove without one for six months. It was only on the first day of a journey that the theatrical performance was produced.

But this chronicle would be incomplete without reference to the sad alternative when the start did *not* come off at first intention. On these inauspicious occasions, possibly from an east wind or oats below sample, everything went wrong. Steamer sidled and pulled prematurely before the traces were 'hitched', while Railway's reserved expression deepened – a sure sign that he wasn't going to pull at all. The other varied his vexatious plungings by backing on to the whipple-tree, or bending outwards, by way of testing the elasticity of the pole.

Nothing could now be done. Persuasion, intimidation, deception, had all been tried previously in vain. The recipe of paterfamilias, as to horse management, was to sit perfectly still with the reins firmly held but moveless, buttoning his gloves with an elaborate pretence of never minding. All known expedients have come to nought long ago. Pushing the wheels, even downhill, is regarded with contempt; leading (except by a lady) scornfully refused. The whip is out of the question. 'Patience is a virtue' – indeed *the* virtue, the only one which will serve our turn. Meanwhile, when people are fairly on the warpath, this dead refusal to budge an inch is a little, just a little, exasperating. Paterfamilias computes, however, that ten minutes' delay can be made up with such steppers. He smiles benignantly as he pulls out a newspaper and asks his wife if she has brought her book. Two minutes, four, five, or is it half an hour? The time seems long. 'Trois cent milles diables!' the natural man feels inclined to ejaculate. He knows that he is sinking fast in the estimation of newly arrived station hands and chance spectators. Eight minutes – Railway makes no sign; years might roll on before *he* would start with an unwilling mate. Nine minutes – Steamer, whose impatient soul abhors inaction, begins to paw. The student is absorbed in his leading article. Ten minutes – Steamer opens his mouth and carries the whole equipage off with one rush. Railway is up and away; half a second later the proprietor folds up his journal and takes them firmly in hand. The children begin to laugh and chatter; the lady to converse; and the journey, long or short, wet or dry, may be considered, as far as horseflesh is concerned, to be *un fait accompli*.

At the end of four years of unclouded happiness (as novelists write of wedded life) this state of literal conjugal bliss was doomed to end. An epidemic of lung disease, such as at intervals sweeps over the land, occurred in Victoria. Railway fell a victim, being found dead in his paddock. Up to this time he had never been 'sick or sorry', lame, tired, or unfit to go. His iron legs, with feet to match, showed no sign of work. In single harness he was miraculous, going mile after mile with the regularity of a steam-engine, apparently incapable of fatigue. I was lucky enough to have a fast, clever grandson of Cornborough to put in his place. He lasted ten years. A half-brother three years more. The old horse was using up his *fourth* running mate, and entering upon his twentieth year *in my service*, when King Death put on the brake.

Not the least noticeable among Steamer's many good qualities was his kindly, generous temper. His was the Arab's docile gentleness with children. The large mild eye, 'on which you could hang your hat' as the stable idiom goes, was a true indication of character. I was a bachelor when I first became his master. As time passed on, Mrs Boldrewood and the elder girls used to drive him to the country town in New South Wales, near which we afterwards dwelt. The boys rode him as soon as they could straddle a horse. They hung by his tail, walked between his legs, and did all kinds of confidential circus performances for the benefit of their young friends. He was never known to bite, kick, or in any way offer harm; and, speedy to the last, with age he never lost pace or courage. 'All spirit and no vice' was a compendium of his character. By flood and field, in summer's heat or winter's cold, he failed us never; was credited, besides, with having saved the lives of two of the children by his docility and intelligence. He was twice loose with the buggy at his heels at night – once without winkers, which he had rubbed off. On the last occasion, after walking down to the gate of the paddock, and finding it shut – nearly a mile – he turned round without locking the wheels, and came galloping up to the door of the house (it was a ball night, and he had got tired of waiting). When I ran out, pale with apprehension, I discovered the headstall hanging below his chest. His extreme docility with children I attribute to his being for many years strictly a family horse, exclusively fed, harnessed, and driven by ourselves. It is needless to say he was petted a good deal: indeed he thought nothing of walking through the kitchen, a brick-floored edifice, when he thought corn should be forthcoming. Horses are generally peaceable with children but not invariably, as I have known of limbs broken and more than one lamentable death occasioned by kicks, when the poor things went too near unwittingly. But the old horse *couldn't* kick. 'I reckon he didn't know how.' And when he died, gloom and grief fell upon the whole family, who mourned as for the death of a dear friend.

(1901)

THE LINE

David Brooks

Late, on the hottest night of the year, he sits by the window. For a long time he searches for a line and at last he finds it, beginning at the tip of his pen and continuing across the page beneath the words *continuing across the page beneath* until it reaches the edge and, independent of ink and human motion, and pausing only briefly as if about to dive, moving thence onto the desk and past the candle and the glass toward the sill.

From there, against the first faint stirrings of a cool breeze from the river, it slips through the wire screen and out across the fuchsias and the lawn. Traversing the pavement, rising above the trees, and following no streets or feasible cross-country route, it passes westward over Roe Street and the Beggar's Lane to the playing-fields and the old stone buildings of the university. Not stopping at these, nor in the cafe quarter, and following roughly the course of the river, it passes through the wide updraught of denser oxygen above the park, directly above the last bedless lovers in an EJ Holden and the pointing arm of the statue of Sir John F, the founding father of the city, and thence across the long, perfect reflection of the Great Port Bridge and into the sleeping suburbs.

After almost one mile of these, just grazing the upper branches of an avenue of flowering gums, it slows and descends, approaching cautiously the third front window of a darkened house four miles or three pages of the city directory from where first it left the orderly confines of the introductory paragraph of a tale for which it may, in truth, have never been intended.

To follow it by car (public transport, needless to say, is unthinkable), one would have – to employ again the city directory – to begin on page 48, in the square designated by the fine blue lines that descend from either side of the letter B, and those which stretch toward the left from the number 53 at the far right-hand margin. Bearing in mind that one's general direction must always be westward, one would then move at first in a southerly direction along Alton Road until Balcott and, turning right at the church with the great rose window, move diagonally across two map squares to where the page joins 47 and, crossing at first Charles Road, Balcott leads into Dean Parade. Now moving directly westward, one traces Dean through four squares of the light blue grid – past the city pool, the council offices and the Ladies College – and passes beneath the freeway into Estuary Road, where the Floral Beach Parade and map 46 begin. Following the Floral Beach Parade diagonally across the upper right, beside Dog Swamp and the Herdsman Cemetery, one finds oneself, having strayed north-westerly, referred to map 36, where the Floral intersects Green Street and turns toward the sea. At Herbert Street one takes a left-hand turn. Moving again southward, one drives beneath flowering gums to a lane beginning, of course, with the letter *I*, and halts at the darkened frontage of number 38, at a considerable disadvantage and at least half an hour behind the line which, unshackled by a pedestrian imagination, has already entered the third window from the left – left open to catch the cool sea breeze – and passed between billowing curtains toward a bed upon which sleeps a woman with soft white skin and auburn hair, her face partly hidden by her furled right arm and a fold of the single sheet. Uninhibited by this last barrier, the line has long since found her, and, not without an initial parabolic digression, proceeded along her left calf and thigh and come to rest, peacefully and without thought of return.

She, of course, knows nothing of this. She has, in fact, been borrowed from Alain Dufort, and was last seen on a balcony above a courtyard lined with palms. All she could tell is that, when she awoke, she had been dreaming of an old man on an esplanade, feeding seagulls that, for their own mysterious reasons, suddenly rose and, banking westward, traced with their soft grey wings an ambiguous message, free of grid or narrative, on a dark sky promising rain.

(1985)

REPUBLIC OF LOVE

Delia Falconer

I, Mary the Larrikin, tart of Jerilderie, have loved for roast beef and I have loved for the feather on a well-trimmed hat. In my room above the hotel bar I have felt a squatter's spurs and sucked once on a bishop's fingers. The perfumes of my thighs have greased many a stockman's saddle and kept him company through lonely nights. Men can nose out my room from thirty miles away, their saddlebags tight and heavy with desire. But of all the men I have ever loved, Ned Kelly, dead three years before they put him in the ground, stole my heart away.

It is hard work loving a dead man: your pillow a gravestone, your arms a confessional. Dead men crawl into your bed at night and evaporate like steam with the rising of the sun. I never saw Kelly in the even light of day. Instead I saw the shadows of candle smoke drift across the smoothness of his hips. I dug my fingertips into the silver squares of window cast upon the muscles of his arms. But I saw enough and felt the rest with my famous mouth and hands. I can tell you that the insides of his thighs had been smoothed by the saddle. He was covered with scars paler than moonlight. He had a foreskin as soft as a horse's inner lip.

322

Mostly we fucked like greedy children trying to hold on to an Indian summer. Our love had ripened out of season, and each full moon hung heavy on the frailest stem of night. But sometimes, in the quiet hour, when his beard rested on my breasts, Kelly told me about the Republic of Love.

In the Republic of Love, said Kelly, there will be no police to eavesdrop on our sleep. We will dream no more in timid whispers but laugh as loud as kookaburras in the dark. Our desires will dive through the hills like flocks of night birds. The dawn will echo with the yapping of our hopes.

In the springtime, when the snows melted, the ground was so damp it rotted beneath a horse's feet. In the morning, clouds clung to the roads like sullen cobwebs. By midday they peeled off the mountainsides and stacked themselves like sodden hay in tiered bales that reached towards a hidden sun. It was a time for wet and stumbling love.

I am an indoor girl myself, but I could read Kelly's body like a map and feel what it was like gullying and ungullying through the deep-scored seams that marked those brilliant hills. After three days' ride, his stirrups had stained the tops of his feet with orange. His wideawake was filled with melted hail up to the edges of its brim. When he hung his trousers by the fireplace, the clouds that had caught in his pockets unfurled and rose up to the corners of the room. His whiskers had been brushed backwards by the stormy winds and stood out from his face. Scratch my beard for me, Mary my love, he said, for it is crawling with lightning. I felt blue sparks crackle beneath my fingertips.

I stood naked before him. He wrapped his cool green sash around my waist and came in close to tie the bow. He said he held all the softness of Ireland wrapped up as a Christmas gift. When we lay on his jacket before the fire to make our clumsy love, I felt mud slide across the surface of my skin. For weeks it bore the purple scent of Salvation Jane.

In the Republic of Love, Kelly said, we will soak beds thick with emerald sheets and curtains. There will be so much bread to go around that we will scoop out the hearts of loaves and use them for our babies' cradles. They will nestle in the warmth of the fresh-baked centres and rock sideways on the curving crusts.

Shortly before we met, Kelly had begun to rustle horses. He would come to me from the hills at night, his belly full of parrot. I knew without asking when he had shot and eaten lorikeet. His lips were as soft as feathers. He sweated rainbows. He played with thoughts on the tip of his tongue and mused with the subtlety of a philosopher between my legs.

Each theft, he said, avenged the times the squatters had impounded the Kellys' cattle for straying onto their glutted pastures. They are slick-lipped, swamp-hearted, rough-bellied toads, said Kelly, who begrudge us even the flies that circle round our heads. They would brand the water in the rain clouds if they could.

I grasped him firmly in my hand and began the movements that would comfort him. He laughed and said the law had squeezed him harder there before. He told me of the arrest when the policeman Lonigan had cupped his fist around his balls and tried to wrench them off, his breathing fast, his face more crimson than a mangel-wurzel. From my work in this room I understood that impulse well. It is police and magistrates, I said, who fall on you like a cattle crush and make each act of love a punishment. They grind you against the mattress until your breath is thinner than a paper-knife. They lust to press you, dry and brittle, between the pages of the police gazette. They threaten to arrest you if you tell.

In the Republic of Love, Kelly told me, you can take any shape your loving chooses. You can fuck like a centaur at midnight and squeal like a poddy calf at noon.

There is one thing I can tell you with certainty. That day at Glenrowan may have been the first time Kelly wore an iron helmet, but it was not the first landscape he had seen as if he was looking up from the bottom of his grave. Before we met he had spent ten years in prison, where he had known the world only as a narrow strip of daylight.

He was born in the shadow of Mount Disappointment. Like the other Irish convicts' sons, he grew thin as a weed from the dusty cracks between the squatters' properties. His mouth set into a hard straight line. He had seen his father's body swell with dropsy before his death. He said it was as if Red Kelly's ankles at last had cracked the phantom shackles that had made them ache since those cold years in Van Diemen's Land. He had watched his mother stumble to unlatch the door with a baby on her hip when the police tried to make the Kellys soft by breaking their nights into tiny pieces. He had felt the slab walls quiver as the policeman Flood pinned his sister Annie with his belly, discharging the seed that was to stretch her taut until she died, weakened by the fleshy issue in her womb.

When he was five, Kelly's mother explained to him that there were no days or seasons on the wrong side of the law. There were only lucky hours, she said, and nights of swift riding when you could slide in and out of the chilly pockets of the moon.

Later he gave up shearing because the sound of the metal reminded him of a warden's scissors clipping his hair down to its roots. He had stopped sawing wood in the Gippsland forests when the milky sun filtering through the treetops made him think of prison bars.

Before I was eighteen, Kelly said, my arse was polished by the court-rooms' wooden benches. My spine grew straight as a prison bunk. I have nine notches in my forehead made by the butt of a policeman's rifle. I think the granite I broke at Beechworth has passed into my blood, for my veins feel as rough as sandpaper.

In Pentridge, in solitary confinement, Kelly spent six weeks with his head covered by a hood. Two slits were cut in the canvas for his eyes. That was when he began to see the landscape inside an angry frame with no soft tomorrows beyond its edges. It gave him ideas. He would turn ploughshares into armour, soldering and riveting the grimness of his gaze.

I stroked his chest and kissed his ear. I knew how it is to feel your body bruise and bend beneath a greater power. To this day my buttocks bear the impressions of floorboards and mattress buttons. I can still read the angry marks made by a grazier's signet ring upon my breasts. I loved Kelly the more for this. I asked him about the Republic of Love.

In the Republic of Love, Kelly replied, the prisons will be emptied and converted into breweries. Their quarries will be thick with waving heads of barley. The husks will drift across the lintels and gateways and wear away their English coats of arms. In the courtyards the smell of hops bubbling will lift away the stench of sweat. Barmaids will trail the scents of their soft perfumes along the dim, grey passages. In the banks, lovers will rut on crackling banknotes. They will roll in the safes until their backs are stained with mortgage inks. Sixpences will stick to them until they shine more silver than a blue-tongue lizard's belly.

The day the Proclamation of Outlawry was passed, Kelly began to notice clods of grave dirt weighing down his trouser hems. He lost his boxer's gait and began to move as if he wore Red Kelly's irons. He said he could feel his soul trailing like a muddy shadow in his horse's wake, catching and tearing on each roughened patch of bark. When he stood in my room, he squinted hard and nodded as we talked. He could not see my breasts and face at once.

That Act had closed even those narrow gaps, thinner than horizons, in which he had once moved. Since they had been ambushed at Stringybark,the Kelly gang no longer held the rights of citizens. The proclamation put into words what they already knew: that they were unwelcome in this land that wore a crown. Any man offended by the sight of them could shoot them in the back. Ellen Kelly would soon be put in jail for giving birth to a bushranger. In his Sunday sermon at Mansfield, the Anglican Bishop declared them dead already and damned to hell.

Odd to find yourself, said Kelly, staring through a dead man's face. Some days the landscapes he rode through looked as drab and frail as photographs that might lift at any moment from their edges. He had sepia nightmares in which he could not find his way from one image to the next, wandering forever in the soft jigsaw clefts of the Puzzle Ranges. On other days he found the dark-blue curves and creases of the hills too beautiful. He lay in the darkness of a cave and saw Aaron Sherritt at the entrance, watching over Joe Byrne while he slept. He could hear clearly Sherritt thinking that the golden hairs on Joe's forearms made them look like angels' wings, while his lips smiled but never opened. Each night more disappointed ghosts joined Red Kelly in the darkness that had begun to press upon the edges of his vision. When he passed a house at dawn, the smell of baking bread would nearly break his heart.

He said he thought of going to America, that free land, where he would race steam locomotives on a piebald horse across the plains.

This was the last time Kelly came to me. His eyes focused beyond my head. He mouthed me like a hungry phantom. He felt every part of me to prove that I existed. His fingers were as cool as apples. He took his green sash from my drawer and placed it on his folded clothes.

When he spoke about the Republic of Love, his head was as heavy as a tombstone on my shoulder.

In the Republic of Love, said Kelly, there will be no fences. People will find new uses for ordinary things. They will cook toast on the rusting faces of branding irons. They will float down creeks on the discarded doors of shops. The telegraph wires will carry only love songs, tapped out in Morse like the rapid beatings of a heart.

Kelly did not see the betrayal in the face of the limping school-teacher who left the Glenrowan Hotel and waved his handkerchief like a salesman's wife at a train full of troopers. In the dock he stared past the crimson face of Judge Redmond Barry, mottled and shaking like a turkey's wattle. I want to believe that he did not flinch as the frail trap of the gallows shivered beneath his feet.

That night the soft head I had felt between my thighs was cut off and shaved bare before the mask-maker's steady hands shaped warm wax around its jaw. The firm muscles around Kelly's lips were torn away and discarded. His heart was stolen by the surgeon as a souvenir. His skull with the five smooth mounds that curved around its base was stroked by an idle policeman's fingers as it weighed down the papers on his desk.

Back in Jerilderie I continued with my whoring, staring beyond the publican's shoulder.

I looked towards the same place as Kelly.

That day, neither of us blinked. If we concentrated hard enough, we could sense each other breathing: feel the wet cages of our ribs pressing into one another: hear the spines of law books splitting beneath our backs: rolling, beyond our senses, into the Republic of Love.

(1995)

NORTH

Tim Winton

He walks the narrow blacktop in the warm dark. The sea is miles behind but he feels it at his back. Above the murky hinterland, stars hang like sparks and ash from a distant bushfire. By dawn his hamstrings are tight and his feet sore in their boots. The pack is snug enough in his back but the swag lashed across it teeters with every stride and butts the top of his head. He trudges into the rising sun until an old truck eases up beside him and an arm motions him to get in.

The man is long and thin with a shapeless hat and stringy grey hair to his shoulders. He looks tired, waits for Fox to speak and then sighs a suit-yourself sigh and just drives. Fox glances behind at the flatbed where several olive trees lie wrapped and lashed beneath a tarp.

They drone through floodplain country and into the beginnings of rich soil where late crops stand brassy in the sun. They veer north into the midlands wheatbelt where harvesters raise clouds of chaff and dust across the rolling hills.

This is it, says the driver at New Norcia.

Thanks, says Fox.

That Darkie could play.

Fox climbs out.

Headin north?

He drags his pack and bedroll off the rusty truckbed.

Fox cinches himself in. The sun is in his face.

It was only a matter of time, the man says. You would've bug-gered off eventually.

Thanks again.

Worth it for the conversation.

Fox walks through the old Spanish monastery town with barely a glance. Town cars and farm utes roll by but he doesn't even bother sticking his finger out. At the outskirts he shrugs his load onto the gravel shoulder and waits. Flies suck the sweat around his eyes, along his neck. In the paddock's remnant stand of gums, cockatoos stir. Eventually a Kenworth hulks up in a gust of airbrakes. He throws his kit up and climbs in.

G'day, says the truckie.

G'day.

This man is the colour of a boiled crab. His nose is thin and ruined. His ears are crisp with lesions.

Great Northern Highway, says the driver.

That's it, says Fox settling back into the smell of sweat and old socks and fried food.

Get yeself a hiding?

Fox grimaces. Hasn't thought how he must still look after swim-ming and walking home.

Face says everything, dunnit.

Yeah.

They ride in silence the rest of the morning with the cricket trickling in like water torture from the radio. The aircon dries the perspiration then chills him. As they lurch inland, the trailers swaying behind them, the country grows dry and low and wheat gives out to sheep paddocks which seem thinner and more marginal until only squat mulga scrub remains; just olive dabs of vegetation spread over stony yellow dirt.

Wildflower country, says the truckie, failing to suppress a fart. Should see it in September. Flowers as far as ye can look.

Fox can't imagine it. He hasn't expected this sudden absence of trees. He's hardly been on the road five hours and already it's just flat dirt out there.

So, what you pissin off from?

People, says Fox.

People in particular, or people in general?

Both.

The truckie takes the hint and contents himself with the cricket match on the radio. It's hard to think of anything more dreary but at least it spares him music.

A steer lies with its legs in the air like an overturned table at the road's edge. Rippling black sheet of birds.

Out of the low scrub a gum rises in the distance and as they pass Fox sees a white cross and a pair of elastic-sided boots. A scene from a Burl Ives song. Old Burl. How the old man loved him. Wrap me up in my stockwhip and blanket.

At the Paynes Find roadhouse Fox sits up in the Kenworth's cab while the bowser pumps diesel into its enormous tanks. He looks out in search of a settlement to go with the name but there's only scrub and stony ground. Eventually the smell of diesel drives him out. He buys a Coke and sits in the sweltering shade while his driver, having made it plain he wants to eat alone, hoes into a baconburger at a table inside.

Caravans towed by Pajeros and Range Rovers pull in from the north and line up for fuel. Old people with baggy shorts and leathery tans cross the oil-tamped dirt of the forecourt to the reeking bogs.

A young bloke in khaki work gear and steel-capped boots comes out of the roadhouse dragging a gust of refrigerated air and cigarette smoke with him.

Sads, he says disgustedly.

Sorry? says Fox finishing his Coke.

Sads, the bloke says, jerking his head at the retirees emerging from the toilets to compare mileages. See Australia and Die.

Fox shrugs.

Some of em do the whole trip. North, then across the top to the Territory. Queensland. Drive south. Come back across the Nullarbor. The big circle. Then they start again. I blame private superannuation. They clog up the road. Where you headed?

Oh, says Fox, up.

Hitchin?

You can tell?

Practice, mate.

Fox looks at the embroidered logo on his workshirt. A gold miner.

Headin back to Magnet in a sec. Give you a lift if you don't mind ridin in the back. Me mate's takin a dump.

Thanks.

The diesel bowser continues to roll its eyes at the Kenworth. The luckless motorists caught behind the truck's trailers wait it out. Fox hauls his gear down from the cubby behind the cab and humps it to the miner's trayback Cruiser.

All afternoon from the windblown tray of the Landcruiser he watches the mulga country gradually transformed by the emergence of granite breakaways. The rocky escarpments come as a relief from the horizontal monotony. Convoys of vans and towed dinghies blow by southward. But for the occasional northbound roadtrain, the traffic is all headed the other way. In the cab they're playing Judas Priest; it's mercifully muted by windrush.

At Mount Magnet the young blokes set him down at a corner that feels like a crossroads of some moment. This is the end of the south. Farm fences are gone and soil has long been replaced by dust or grit. The Indian Ocean is hours to the west. On the road sign, towns have three- or four-digit distances. He tries to imagine the gibber plains and red dunes to the east, the impossible amplitude of the continent. They say it's empty and the idea draws him but he can't get his mind around it. Thinks of the north the old man spoke of with pride and fear in his voice, the rugged stone ranges, the withering heat, the ceaseless blasting and digging, the epic drinking that made the boozy south seem temperate, the cattle herds pounding red dust skyward and the seasons discounted to plain Wet or Dry.

He hoists his kit and considers his options. It's not too late to steer seaward to Highway 1 and head north along the coast, but he has momentum now and he knows the inland route will take him past Wittenoom and the mine that orphaned him. He plumps for pressing on.

He pulls the bankroll from his pack and stuffs a few notes into his shorts to buy food. He crosses the wide, empty street to the BP station and orders himself a meal. While he sits black kids come and go. They buy Cokes and icecream and stand out on the tarmac to tease each other and mug at him through the window. Later he straps himself to his load and they follow him a little way, giggling, cheeky and loud as cockatoos.

Nobody stops so he walks to burn the time. The sun gets low but the heat seems to abide in the land. On the other side of town at sunset with no chance of a lift in such gloom, he veers into the scrub to find a place to camp.

He heads for a granite outcrop that he spies over the mulga and there he finds a decent patch of dirt. He unrolls his swag and collects sticks before the night closes in. The fire he lights is more for illumination than anything else. Having eaten not long back he doesn't bother to cook. By the glow of his little fire he examines the contents of his pack, the dried food, the billycan, lighter, torch, two changes of clothes, spare socks, waterbottles, pocket knife, a boning knife and steel, the floppy hat he's forgotten to wear all day, sunscreen, repellent. He carries a few first aid supplies. Band-Aids of course. Tweezers, Betadine. But no book, not a one. It's a bad oversight. He wants to be alone, God knows, but not without something to read.

He's sore now and his skin itches all over where scabs have formed. His nose is peeling and his lips cracked. He pulls his boots off and feels the blisters on his toes where the skin is still soft.

He doesn't think of Georgie Jutland. She hovers, of course, like something you can't quite believe in, but he doesn't let himself think of her. Stretched on his swag with the sheet half off, he thinks of himself in the paddock this morning kneeling with the knife to cut the end from a melon and slide his hand in, his arm to the elbow. It was hot from the sun and sweet, winy as the sea he'd been dreaming of, and days past eating. He took a mouthful to feel it fizz a little on his tongue. Even now he imagines he tastes that fermenting sweetness. It was the last thing he did before pulling his money from the stone on the hill and setting out. He doesn't know why he did it, though it was true that his mouth was parched from the night and day before and from what he'd decided to do. It was the sacrament he couldn't admit to. Just goodbye, that's all. A spitting of seeds, a quick turning for the hill.

Neither melancholy nor creeping anxiety keep him awake tonight. The farm could be burning but he sleeps. Last thing he hears is the curlew.

—·—

The sky is still layered pink and grey when the seventies-model Bedford van pulls over in a gale of dust and music. He steps up to the door and pulls it open and the aircon and the thumping bass blast him head-on. The driver is in his twenties with sunbleached dreadlocks and flat blue eyes, the very picture of a surfer.

Got any juice money? he yells across the music.

I spose.

Orright, then.

Fox reefs the side door open and throws in his gear. It's pandemonium in there. A naked foam mattress with bites out of it and a sheet skewed halfway across it. On top are cheap PVC stuffbags, a fishing rod, jaffle iron, Igloo esky, camp oven, wank mags, a bong made from garden hose and a Mr Juicy bottle. A carton of Victoria Bitter has burst and cans lie all about.

He climbs into the passenger seat and feels the van surge away. Holden motor, you can bet on it.

Where you goin? says the driver, turning the tapedeck down a notch.

Wittenoom.

Fuck. Ghost town, innit?

Fox shrugs.

I'm not a tidy packer, says the surfer who catches him looking back at the shambles in the back. Only bought it last night. Well, won it as a matter of fact.

How?

By bein better than the other bloke, of course, he said with a hoarse laugh.

The van stinks of mull smoke and dirty clothes and the chilled air pouring from the vents smells mouldy. Fox's boots settle into a snarl of junkfood containers, beercans, crushed maps, and plastic bags. At the uncommon bends in the two-lane, a half-full Southern Comfort bottle rolls against one ankle.

Rusty, says the driver.

Lu, he offers reluctantly.

The music hammers at him; he feels it at the back of his throat. Steely Dan, their best album. Full of angular licks and slick changes, lyrics that peck at you. But he doesn't want to hear it. Music unstitches him now; he can do without it.

They drive hard into the morning. The tape restarts itself over and over. Rusty, it seems, hardly hears it. The country spreads out into salt lakes and vast baked pans wherein tiny islands of mallee hold up. They blow through the old mine-town of Cue where diggings and slagheaps become landscape.

At Meekatharra the earth is red. It stains the tar streets and the vehicles and buildings along them. Rusty veers into a service station and looks expectantly at Fox. It takes a moment to realise he wants money.

You fill it and I'll buy breakfast.

I've eaten, says Fox, though his billy tea and muesli bar are long behind him.

Rusty takes three twenties from him and limps inside while Fox pumps the tank full. There's something about Rusty that strikes him as odd. Sees him limp from the restaurant to the toilets. On the way back to the glass doors his gait seems milder. When he comes back he hands Fox a burger and a bag of doughy fries and he drops a carton of similar delicacies onto the seat. Fox registers the clonk of Rusty's shin as he climbs in. Rusty looks at him with a sudden ferocity.

Artificial, orright? I'm a fuckin pegleg.

Oh.

Yeah, friggin oh.

Rusty pulls a monster rollie from his pocket, a roach the size of a turd. He lights up and wheels them out into the street.

Some dickhead in his Range Rover backed into me, says Rusty. Out the front of the Margaret River tavern. I was sittin on me car. He reverses up, pins me at the knee, totally friggin crushes it. Some fancypants lawyer from Cottesloe.

I spose you were surfing at Margaret River.

Not anymore. And that prick gets himself a bunch of hot-shot mates and they do me out of a decent pay-out.

Out on the highway Rusty opens it up and the Bedford's transmission gulps.

Automatic, he says. Cripple-friendly.

The van gets up so much speed that it floats, seems to hydroplane across the water mirages on the road.

Ever felt bitter? says Rusty not noticing that Fox has killed the stereo. You look the contented type.

That's me.

Fox watches him toke on the joint with all the pleasure of a man siphoning petrol. The van fills with smoke but it's too hot outside to crank down a window. Right at the dag-end of his smoke he offers Fox a puff but he declines.

Chuck me that Woolworths bag behind the seat, will ya?

Fox pivots and pulls the bag onto the seat between them.

Got some good gear in Geraldton.

Fox nods.

Well, take a look.

He opens the plastic bag and sees a jumble of tubes, bottles, cellophane sachets. There are boxes of prescription drugs in there and several syringes.

Starting a pharmacy, says Fox.

My oath.

All day Rusty grips the wheel but his pace is erratic. The break-neck speed of the morning gives out to fitful surges and lulls by midday. Now and then they pull over so he can stuff a morphine suppository. In the afternoon Fox offers to drive but he's rebuffed and Rusty pilots the van at a pace that has triple-trailer roadtrains honking as they overtake in slipstream blasts that shove the Bedford aside.

Almost without noticing the transition, Fox sees that the country has become vivid, dramatic. The midwest is behind them. This is the Pilbara. Everything looks big and Technicolor. Ahead the stupendous iron ranges. There are trees again. This land looks dreamt, willed, potent.

Fark, says Rusty apropos of nothing.

At Newman they drive, lost for a while, through the big mine-town's circuitous streets. There are lush lawns here and flowers, mists of pumped water that soften the lines of neat bungalows and company shops. On one corner a Haulpak truck towers over the suburb. Water, iron ore, money.

Eventually Fox coaches Rusty back out onto the highway which climbs into the Opthalmia Ranges whose bluffs and peaks and mesas rise crimson, black, burgundy, terracotta, orange against the cloudless sky. Gully shadows are purple up there and the rugged layers of iron lie dotted with a greenish furze of spinifex. You sense hidden rivers. Your ears pop with altitude. Closer to the road, on scree slopes the colour of dry blood, the smooth white trunks of snappy gums suspend crowns of leaves so green it's shocking. Mobs of white cockatoos explode from their boughs. The colours burn in his head. Wide bends reveal the country behind darkened by the shadows of late afternoon. Fox feels his head slump back on his neck. He comes from low, dry, austere country, limestone and sand and grasstrees. Apart from the sea itself the only majestic points at home are the sculpted dunes. Even the graceful tuart tree seems dowdy up here.

Jesus, that's me done, says Rusty veering off into a roadside scrape where a snappy gum and a few tufts of scrub mark a rough lookout.

Fox realises that twilight has fallen. He's a little stoned from the smoke in the van. The sky is puce, the peaks and crags of the iron ranges black against it.

Rusty kills the motor, throws the door open and hot, clean air rushes in. It feels velvety. Rusty pisses on the dirt.

Fox climbs out into the still heat of evening.

They break up dead wood for a fire and by dark the billy is boiling. Fox throws tea leaves into the water but lets the tea stand so long Rusty picks it up and takes it to the van where they've left the mugs. Fox feels tired and passive; he doesn't care.

Spose you want me to cook, too, eh? calls Rusty.

I don't mind.

Need a pep-up?

Just a cuppa. Maybe a beer later.

No worries!

When Rusty brings the tea back it tastes coppery, worse than stewed.

Here, says Rusty, almost jovial. He tips a bit of Southern Comfort into each mug. Rusty's chronic tonic.

Fox sips his bitter tea and stares at the dance of flames. The drone of the road seems to vibrate in him still. The night is thick as a blanket.

Why Wittenoom? asks Rusty.

Fox tells him about the old man and the asbestos mine. The mesothelioma and the monumental bastardry of the cover-up.

There was a Midnight Oil song, right?

Fox nods. He doesn't mention the dying, the actual way he went. The yellow slaughteryard eyes, the horrible swelling trunk. The falling down and liquid shitting and desperate respiration. In the end it was hospital. Lying there like a man being held down in a tub of water. Neck straining at the end of him as though he might get his head out and take a clean breath if only he pushed hard enough. But he was drowning anyway. And Fox sitting at the bedside too young to drive legally. Darkie and Sal waiting down in the carpark.

For revenge, says Rusty, I could understand it. But from what I heard there's nothin there, no one.

Rusty seems a long way off.

He said it was God's own country up here, says Fox. And I was headin north anyway—

What, *further* north?

Yeah, all the way.

Take you to Broome if you shout me the juice.

Fox shrugs. Orright, he murmurs. Spose it'd give the trip some shape.

Shape. Yeah. That's what I'm after. I'm gonna get shaped up in Broome.

Yeah? How's that?

Rusty starts grilling a couple of T-bones on an old fridge rack. Fox feels like he's looking at him from the other end of a drainpipe. Out beyond the firelight there's only blackness.

341

My fella in the Range Rover. He's in Broome this month.

How d'you know?

I paid someone.

Shit.

Mate, he purrs conspiratorially. I'm all organised. Gonna give *his* trip a new shape.

My lips are numb, says Fox at the very moment he thinks it.

Rusty snickers.

You put something in the tea.

Relax.

Shit.

Fox listens to the thousand tiny sounds of the hissing fat, the throbbing coals, the beef bones expanding in the heat.

Here.

Fox suddenly contemplates a hot steak on a torn strip of cardboard. His leg burns. He feels it, feels it.

Rusty's gnawed bone drops into the fire before Fox picks his up to begin. A sprinkle of ash settles on him as he eats.

When he's finished he turns to see Rusty in the open door of the Bedford with his jeans around his knees and a needle shoved into his thigh.

Morphine made me an orphine, says Rusty. So what's your excuse?

From a long way off the sound of a car. It's more road roar than engine noise; it rolls against the gorges and returns like backwashing surf. Fox sits and listens, watches Rusty as if through the wrong end of a telescope until lights bleach the mesa ahead and a motor eases into a coasting deceleration and a vicious grate of gears. In a blaze of headlights something pulls in nearby. As it wheels around on the gravelly pad Fox sees it's an old stationwagon, an EK. Someone, a woman, calls out.

Mind if we camp over here?

Suit yourself, says Rusty.

The car pulls away a few yards and the engine dies and the interior light appears yellow and feeble as doors open.

A man and two women wander over to the fire stretching and groaning as they come. The man has wild hair and a beard. Elastic-waisted pants, a shimmery waistcoat over his bare chest. They're barefoot. The women wear baggy cotton dresses, and jangly bangles.

G'day, says the man.

Where you headed? says Rusty.

Perth. Comin back from Darwin.

Long way.

Fox looks carefully at each woman's face. The fire twitches in their eyes; it lights up the studs in their noses and brows. They seem young, eighteen, twenty.

Quiet, isn't it? says one. Her arms in the sleeveless dress look downy.

Can we cook on your fire? says the other. Her hair is thick and tight with curls and it hangs down to her elbows and glistens in the firelight.

They bring a cast-iron pot already full of rice and vegetables to the edge of the coals and stir the slurry with a long steel spoon. Fox watches with a tired detachment.

Woman crouches, stirring, hair lit in flickers. Someone offers him the bong but he barely notices. Steely Dan in the Bedford. Lips tingle with pins and needles.

You don't say much, says the man.

Superior being, says Rusty.

We can dig that, says the girl with all the hair.

Fox gets up with infinite care and pukes his steak into the dirt behind the Bedford. When he straightens himself he discovers that he still has the greasy bone in his hand and he hoiks it into the darkness. Unsteady and slimed with sweat, he hauls his swag out of the van and drags it a little way beyond the firelight where he lies on the canvas and watches the dandruff drift of the sky.

The earth thrums beneath him, stirs with a thousand grinding clanks and groans like the deck of a ship in heavy weather. He feels it twist and flex and murmur and, deep down, between rivety stones, there's an endlessly repetitive vibration like a piston-chant foghorn drone. *Whorrr, whorrrr, whorrrrr.*

He surges in and out of darkness, sleep, stupor.

Two of them – Rusty and the girl with all the hair – backlit by the fire. On her knees in the dirt. Something glitters on her tongue. The surfer's dry crow laugh. Her hair in his fists.

Fox lies back with his throat scorched. The ground purrs against his skull. The dark, the hiss of static.

Sometime then, later perhaps, the girl or a girl is over the fender of the stationwagon, hair and arms lolling with Rusty upright and jerking like a shot man. Then so much yelling.

A small creature with eyes ablaze trembles beside his swag a moment and flees.

Silhouettes blur past the fire with screams propelling them. Fox rises incrementally to an elbow and summons a cry that never comes. Convulsion and confusion in the flickering half-light. The bearded man shirtless. Great gout of sparks as something crashes into the fire.

My pack, Fox thinks. I should have kept it by me.

The sound of breaking glass. Men and women screaming. And in the last seeable moment of the night, the sight of Rusty beating the stationwagon with his unstrapped leg like a madman flogging a dog. Fox falls back with flares and flashes beneath his eyelids. They crackle and buzz like neon. He sleeps, it seems. Lights out.

Fox wakes with the hot sun on his face, and when he shifts onto his side he sees a girl facedown in the dirt beside him, her cracked heels, the down on the back of her thighs a mist in the morning light. She smells of patchouli and sweat. The pattern of her cotton dress is a field of tiny shells in purple and white. For a long time he considers touching her but is afraid of what he might find; she's only half an arm away and his hand flutters back and forth until she finally breaks into a snore and his hand falls in relief. A posse of cockatoos passes shrieking overhead and the girl stirs. Her small, crushed and dirty face emerges.

Hello.

Hello, he croaks.

She rests her head on the edge of his swag. There are sticks in her hair and smears of red grime across one cheek. Her breath is bitter.

I'm Nora.

He nods and sees beyond her that the other car is gone. Rusty's arm hangs from the open door of the Bedford and his leg lies on the dirt nearby.

All around, the country is high and red. When Fox gets up he sees stars and his lips prickle. He finds a drum of water at the rear of the van and drinks greedily from it. He reaches into his pack, to discover that he hasn't been robbed.

Fox drives them through the gorge country. He feels like he's driving through a movie. A western. Mesas, buttes. Cliffs, gulches. Nora sits with lips parted, breathing through her mouth, only half awake. They don't talk. He feels queasy and anxious, uncertain about last night's proceedings but alive to the fact that she doesn't want to talk about it or anything else. From the moment they got up she's just acted as though she's along for the ride. He drives while Rusty sleeps in the back. The surfer wakes when they hit the rugged corrugations at the turn-in to Wittenoom.

In the gutted old settlement Fox steers them up paved streets with footpaths and remnant gardens but no houses. Almost everything has been pulled down and carted off to stop people living here. Front steps and concrete pads lie bare. Here and there a set of house stumps, a driveway. A forlorn school sign. Sections of low neighbourly fence, exotic trees, trellises with bougainvillea and jasmine wound through. A few people seem to have persisted but mostly it's just empty streets and health warnings. At the end of the last bare lane Fox pulls up on the cracked blacktop and gazes out at the canyon wall. Back up in there, he supposes, was where they mined the blue asbestos with it billowing in drifts all round them. When the old man was a sandy-haired young fella with a bookish wife at home and some land down south he had an eye on.

The Bedford idles. Above them the gorge rises like a breaking wave, red, purple, black.

Didn't expect it to be beautiful, says Fox, not meaning to say it aloud.

It's not, says Rusty. It's fuckin hot and dusty and the coons are welcome to it.

The girl looks back at Rusty then at Fox; she blinks.

Fox realises he's seen enough; more to the point he wants to go now.

346

The girl opens the door, climbs out and squats. Her piss bores against the stony earth.

Fucksake, growls Rusty.

Fox turns to look at him but says nothing. Rusty lies back on the foetid jumble in his leopard-skin jocks with his stump blunt and angry looking.

I'm hungry, says Nora climbing in and shutting the door on the heat. I could eat a horse.

Eat me, says Rusty.

You're a pig.

And it's my truck you're in, so fuckin watch yer mouth.

Fox turns the van around and winds his way back down the empty streets, busy driving to keep himself from saying anything.

What? yells Rusty. That's it? You come this far and that's all you wanna see? This is the place that killed his father and five minutes and a dose of hippy piss is all he gives it?

The girl looks at Fox, he can feel it but he doesn't meet her gaze as he drives on past the remnant dwellings of the diehards and out onto the corrugated red track to the highway.

Yer ole man must be proud.

Shut up, will you? says the girl over the battering of the suspension.

Suck my stump.

Yeah, sure.

And I'll fuck your big hippy rump.

God, you're low.

I'll pump and I'll pump and I'll pump and I'll pump—

Fox stuffs Steely Dan back into the deck and drowns Rusty out. After a time he sees the surfer in the rear-view mirror with a syringe stuck high in his leg again, lurching with the sway of the vehicle, and ten minutes later he's lolling back with his hand on his cock mouthing the words to the music.

Through the deep red ranges they clatter, below stony foothills stippled with snappy gums whose limbs are mere whiskers on the jowls of the great bluffs and buttes above them. Up there the clefts harbour shadows black enough to unnerve him. Sit here looking long enough, he thinks, and those shadows'd suck the mind right out of you. Just one indrawn breath from all those gill-like fissures. These ranges look to him like some dormant creature whose still-ness is only momentary, as though the sunblasted, dusty hide of the place might shudder and shake itself off, rise to its bowed and saurian feet and stalk away at any moment.

His thoughts reel on until at a sharp bend in the road Fox sees a solitary termite mound whose black shadow beats a path to its door. A moment later there are others, a whole colony of them. He brings the Bedford to a sliding halt.

You alright? says the girl Nora as he climbs out.

I just want to see this, he says as their pastel dust wake boils up and overtakes them. I'll only be a sec.

The hot air is thicker than dust. He strides out through bunches of spinifex to stand among the red monoliths. He puts his hands on the first one he comes to and feels the rendered form of the thing, traces the creases at its sides, hot to the touch. A spinifex pigeon takes wing nearby. The Bedford's horn begins to honk.

At the huge, bleak roadhouse the girl asks for rice. The woman behind the counter smirks. Back out on the highway Nora eats her pasty with a look of martyrdom. Back on his mattress Rusty sits with a silver thread of drool suspended from his chin.

They come down out of the brilliant gorges onto a vast savannah.

They cross the Fortescue River, and iron nubs and boulders begin to jut from the grassland.

Fox wonders if he should have made more of the stop at Wittenoom. He could have gone up to the minehead. But the old man would have thought him a bloody idiot. All that asbestos puffing up at every step. Be like an insult. Let the dead bury their dead – isn't that what he said?

For a long time he wants to talk to the girl, figure out what's what, but she seems impervious as a lizard to his frequent looks. Eventually when he's given up, she speaks.

He your mate?

You must be jokin, he says. I was just hitchin.

She nods and puts her bare feet on the dash. Air balloons her dress. She pegs it down with her hands.

You orright? he murmurs.

She shrugs.

D'you know where your friends went?

Perth, I guess. Amber had to get her kid.

Is that where you're headin?

Yeah.

Well, you're goin the wrong way. You know that?

She doesn't move.

Shit, he says.

A windblown tear rides off her cheek into her hair.

How old are you? he asks.

Sixteen.

God.

God? she laughs bitterly. God is sixteen. And she's a girl.

Well.

And men fuck her to death every day.

Look, he says, bewildered. We'll drop you at the next town.

You can get a bus. Port Hedland, I spose. You'll probably catch your mates.

The girl says nothing. Fox begins to notice graffiti on every outcrop.

The Great Northern Highway finally ends at the junction with Highway 1. Fox makes the turn. The low flat floodplain is bleached yellow, the colour of a dried biscuit. It feels coastal but the sea is not in sight. This stretch of road is festooned with shredded radials, beasts, beercans.

Welcome, Nora says, to the land of the big white bogan.

What?

Rednecks.

They plough on but the van feels motionless on the shimmering plain. Boredom eats at Fox. He writhes in his seat.

After the longest time, maybe half an hour, the saltpiles of Port Hedland rise above the plain. In the desolate outskirts of the iron port, a badlands of power pylons, railyards, steel towers and smokestacks, they pull into a roadhouse whose dirt forecourt is black with spilled diesel. Disassembled road-trains. Pre-fab buildings stained with iron dust. Hitchhikers sleeping beside cartons of Emu Bitter.

Fox pulls up beside the pump and peels off some money.

Here, he murmurs to Nora before Rusty stirs. Just hitch into town if the bus doesn't stop here.

She nods. She smells of mouldy towel. She takes the money and climbs out. The door closes with a thump.

Fuck, I need a piss, says Rusty. Where are we?

Hedland.

Shithole.

Been here before?

Nah. Where's the chick?

Gone for a leak, says Fox. Want me to fill it?

I'm not keepin you on for the company.

Fox gets out and pumps petrol while Rusty straps his leg on. They meet at the register.

Get some of that steak, says Rusty pointing out a whole vacuum-sealed fillet behind a beaded glass door. She likes meat, that chick.

Buy it yourself, says Fox, wishing he'd been the one to hide in the toilet. If it wasn't for the girl he'd be bailing out here. A child with a steaming plate of chips before her stares at Rusty's prosthesis. Under fluorescent lights it gleams a shocking pink against his floral board shorts.

No money.

It's too big.

Rusty scratches his scalp through the musty furrows of his dreadlocks. Through the window Fox sees Nora climbing back into the Bedford. The miserable dumpy girl behind the register sighs dramatically.

We'll have the porterhouse, love. Ring it up.

Fox pays and carries the meat out cold against his chest.

Nora doesn't even look at him as he climbs in.

He drives, his anger giving out to desolation. The two-storey roadsigns don't help. Perth is 1650 kilometres south and Kununurra the same distance north. Halfway feels like no way.

For a while there is the consolation of the grand mesas that rise from the ravaged floodplain but they give out onto the same dreary flatlands with grim, narrow creeks.

Fox drives with odd flashes erupting behind his eyes.

The De Grey River, brown and wide on its tree-strewn banks, gives a moment's respite as they fly across the bridge.

Rusty rolls a joint and shares it with Nora. She tokes on it with feeling. Fox's lips tingle and for a few minutes one of his legs trembles. No one speaks. The fungal smell of dope fills the van.

Fox drives.

The two in the back rustle in the stash bag.

The plain, the plain, the plain.

Rusty begins to sneeze.

Fox knows it's cattle country by the dead bullocks, but he hasn't seen a live beast yet. This far north there are no fences. He has cramps with the flashes now.

All along the roadside are the remains of campfires, strewn empties, rubbish. From the north the Landcruisers and Cherokees drag their loads. It's like a column of well-heeled refugees. Fox needs to stop. He has to get out.

At Pardoo he pulls in. It's just a fuel pump and van park. He climbs out and reefs his kit from under the surfer in the back. Rusty lolls, slit-eyed. The pack smells of him as Fox pulls it on.

You wamme to fill it? asks a crewcut woman through her teeth.

That turn-off go to the coast? says Fox.

Yeah. You want petrol or not?

Ask him.

Thanks for nothin, says Nora.

Fox walks fast until he finds a rhythm. The air is woolly. Sweat leaves him purblind. He thinks of the hat but the sun is low. The mulga scrub is thin and burnt on the gravel track either side of him. There are no trees in sight. He is the tallest thing on the plain.

After a long time he hears a motor and the sound of spitting gravel. He moves over, doesn't stick his hand out. Hears the vehicle slow behind him.

You forgot something, says the girl from the driver's window.

It hits him in the belly and knocks him winded to his knees and when the van finishes its dirt spraying U-turn and its brief wallow in the mulga scrub on its way back to the highway, he finds the vacuum-sealed parcel of porterhouse in the dust by his knees. He gets his breath back. He picks it up, hauls himself upright and presses on into the sunset and the gathering mosquitoes.

From *Dirt Music* (2001)

LONE PINE

David Malouf

Driving at speed along the narrow dirt highway, Harry Picton could have given no good reason for stopping where he did. There was a pine. Perhaps it was that – its deeper green and conical form among the scrub a reminder out here of the shapeliness and order of gardens, though this particular pine was of the native variety.

May was sleeping. For the past hour, held upright by her seat-belt, she had been nodding off and waking, then nodding off again like a comfortable baby. Harry was used to having her doze beside him. He liked to read at night, May did not. It made the car, which was heavy to handle because of the swaying behind of the caravan, as familiar almost as their double bed.

Driving up here was dreamlike. As the miles of empty country fell away with nothing to catch the eye, no other vehicle or sign of habitation, your head lightened and cleared itself – of thoughts, of images, of every wish or need. Clouds filled the windscreen. You floated.

The clouds up here were unreal. They swirled up so densely and towered to such an infinite and unmoving height that driving, even at a hundred k's an hour, was like crawling along at the bottom of a tank.

A flash of grey and pink flared up out of a dip in the road. Harry jerked the wheel. Galahs! They might have escaped from a dozen backyard cages, but were common up here. They were after water. There must have been real water back there that he had taken for the usual mirage. Like reflections of the sky, which was pearly at this hour and flushed with coral, they clattered upwards and went streaming away behind.

'May,' he called. But before she was properly awake they were gone.

'Sorry, love,' she muttered. 'Was it something good?'

Still half-asleep, she reached into the glovebox for a packet of lollies, unwrapped one, passed it to him, then unwrapped another and popped it into her mouth. Almost immediately she was dozing again with the lolly in her jaw, its cherry colour seeping through into her dreams.

They were on a trip, the first real trip they had ever taken, the trip of their lives.

Back in Hawthorn they had a paper run. Seven days a week and twice on weekdays, Harry tossed the news over people's fences on to the clipped front lawns: gun battles in distant suburbs, raids on marijuana plantations, bank holdups, traffic accidents, baby bashings, the love lives of the stars.

He knew the neighbourhood – he had to: how to get around it by the quickest possible route. He had got that down to a fine art. Conquest of Space, it was called, just as covering it all twelve times a week in an hour and a quarter flat was the Fight against Time. He had reckoned it up once. In twenty-seven years bar a few months he had made his round on ten thousand seven hundred occasions in twelve thousand man-hours, and done a distance of a hundred thousand miles. That is, ten times round Australia. Those were the figures.

But doing it that way, piecemeal, twice a day, gave you no idea of what the country really was: the distances, the darkness, the changes as you slipped across unmarked borders.

Birds that were exotic down south, like those galahs, were everywhere up here, starting up out of every tree. The highways were a way of life with their own population: hitch-hikers, truckies, itinerant fruit-pickers and other seasonal workers of no fixed address, bikies loaded up behind and wearing space helmets, families with all their belongings packed into a station wagon and a little girl in the back waving or sticking out her tongue, or a boy putting up two fingers in the shape of a gun and mouthing Bang, Bang, You're Dead, kids in panel-vans with a couple of surfboards on the rack chasing the ultimate wave. Whole tribes that for one reason or another had never settled. Citizens of a city the size of Hobart or Newcastle that was always on the move. For three months (that was the plan), he and May had come out to join them.

Back in Hawthorn a young fellow and his wife were giving the paper run a go. For five weeks now, their home in Ballard Crescent had been locked up, empty, ghosting their presence with a lighting system installed by the best security firm in the state that turned the lights on in the kitchen, just as May did, regular as clockwork, at half-past five; then, an hour later, lit the lamp in their living-room and flicked on the TV; then turned the downstairs lights off again at nine and a minute later lit the reading lamp (just the one) on Harry's side of the bed in the front bedroom upstairs.

Harry had spent a good while working out this pattern and had been surprised at how predictable their life was, what narrow limits they moved in. It hadn't seemed narrow. Now, recalling the smooth quilt of their bed and the reading lamp being turned on, then off again, by ghostly hands, he chuckled. It'd be more difficult to keep track of their movements up here.

There was no fixed programme – they took things as they came. They were explorers, each day pushing on into unknown country. No place existed till they reached it and decided to stop.

'Here we are, mother,' Harry would say, 'home sweet home. How does it look?' – and since it was seldom a place that was named on the map they invented their own names according to whatever little event or accident occurred that made it memorable – Out-of-Nescaf Creek, Lost Tin-opener, One Blanket Plains – and before they drove off again Harry would mark the place on their road map with a cross.

This particular spot, as it rose out of the dusk, had already named itself. Lone Pine it would be, unless something unexpected occurred.

'Wake up, mother,' he said as the engine cut. 'We're there.'

Two hours later they were sitting over the remains of their meal. The petrol lamp hissed, casting its light into the surrounding dark. A few moths barged and dithered. An animal, attracted by the light or the unaccustomed scent, had crept up to the edge of a difference they made in the immemorial tick and throb of things, and could be heard just yards off in the grass. No need to worry. There were no predators out here.

Harry was looking forward to his book. To transporting himself, for the umpteenth time, to Todgers, in the company of Cherry and Merry and Mr Pecksniff, and the abominable Jonas – he had educated himself out of Dickens. May, busily scrubbing their plates in a minimum of water, was as usual telling something. He did not listen.

He had learned over the years to finish the Quick Crossword while half tuned in to her running talk, or to do his orders without making a single blue. It was like having the wireless on, a comfortable noise that brought you bits and pieces of news. In May's case, mostly of women's complaints. She knew an inordinate number of women who had found lumps in their breast and gone under the knife, or lost kiddies, or had their husbands go off with younger women. For some reason she felt impelled to lay at his feet these victims of life's grim injustice, or of men's unpredictable cruelty, as if, for all his mildness, he too were one of the guilty. As, in her new vision of things, he was. They all were.

Three years ago she had discovered, or rediscovered, the church – not her old one, but a church of a newer and more personal sort – and had been trying ever since to bring Harry in.

She gave him her own version of confessions she had heard people make of the most amazing sins and of miraculous conversions and cures. She grieved over the prospect of their having, on the last day, to go different ways, the sheep's path or the goat's. She evoked in terms that distressed him a Lord Jesus who seemed to stand on pretty much the same terms in her life as their cats, Peach and Snowy, or her friends from the Temple, Eadie and Mrs McVie, except that she saw Him, Harry felt, as a secret child now grown to difficult manhood that she had never told him about and who sat between them, invisible but demanding, at every meal.

Harry, who would have defended her garrulous piety against all comers, regarded it himself as a blessed shame. She was a good woman spoiled.

Now, when she started up again, he vanished into himself, and while she chattered on in the background, slipped quietly away.

Down the back steps to his veggies, to be on his own for a bit. To feel in his hands the special crumbliness and moisture of the soil down there and watch, as at a show, the antics of the lighting system in their empty house, ghosting their lives to fool burglars who might not be fooled.

Harry woke. His years on the paper run had made him a light sleeper. But with no traffic sounds to give the clue, no night-trains passing, you lost track. When he looked at his watch it was just eleven.

He got up, meaning to slip outside and take a leak. But when he set his hand to the doorknob, with the uncanniness of a dream-happening, it turned of its own accord.

The young fellow who stood on the step was as startled as Harry was.

In all that emptiness, with not a house for a hundred miles in any direction and in the dead of night, they had come at the same moment to opposite sides of the caravan door: Harry from sleep, this youth in the open shirt from – but Harry couldn't imagine where he had sprung from. They faced one another like sleepers whose dreams had crossed, and the youth, to cover his amazement, said 'Hi' and gave a nervous giggle.

He was blond, with the beginnings of a beard. Below him in the dark was a woman with a baby. She was rocking it in a way that struck Harry as odd. She looked impatient. At her side was a boy of ten or so, sucking his thumb.

'What is it?' Harry asked, keeping his voice low so as not to wake May. 'Are you lost?'

He had barely formulated the question, which was meant to fit this midnight occasion to a world that was normal, a late call by neighbours who were in trouble, when the young man showed his hand. It held a gun.

Still not convinced of the absolute reality of what was happening, Harry stepped back into the narrow space between their stove and the dwarf refrigerator, and in a moment they were all in there with him – the youth, the woman with the baby, the boy, whose loud-mouthed breathing was the only sound among them. Harry's chief concern still was that they should not wake May.

The gunman was a good-looking young fellow of maybe twenty. He wore boardshorts and a shirt with pineapples on a background that had once been red but showed threads now of a paler colour from too much washing. He was barefoot, but so scrubbed and clean that you could smell the soap on him under the fresh sweat. He was sweating.

The woman was older. She too was barefoot, but what you thought in her case was that she lacked shoes.

As for the ten-year-old, with his heavy lids and open-mouthed, asthmatic breathing, they must simply have found him somewhere along the way. He resembled neither one of them and looked as if he had fallen straight off the moon. He clung to the woman's skirt, and was, Harry decided, either dog-tired or some sort of dill. He had his thumb in his mouth and his eyelids fluttered as if he was about to fall asleep on his feet.

'Hey,' the youth said, suddenly alert.

Down at the sleeping end, all pink and nylon-soft in her ruffles, May had sat bolt upright.

'Harry,' she said accusingly, 'what are you doing? Who are those people?'

'It's all right, love,' he told her.

'Harry,' she said again, only louder.

The youth gave his nervous giggle. 'All right,' he said, 'you can get outa there.'

Not yet clear about the situation, May looked at Harry.

'Do as he says,' Harry told her mildly.

Still tender from sleep, she began to grope for her glasses, and he felt a wave of odd affection for her. She had been preparing to give this young fellow a serve.

'You can leave those,' the youth told her. 'I said *leave 'em*! Are you deaf or what?'

She saw the gun then, and foggily, behind this brutal boy in the red shirt, the others, the woman with the baby.

'Harry,' she said breathlessly, 'who *are* these people?'

He took a step towards her. It was, he knew, her inability to see properly that most unnerved her. Looking past the man, which was a way also of denying the presence of the gun, she addressed the shadowy woman, but her voice had an edge to it. 'What is it?' she asked. 'Is your baby sick?'

The woman ignored her. Rocking the baby a little, she turned away and told the youth fiercely: 'Get it over with, will ya? Get 'em outa here.'

May, who had spoken as woman to woman, was deeply offended. But the woman's speaking up at last gave life to the boy.

'I'm hungry,' he whined into her skirt. 'Mummy? I'm hungreee!' His eye had caught the bowl of fruit on their fold-up table. 'I wanna banana!'

'Shuddup, Dale,' the woman told him, and put her elbow into his head.

'You can have a banana, dear,' May told him.

She turned to the one with the gun.

'Can he have a banana?'

The child looked up quickly, then grabbed.

'Say ta to the nice lady, Dale,' said the youth, in a voice rich with mockery.

But the boy, who really was simple-minded, lowered the banana, gaped a moment, and said sweetly: 'Thank you very much.'

The youth laughed outright.

'Now,' he said, and there was no more humour, 'get over here.'

He made way for them and they passed him while the woman and the boy, who was occupied with the peeling of his banana, passed behind. So now it was May and Harry who were squeezed in at the entrance end.

'Right,' the youth said. 'Now—' He was working up the energy in himself. He seemed afraid it might lapse. 'The car keys. Where are they?'

Harry felt a rush of hot anger.

Look, feller, he wanted to protest, I paid thirty-three thousand bucks for that car. You just fuck off. But May's hand touched his elbow, and instead he made a gesture towards the fruit bowl where the keys sat – now, why do we keep them there? – among the apples and oranges.

'Get 'em, Lou.'

The woman hitched the baby over her shoulder so that it stirred and burbled, and was just about to reach for the keys when she saw what the boy was up to and let out a cry. 'Hey you, Dale, leave that, you little bugger. I said leave it!'

She made a swipe at him, but the boy, who was more agile than he looked, ducked away under the youth's arm, crowing and waving a magazine.

'Fuck you, Dale,' the woman shouted after him.

In her plunge to cut him off she had woken the baby, which now began to squall, filling the constricted space of the caravan with screams.

'Shut it up, willya?' the youth told her. 'And you, Dale, belt up, or I'll clip y' one. Gimme that.' He made a grab for the magazine, but the boy held on. 'I said, give it to me!'

'No, Kenny, no, it's mine. I found it.'

They struggled, the man cursing, and at last he wrenched it away. The boy yowled, saying over and over with a deep sense of grievance: 'It's not fair, it's not fair, Kenny. I'm the one that found it. It's mine.'

Harry was flooded with shame. The youth, using the gun, was turning the pages of the thing.

'Someone left it in a cafe,' Harry explained weakly. 'Under a seat.'

The youth was incensed. He blazed with indignation. 'See this, Lou? See what the kid found?'

But the woman gave him only the briefest glance. She was preoccupied with the baby. Moving back and forth in the space between the bunks, she was rocking the child and sweet-talking it in the wordless, universal dialect, somewhere between syllabic spell-weaving and an archaic drone, that women fall into on such occasions and which sets them impressively apart. The others were hushed. May, lowering her voice to a whisper, said: 'Look here, if you're in some sort of trouble – I mean—' She indicated the gun. 'There's no need of that.'

But the youth had a second weapon now. 'You shut up,' he told her fiercely. 'Just you shut up. You're the ones who've got trouble. What about this, then?' and he shook the magazine at her.

She looked briefly, then away. She understood the youth's outrage because she shared it. When he held the thing out to her she shook her head, but he was implacable.

'I said, look!' he hissed.

Because of the woman's trouble with the baby he had lowered

his voice again, but the savagery of it was terrible. He brandished the thing in her face and Harry groaned.

'Is this the sort of thing you people are into?'

But the ten-year-old, excited now beyond all fear of chastisement, could no longer contain himself.

'I seen it,' he crowed.

'Shuddup, Dale.'

'I seen it . . .'

'I'll knock the bloody daylights out of you if you don't belt up!'

'A cunt, it's a cunt. Cunt, cunt, cunt!'

When the youth hit him he fell sideways, howling, and clutched his ear.

'There,' the youth said in a fury, swinging back to them, 'you see what you made me do? Come here, Dale, and stop whinging. Come on. Come on here.' But the boy had fled to his mother's skirts and was racked with sobs. The baby shrieked worse than ever. 'Jesus,' the youth shouted, 'you make me sick! Dale,' he said, 'come here, mate, I didn't mean it, eh? Come here.'

The boy met his eye and after a moment moved towards him, still sniffling. The youth put his hand on the back of the child's neck and drew him in. 'There,' he said. 'Now, you're not hurt, are you?' The boy, his thumb back in his mouth, leaned into him. The youth sighed.

'Look here,' May began. But before she could form another word the youth's arm shot out, an edge of metal struck her, and 'Oh God,' she said as she went down.

'That's enough out of you,' the youth was yelling. 'That's the last *you* get to say.'

She thought Harry was about to move, and she put out her hand to stop him. 'No, no,' she shouted, 'don't. It's all right – I'm all right.' The youth, in a kind of panic now, was pushing the gun into the soft of Harry's belly. May, on her knees, tasted salt, put her fingers to her mouth and felt blood.

'All right, now,' the youth was saying. He was calming himself, he calmed. But she could smell his sweat. 'You can get up now. We're going outside.'

She looked up then and saw that it made no difference that he was calm. That there was a baby here and that the mother was concerned to get it to sleep. Or that he was so clean-looking, and strict.

She got to her feet without help and went past him on her own legs, though wobbling a little, down the one step into the dark.

The tropical night they had stepped into had a softness that struck Harry like a moment out of his boyhood.

There were stars. They were huge, and so close and heavy-looking that you wondered how they could hold themselves up.

It seemed so personal, this sky. He thought of stepping out as a kid to take a piss from the back veranda and as he sent his jet this way and that looking idly for Venus, or Aldebaran, or the Cross. I could do with a piss right now, he thought, I really need it. It's what I got up for.

They were like little mirrors up there. That's what he had some-times thought as he came out in the winter dark to load up for his round. If you looked hard enough, every event that was being enacted over all this side of the earth, even the smallest, would be reflected there. Even this one, he thought.

He took May's hand and she clutched it hard. He felt her weight go soft against him.

The youth was urging them on over rough terrain towards a patch of darker scrub further in from the road. Sometimes behind them, but most often half-turned and waiting ahead, he could barely contain his impatience at their clumsiness as, heavy and tender-footed, they moved at a jolting pace over the stony ground. When May caught her nightie on a thorn and Harry tried to detach it, the youth made a hissing sound and came back and ripped it clear.

No words passed between them. Harry felt a terrible longing to have the youth speak again, say something. Words you could measure. You knew where they were tending. With silence you were in the open with no limits. But when the fellow stopped at last and turned and stood waiting for them to catch up, it wasn't a particular point in the silence that they had come to. A place thirty yards back might have done equally well, or thirty or a hundred yards further on. Harry saw with clarity that the distance the youth had been measuring had to do with his reluctance to get to the point, and was in himself.

The gun hung at the end of his arm. He seemed drained now of all energy.

'All right,' he said hoarsely, 'this'll do. Over here.'

It was May he was looking at.

'Yes,' he told her. 'You.'

Harry felt her let go of his hand then, as the youth had directed, but knew she had already parted from him minutes back, when she had begun, with her lips moving in silence, to pray. She took three steps to where the youth was standing, his face turned away now, and Harry stretched his hand out towards her.

'May,' he said, but only in his head.

It was the beginning of a sentence that if he embarked on it, and were to say all he wanted her to know and understand in justification of himself and of what he felt, would have no end. The long tale of his inadequacies. Of resolutions unkept, words unspoken, demands whose crudeness, he knew, had never been acceptable to her but which for him were one form of his love – the most urgent, the most difficult. Little phrases and formulae that were not entirely without meaning just because they were common and had been so often repeated.

She was kneeling now, her nightie rucked round her thighs. The youth leaned towards her. Very attentive, utterly concentrated. Her fingers touched the edge of his pineapple shirt.

Harry watched immobilised, and the wide-eyed, faraway look she cast back at him recalled something he had seen on television, a baby seal about to be clubbed. An agonised cry broke from his throat.

But she was already too far off. She shook her head, as if this were the separation she had all this time been warning him of. Then went back to *him*.

He leaned closer and for a moment they made a single figure. He whispered something to her that Harry, whose whole being strained towards it, could not catch.

The report was sharp, close, not loud.

'Mayyeee,' Harry cried again, out of a dumb, inconsolable grief that would last now for the rest of his life, and an infinite regret, not only for her but for all those women feeling for the lump in their breast, and the ones who had lost kiddies, and those who had never had them and for that boy sending his piss out in an exuberant stream into the dark, his eyes on Aldebaran, and for the last scene at Todgers, that unruly Eden, which he would never get back to now, and for his garden choked with weeds. He meant to hurl himself at the youth. But before he could do so was lifted clean off his feet by a force greater than anything he could ever have imagined, and rolled sideways among stones that after a moment cut hard into his cheek. They were a surprise, those stones. Usually he was careful about them. Bad for the mower.

He would have flung his arms out then to feel for her comfortable softness in the bed, but the distances were enormous and no fence in any direction.

Her name was still in his mouth. Warm, dark, filling it, flowing out.

The youth stood. He was a swarming column. His feet had taken root in the earth.

Darkness was trembling away from the metal, which was hot and hung down from the end of his arm. The force it contained had flung these two bodies down at angles before him and was pulsing away in circles to the edges of the earth.

He tilted his head up. There were stars. Their living but dead light beat down and fell weakly upon him.

He looked towards the highway. The car. Behind it the caravan. Lou and the kids in a close group, waiting.

He felt too heavy to move. There was such a swarming in him. Every drop of blood in him was pressing against the surface of his skin – in his hands, his forearms with their gorged veins, his belly, the calves of his legs, his feet on the stony ground. Every drop of it holding him by force of gravity to where he stood, and might go on standing till dawn if he couldn't pull himself away. Yet he had no wish to step on past this moment, to move away from it into whatever was to come.

But the moment too was intolerable. If he allowed it to go on any longer he would be crushed.

He launched himself at the air and broke through into the next minute that was waiting to carry him on. Then turned to make sure that he wasn't still standing there on the spot.

He made quickly now for the car and the group his family made, dark and close, beside the taller darkness of the pine.

(2000)

A HAPPY STORY

Helen Garner

I turn forty-one. I buy the car. I drive it to the river bank and park it under a tree. The sun is high and the grass on the river bank is brown. It is the middle of the morning. I turn my back on the river and walk along the side of the Entertainment Centre until I find a door. I am the only person at the counter. The air inside is cool. The attendant has his feet up on a desk in the back room. He sees me, and comes out to serve me.

'Two tickets to Talking Heads,' I say.

He spins the seating plan round to face me. I look at it. I can't understand where the band will stand to play. I can't believe that the Entertainment Centre is not still full of water, is not still the Olympic Pool where, in 1956, Hungary played water polo against the USSR and people said there was blood in the water. What have they done with all the water? Pumped it out into the river that flows past two hundred yards away: let it run down to the sea.

I buy the tickets. They cost nearly twenty dollars each. I drive home the long way, in my car which is almost new.

I give the tickets to my kid. She crouches by the phone in her pointed shoes. Her friends are already going, are going to Simple

Minds, are not allowed, have not got twenty dollars. It will have to be me.

'I can't *wait*,' says my kid every morning in her school uniform. The duty of going: I feel its weight. 'What will you wear?' she says.

I'm too old. I won't have the right clothes. It will start too late. The warm-up bands will be terrible. It'll hurt my ears. I'll get bored and spoil it for her. I'll get bored. I'll get bored. I'll get bored.

I sell my ticket to my sister. My daughter tries to be seemly about her exhilaration. My sister is a saxophone player. Her hair is fluffy, her arms are brown, she will bring honour upon my daughter in a public place. She owns a tube of waxed cotton ear-plugs. She arrives, perfumed, slow-moving, with gracious smiles.

We stop for petrol. My daughter gets out too, as thin as a clothes peg in narrow black garments, and I show her how to use the dip-stick. My sister sits in the car laughing. 'You look so like each other,' she says, 'specially when you're doing something together and aren't aware of being watched.'

On Punt Road the car in front of us dawdles.

'Come on, fuckhead,' says my sister.

I accelerate with a smooth surge and change lanes.

'Helen!' says my sister beside me. 'I didn't know you were such a *reckless driver!*'

'She's not,' says my daughter from the back seat. 'She's only faking.'

My regret at having sold the ticket does not begin until I turn right off Punt Road into Swan Street and see the people walking along in groups towards the Entertainment Centre. They are happy. They are going to shout, to push past the bouncers and run down the front to dance. They are dressed up wonderfully, they almost skip as they walk. Shafts of light fire out from the old Olympic Pool into the darkening air. Men in white coats are waving the cars into the parking area.

'We'll get out here,' says my sister.

They kiss me goodbye, grinning, and scamper across the road. I do a U-turn and drive back to Punt Road. I shove in the first cassette my hand falls on. It is Elisabeth Schwarzkopf: she is singing a joyful song by Strauss. I do not understand the words but the chorus goes '*Habe Dank!*' The light is weird, there is a storminess, it is not yet dark enough for headlights. I try to sing like a soprano. My voice cracks, she sings too high for me, but as I fly up the little rise beside the Richmond football ground I say out loud, 'This is it. I am finally on the far side of the line.' *Habe Dank!*

(1985)

NOTES ON THE AUTHORS

Barbara Baynton (1857–1929) was born in Scone, NSW. The author of the novel *The Human Toll*, and a contributor to *The Bulletin*, she is most famous for her short story collection *Bush Studies* (1902), which offers an unromantic vision of the harshness of life in the Australian bush, especially for women. She became Lady Headley upon her brief 1921 marriage to Rowland George Alanson-Winn, fifth baron Headley.

Rolf Boldrewood (1826–1915) was the pen name of Thomas Alexander Browne, who arrived in Australia in 1831 when his father, a sea captain, delivered a cargo of convicts to Hobart Town. He worked as a headmaster, then pastoralist and justice of the peace, earning extra income through articles and serialised novels. His most well-known work is the bushranging novel *Robbery Under Arms* (1888).

As well as a short-fiction writer (*The Book of Sei*, *Sheep and the Diva*, *Black Sea*), **David Brooks** is a poet (*Walking to Point Clear*, *Urban*

Elegies, The Balcony) and novelist (*The House of Balthus, The Fern Tattoo*). His work has been widely anthologisd, and has been translated into several languages. He teaches Australian Literature at the University of Sydney, where he also directs the Graduate Program in Creative Writing, and is co-editor of *Southerly*.

Robert Bropho is a Nyungah elder from Western Australia. He is the author of *Fringedweller*.

Peter Carey was born in 1943 in Bacchus Marsh, Victoria where his parents ran a car dealership. After a successful career in advertising, he began to write acclaimed short stories and novels. Two – *Oscar and Lucinda* and *The True History of the Kelly Gang* – have won the Booker Prize. He lives in New York.

Robert Drewe was born in Melbourne and grew up on the West Australian coast. His ten novels and story collections, and his prize-winning memoir *The Shark Net*, have been widely translated, won many national and international awards, and been adapted for film, television, radio and the theatre around the world.

Delia Falconer is the author of two novels, *The Service of Clouds* (1997) and *The Lost Thoughts of Soldiers* (2005, republished as *The Lost Thoughts of Soldiers and Selected Stories* in 2006.) Her award-winning essays and short stories have been widely anthologised, including in *The Penguin Century of Australian Stories*. She lives in Sydney.

Miles Franklin was the pen name of Stella Maria (Marian) Sarah Miles Franklin (1879–1954) who also wrote as 'Brent of Bin Bin'. Her novels, including *My Brilliant Career* (1901) and *My Career*

Goes Bung (1946), are notable for their early feminism and nationalism. Her bequest still funds the Miles Franklin Literary Award, Australia's most prestigious literary prize.

Helen Garner was born in Geelong in 1942. Her award-winning books include novels, stories, screenplays and works of non-fiction including *The First Stone* (1995) and *Joe Cinque's Consolation* (2004). *The Spare Room* (2008) is her first work of fiction for fifteen years.

Author and essayist **William Gosse Hay** (1875–1945) was born in Adelaide. His works include the novels *Herridge of Reality Swamp* (1907), *Captain Quadring* (1912) and *The Escape of the Notorious Sir William Heans* (1919), along with *An Australian Rip Van Winkle and Other Pieces*, a collection of essays and stories.

Dorothy Hewett (1923–2002) grew up on an isolated wheat farm in Western Australia. By the time she was twenty she was a prize-winning playwright and poet. She was the author of three novels, an autobiography, thirteen plays and twelve collections of poetry.

Robert Hughes was born in Australia in 1938. He lived in Italy and Britain in the 1960s, but in 1970 made his home in America, where he was appointed art critic for *Time*. His books include monographs on the painters Lucian Freud and Frank Auerbach, a history of Australian art, *Heaven and Hell in Western Art* (1969), *The Shock of the New* (1981), *The Fatal Shore* (1987), a collection of reviews, *Nothing if Not Critical* (1990), *Barcelona* (1992) and a book of social criticism, *The Culture of Complaint* (1995). Prior to *Things I Didn't Know*, his most recent book was a biography of Goya.

Linda Jaivin is the author of five novels, including the international bestseller *Eat Me* and *The Infernal Optimist,* as well as the collection of essays *Confessions of an S&M Virgin* and the China memoir *The Monkey and the Dragon.* She doesn't drive but she knows how to travel.

Clive James is the author of more than thirty books. As well as essays and novels, he has published collections of literary and television criticism, travel writing and verse, plus four volumes of autobiography. As a television performer he has appeared regularly for both the BBC and ITV, most notably as writer and presenter of the *Postcard* series of travel documentaries. He helped to found the independent television company Watchmaker, and the Internet enterprise Welcome Stranger, one of whose offshoots is a multimedia personal website, www.clivejames.com. In 1992 he was made a Member of the Order of Australia, and in 2003 he was awarded the Philip Hodgins Memorial Medal for literature.

Malcolm Knox is the author of seven books including the novels *Summerland, A Private Man* and *Jamaica.* His worst childhood memories are of sitting in the back of his parents' car in summer on the Pacific Highway and needing to go to the toilet.

David Malouf was born in Brisbane in 1934. He is the author of several collections of poetry and short stories, and ten works of fiction including *Johnno, The Great World* and *Remembering Babylon,* which won the first Dublin International IMPAC Prize. He lives in Sydney.

Gillian Mears grew up on the NSW north coast. Writing since she was twenty, she has received many prizes and awards including the

Australian/Vogel Literary Award in 1990 for her novel *The Mint Lawn*. Her other books include *Fineflour* and *The Grass Sister*. Her most recent book is the collection of short stories *A Map of the Gardens*. It was awarded the Steele Rudd Award in 2003.

Major Sir Thomas Livingston Mitchell (1792–1855) was surveyor-general of NSW. From 1831–32 he led an exploratory expedition to the north of the state, and two to the west in 1835 and 1836. His account of these journeys was published as *Three Expeditions Into the Interior of Eastern Australia*.

Frank Moorhouse is the author of the prize-winning historical novels, *Grand Days* and *Dark Palace* which have as their background the rise of modern diplomacy and the failure of the League of Nations to prevent World War II. In 2007 his essay 'The Writer in a Time of Terror' won both the Walkley Award and Alfred Deakin prize for Best Essay. Random House is currently republishing Frank Moorhouse's twelve earlier books as 'The Moorhouse Collection'.

D'Arcy Niland (1917–1967) was a prolific writer of short stories, radio scripts and jingles and began to write novels in 1948. He and his wife, novelist Ruth Park, often wrote passionately about the lives of the working classes. Niland's best-loved novel is *The Shiralee* (1955), an international bestseller, which was made into a film in 1957.

Peter Rose grew up in country Victoria. He is the author of five poetry collections, a novel, *A Case of Knives* (2005), and a family memoir, *Rose Boys* (2001), which won the National Biography Award in 2002. During the 1990s he was Oxford University Press's trade and reference publisher. He is currently the editor of *Australian Book Review*.

Christina Stead (1902–1983) was born in Sydney. She was the author of several short-story collections and novellas, and eleven novels including *Seven Poor Men of Sydney, House of All Nations, The Man Who Loved Children* and *For Love Alone*. She left Australia in 1928 and did not return until 1969.

Theodor George Henry Strehlow (1908-1978) was the youngest child of German-born Lutheran missionaries, Friedericke Johanna Henriette and Carl Friedrich Theodor Strehlow, who took over the Finke River Mission at Hermannsburg in the Northern Territory in 1894. Growing up among the Western Aranda, T. G. H. Strehlow later became a linguist and scholar of Aboriginal culture. In 1922, Carl Strehlow, suffering from dropsy, endured an agonising journey toward medical help in Adelaide in a horse-drawn cart, which ended at Horseshoe Bend. T. G. H. Strehlow's book, *Journey To Horsehoe Bend*, recalls this nightmare journey.

Roberta Sykes was born in the 1940s in Townsville and is one of Australia's best known activists for Aboriginal rights. She received both her Masters and Doctorate of Education at Harvard University, has been a consultant to the NSW Department of Corrective Services, including the Royal Commission into Aboriginal Deaths in Custody, was the Chairperson of the Promotions Appeals Tribunal at the ABC, and is the author of several books, including *Love Poems And Other Revolutionary Actions* (1979), *Mumshirl* (1981) and the three-book autobiography *Snake Dreaming*. She has contributed to or co-authored numerous publications, journal articles, conference papers and screenplays.

Kylie Tennant (1912–1988) was a novelist, playwright, historian and short-story writer. She was best known for her interest in people on the fringes of Australian society and her immersion method of research. She camped with the unemployed on Australia's roads during the Great Depression – an experience she mined for her best-loved novel, *The Battlers* – travelled with itinerant beekeepers, and spent time with Aboriginal communities.

Brenda Walker has written four novels. The most recent is *The Wing of Night*, which was shortlisted for the Miles Franklin Award in 2006 and won the Nita B. Kibble Award in 2006 and the Asher Award in 2007. She is an Associate Professor in English and Cultural Studies at the University of Western Australia.

Patrick West lives on the Gold Coast and is Senior Lecturer in Writing in the School of Arts at Griffith University. He publishes essays, literary journalism and short fiction and is currently co-writing a feature-length screenplay.

Tara June Winch was born near Sydney in 1983. She is of Wiradjuri, Afghan and English heritage. Her first novel, *Swallow the Air*, has won the David Unaipon Award for Indigenous Writers, the Victorian Premier's Literary Award for Indigenous Literature, the NSW Premier's Literary Award for New Writing, the Dobbie Award for Women's First Writing, and has been shortlisted for the *Age* Book of the Year and the Queensland Premier's Literary Award. She is ambassador for Indigenous Literacy Day, sits on the Australia Council Board for Aboriginal and Torres Strait Islander Arts, works as a freelance writer and lives with her darling daughter Lila on the beach. Tara was named a *Sydney Morning Herald* Best Young Australian Novelist in 2007.

Tim Winton is the author of twenty books for adults and children. He has won the Miles Franklin award three times and has twice been shortlisted for the Booker Prize. His latest novel is *Breath*, published by Penguin in 2008.

ACKNOWLEDGEMENTS

I wish to thank Sandy Webster for the idea and Robert Sessions for his enthusiastic support of this project. My thanks also to Peg McColl and Jessica Crouch at Penguin Books, and Martin Thomas for pointing me to 'The Search for Mr Cunningham'.

The editor and publisher are grateful to the following writers, agents and publishers for permission to reproduce their stories in this anthology:

'The Line' by David Brooks, from *The Book of Sei*, Hale & Iremonger, Sydney, 1985.

'The Great Journey of the Aboriginal Teenagers' by Robert Bropho, from *Issue Magazine*, vol. 1, issue 3, Spring/Summer 1985. Reproduced by permission of UQP.

'American Dreams' by Peter Carey, copyright © 1974 Peter Carey. Reproduced by permission of the author c/o Rogers, Coleridge & White Ltd., 20 Powis Mews, London W11 1JN.

'The Bodysurfers' by Robert Drewe, from *The Bodysurfers*, Penguin Books, Camberwell, 2008. Reprinted by permission of the author.

'Republic of Love' by Delia Falconer, from *The Lost Thoughts of Soldiers and Selected Stories*, Picador, Sydney, 2006. Reproduced by permission of Pan Macmillan Australia.

'A Happy Story' by Helen Garner, from *Postcards from Surfers*, McPhee Gribble Publishers, Fitzroy, 1985. Reproduced with permission by Penguin Group (Australia).

'Nullarbor Honeymoon' by Dorothy Hewett, reprinted from *A Baker's Dozen*, Penguin Books, Ringwood, 2001, by permission of Kate Lilley for the Estate.

Extract from *Things I Didn't Know* by Robert Hughes, published in 2008, reprinted by permission of Random House Australia.

Extract from *Eat Me* by Linda Jaivin, Text Publishing, Melbourne, 1995.

Extract from *Unreliable Memoirs* by Clive James © 1980, reproduced by permission of PFD (www.pfd.co.uk) on behalf of Clive James.

Extract from *Summerland* by Malcolm Knox, published in 2000, reprinted by permission of Random House Australia.

'Lone Pine' by David Malouf, copyright © 2000 David Malouf. Reproduced by permission of the author c/o Rogers, Coleridge & White Ltd., 20 Powis Mews, London W11 1JN.

'The Burial and the Busker' by Gillian Mears, from *Fineflour*, University of Queensland Press, St Lucia, 1990.

'Across the Plains, Over the Mountain, and Down to the Sea' by Frank Moorhouse, from *Futility and Other Animals*, Gareth Powell Associates, Sydney, 1969. Reprinted by permission of the author.

Extract from *The Shiralee* by D'Arcy Niland, Angus & Robertson, Sydney, 1955. Reprinted by permission of the estate of D'Arcy Niland.

Extract from *Rose Boys* by Peter Rose, Allen & Unwin, Crows Nest, 2001. Reprinted by permission of Allen & Unwin.

'The Milk Run' by Christina Stead, from *Ocean of Story: The Uncollected Stories of Christina Stead*, Viking, Ringwood, 1985. Reproduced with permission by Penguin Group (Australia).

Extract from *Journey to Horseshoe Bend* by T. G. H. Strehlow, Sydney, Angus & Robertson, 1969. Reproduced by permission of Strehlow Research Centre, Alice Springs.

Extract from *Snake Cradle* by Roberta Sykes, Allen & Unwin, St Leonards, 1997. Reprinted by permission of Allen & Unwin.

Extract from *The Battlers* by Kylie Tennant, Gollancz, London, 1941. Reprinted by permission of HarperCollins Publishers.

Extract from *The Wing of Night* by Brenda Walker, Viking, Camberwell, 2006. Reproduced by permission of Penguin Group (Australia).

Extract from *Swallow The Air* by Tara June Winch, University of Queensland Press, St Lucia, 2006.

'Nhill' by Patrick West, from *The Best Australian Stories 2006*, edited by Robert Drewe, Black Inc, Melbourne, 2006.

Extract from *Dirt Music* by Tim Winton, Picador, Sydney, 2001. Reprinted by permission of Pan Macmillan Australia.

The Penguin Century of Australian Stories
Edited by Carmel Bird

This landmark collection brings together the best Australian short stories written in the twentieth century.

From early bush life to contemporary urban existence, *The Penguin Century of Australian Stories* celebrates our finest writers in all their modes: the lively comic fiction of Henry Lawson and Steele Rudd, the distinctive imaginations of Christina Stead and Patrick White, the experimental style of Peter Carey, and the highly lyrical prose of Brenda Walker and James Bradley.

Selected by Carmel Bird, these stories mirror the concerns of Australia's past and present. *The Penguin Century of Australian Stories* will enlighten and entertain for many years to come.